KITCHENER
An Illustrated History

John English and Kenneth McLaughlin

The history of Kitchener is unique among cities in southern Ontario. Although Kitchener shares so much of the character of the region today, its past was considerably different. Until 1916, Kitchener was Berlin, "Canada's German capital." Over two-thirds of the residents were of German origin; many retained strong traces of that past. These became controversial when Canada fought two wars against Germany. By the middle of the First World War, the idea of "a patch of Germany" in the heart of southern Ontario became untenable. Berlin became Kitchener, but not without a battle which split the small city.

This is the first scholarly history of Kitchener. Based on wide-ranging research, it illustrates how a community so unlike its neighbours became a part of the broader Canadian community in the twentieth century. Much of the information is new, and many myths are punctured. The romantic mists which have surrounded the story of the early Mennonite settlers are lifted. The full story of the great controversies of the First World War is told for the first time. The impact of the Depression and the extraordinary economic boom which accompanied the Second World War are analyzed. Kitchener's sometimes-eccentric politicians are seen, not as deviations, but as representatives of a long tradition of civic populism.

Over 100 photographs accompany the text. Maps and tables further illuminate Kitchener's development. *Kitchener: An Illustrated History* will be of interest, not only to its residents, but also to Canadians generally who are interested in the history of multiculturalism and the transition from rural to urban Canada. This book illustrates the difficulties as well as the rewards of maintaining distinct cultural traditions. The problems it identifies concern many Canadians today.

John English *Department of History, University of Waterloo, is the author of* The Decline of Politics: The Conservatives and the Party System, Robert Borden: His Life and World, *and co-author of* Canada Since 1945: Power, Politics, and Provincialism.

Kenneth McLaughlin *Head of the History Department, St. Jerome's College, University of Waterloo, has been co-editor of* Ontario History. *He is also active in preserving Ontario's architectural heritage.*

KITCHENER
An Illustrated History

KITCHENER
An Illustrated History

John English and Kenneth McLaughlin

Wilfrid Laurier University Press

Canadian Cataloguing in Publication Data

English, John, 1945-
   Kitchener : an illustrated history

Bibliography: p.
Includes index.
ISBN 0-88920-137-4 (bound). — ISBN 0-88920-141-2 (pbk.)

1. Kitchener (Ont.) — History. I. McLaughlin,
Kenneth, 1943-   II. Title.

FC3099.K5E64 1983   971.3'45   C83-098930-7
F1059.5.K5E64 1983

Copyright © 1983

WILFRID LAURIER UNIVERSITY PRESS
Waterloo, Ontario, Canada   N2L 3C5

83 84 85 86 4 3 2 1

Cover design by Polygon Design Limited, incorporating
Peter Etril Snyder's print of the Joseph Schneider House

To

Grace Schmidt

and the tradition she represents

CONTENTS

LIST OF TABLES

PREFACE

For generations, one of the main forms of Canadian historical writing has been biography. Indeed, it is sometimes said that Canadian historians and writers have elevated this form to standards rarely equalled elsewhere. This tradition is also apparent in the writing of "urban biography." There is in this country a long list of volumes that claim to be urban biographies and that attempt to capture the personality of a particular community. Unfortunately, many of these volumes are of interest mainly to local residents since the authors usually only chronicle local events and emphasize the greatness of community achievements. Until recently, urban biographers rarely asked searching questions about the process of urbanization, contenting themselves with elaborate accounts of the first settlers to establish ties with a glorious past. This is not to deny that these volumes are useful in the search for historical understanding; they are. The "antiquarian" writers base their work on the assumption that specific towns and cities have distinct personalities, and this is a tradition that still has value. As well, local histories serve as valuable sources. They provide outlines of past events and often suggest subjects for further study.

For all its value, however, antiquarian local history remains parochial; and, in an age when the purpose of history is no longer to glorify the past but to enable a society to understand itself, new approaches are necessary. A more sophisticated methodology must be adopted, one that includes more interpretation and analysis of historical events, exploration into the causes of social change, the study of the relationship among the several dimensions of human experience (economic, political, social, demographic, and spatial), and the use of the relevant tools and concepts developed by the social sciences. In addition, as H. J. Dyos noted, the urban historian has to be concerned with the historical process of urbanization, "a process which envelops an enormous range of places, not only within one country, but across the face of the globe." The challenge is to relate this complex process to the specific experience of particular places; to use the particularity of the place to illustrate the generalities of the process, and vice versa. In this way local history ceases to be parochial and becomes part of the larger story.

The authors of this volume have accepted these challenges, for this history of Kitchener not only examines all aspects of community development but relates the parts to a larger context. While Professors English and McLaughlin have discovered Kitchener's distinct personality, they have also provided analysis that lifts the narrative of the city's experience to the level where it elucidates questions that are of concern to Canadians generally. These questions include such issues as ethnic relationships, regionalism, provincial-municipal interaction, social mobility, labour-management relationships, urban planning, and general economic development.

The authors' text is also enhanced by a fine collection of illustrations. This illustrative material is not only visually enjoyable, it also plays an essential part in recreating and understanding the past. While photographs and maps cannot by themselves replace the written word, they can be used as a primary source in a way equivalent to more traditional sources. The illustrations in this volume capture the images of a wide variety of situations in Kitchener, allowing our generation to understand better the forms, structures, fashions, and interrelationships of earlier periods.

There is, finally, one other noteworthy feature of this volume in particular and good urban biography in general. It is to be hoped that the residents of Kitchener will, as an important part of their process of planning for the future, turn to their history. Progress is, after all, related to the legacy of the past, just as a city is related to the larger society. The goal of "looking backwards" is to seek to understand and use the past in a creative way. Thus, the value of volumes such as this history of Kitchener is that by outlining and analyzing how the city worked in the past—by examining its successes and failures—citizens can better understand how they got to where they are today. It is also to be hoped that an awareness of their history will assist the residents of Kitchener in deciding for themselves what they can do to control and plan future urban development.

The use of the past in the service of the future must, however, be based on a clear understanding of the limits of the exercise. The past is usable not as a clear guide for shaping the city or even as a means of delimiting a particular range of alternatives. It is, rather, to be used as an active part of the context within which decisions are made. In framing urban policy, policy makers, whether they are municipal politicians, planners, or citizens generally, usually have preconceived notions of the past, or at least what they think was the past. As a result, policies are often misguided or inadequate. True policy is a decision about where a city wants to go, a decision based on a sensitive appreciation and consciousness of where it has been. It is in the past that the community will find a reservoir of information and insights. In some ways, this reservoir suffers from the fact that, if it is good history, it is not specifically designed to serve any particular policy concern. But its very variety allows history to serve the community in multiple ways. And, given the challenges of our current era, communities need policies that will deal with conditions of variety and diversity.

Alan F. J. Artibise
Director
Institute of Urban Studies
University of Winnipeg

INTRODUCTION

Standing at Kitchener's major intersection of King and Queen Streets, a casual visitor might well agree with John Kenneth Galbraith's observation that the southern Ontario countryside is "devoid of topographic, ethnic or historical interest." The clutter of Kitchener's downtown reminds one of so many other smaller North American cities where bright façades fitfully cover up weary structures and familiar brand names compete for the passerby's attention, sometimes in flashing neon, sometimes with great bargains. From the corner of King and Queen, the streets seem to lead to more of the same. There are no mountain vistas or sweeping river valleys at the pavement's end. Nor are there ethnic neighbourhoods alive with the foreign chatter and aromas that one finds in Toronto, Vancouver, and other large cities where newcomers cluster.

To a modern observer, then, the topography of the area is unremarkable, and ethnic variety is not striking. There are also few traces of Kitchener's history. For Kitchener, as for most southern Ontario cities, economic progress required that the old give way quickly to the new. Reminders of Kitchener's civic life a century ago are rare. There are some remnants, but they do not suggest a stirring past. Kitchener, therefore, would seem to merit the brusque dismissal Galbraith gave the southern Ontario region. In fact, it does not.

Kitchener today may seem like its southern Ontario neighbours, but its past was significantly different. It began as a settlement of Mennonites, a people who rejected the worldly values of British North America. It soon became Berlin, a haven for German immigrants to British North America. These Germans brought with them special skills and knowledge as well as their own cultural traditions. By the 1880s, Berlin was Canada's "German capital," and, like Germany itself, Berlin's economic success was widely attributed to the industry and community pride of its people. Berlin was different from its overwhelmingly British neighbours, such as Guelph, Brantford, and London; and in those times it was proud of its different ways.

In the twentieth century, however, Canada fought two wars with Germany. In the First World War the fight was against "Germanness" as well as against Germany. Berlin, which in prewar days had loudly proclaimed its distinctiveness, became Kitchener in 1916. The decision to take the name of Britain's most famous warrior split the community. In the last years of the First World War, Kitchener was an angry city, unsure of its future and resentful of the way in which the outside world was imposing change upon it.

After the war the resentment disappeared, but the changes did not. Kitchener's history after 1920 testifies to the effectiveness of modern communications and education in breaking down traditional differences or, stated pejoratively, in stifling unusual growth. Kitchener became much more like the province surrounding it. In the Second World War Kitchener rallied as enthusiastically as its neighbours to the Canadian cause. In the postwar era it shared fully in the remarkable economic growth of the central Ontario region. In the late 1960s and early 1970s, as Canada began to boast about its multicultural tolerance and variety, Kitchener once more expressed its German identity through a rollicking, annual Oktoberfest. Those who recalled earlier, harder times must have seen much irony in the fact that Kitchener again proclaimed its Germanness—in the first decade in its history when those of British origin exceeded those of German origin. Kitchener had thrived not by emphasizing its differences but by adapting to the community around it.

We hope that readers of this book will come to understand why this southern Ontario city chose to change as it did.

Our interest in Kitchener derives from our familiarity with the community as we grew up. In 1974 we were asked to teach a course in local history; we realized then that Kitchener was an especially interesting subject to study because of its German background. The study of Kitchener also raised broader questions about cultural change and Canadian urban development. The National Museum of Man gave us financial support to begin work on this book. The work of the Waterloo Historical Society in preserving the records of Kitchener's past made our task much easier. The Kitchener Public Library preserves those records and extends to researchers the fullest co-operation and courtesy. We owe a particular debt to Lynn Matthews, the chief librarian, and to Grace Schmidt, who, besides being a splendid librarian, is a remarkable repository of knowledge about Kitchener's past. We would also like to thank Susan Hoffman and Ryan Taylor for their help at the library. Several others have helped us with our research. Archie Gillies gave us access to the valuable records of the Kitchener Chamber of Commerce. The staff of the City Clerk's office was especially helpful in providing access to Kitchener's civic records.

Our footnotes reveal the great debt we owe to our students. To all of those we sent to the library basement to pore over old newspapers and files, we would like to extend our thanks. A number of students were particularly helpful: Gordon Cale, John Carter, Robert Cornish, Teresa Deppisch, Jeannie Gillespie, Mark Godin, Marianne Huber, Rosanne Polillo, Tom Schaefer, Dennis Stoetz, Annamaria Tessaro, Bonnie Tough, and Ron Welker. Patricia Myers and Peter Schmalz were most helpful research assistants. Catherine Barclay worked for one and a half summers as our research assistant and typist. Without her valuable work, this overdue book would have taken even longer. All of the above were not only good students but good company. We appreciate them for both qualities.

Susan Burke of the Joseph Schneider House and Jane Humphries and Alexandra Konstantos-Mustakas of Woodside were helpful with details about the 1850s and the 1890s. Wendy Collishaw gave us information from her research on Kitchener's architectural history. Gail Heideman, Kathy Sage, and Laura Moyer managed to make clean type out of clumsy scrawl. From the project's beginning, our institutions, the University of Waterloo and St. Jerome's College, and our colleagues there have assisted us. The book has had the blessing of two priests, our good friends, Norm Choate, President of St. Jerome's College, and the late Hugh MacKinnon, the former chairman of the History Department at the University of Waterloo. We thank them for their support and remember Hugh fondly.

Editorial assistance for the volume came from Alan Artibise, who has contributed a preface to the book. Alan's exceptional knowledge of Canadian urban history was invaluable in keeping us upon the academic path he treads so surely. Peter Rider of the National Museum of Man also helped us with pertinent comments. Diane Mew spent many hours on this manuscript. Like all authors who have worked with Diane, we can testify to her extraordinary sense of what can make a manuscript better. This book is much better because of the time she gave it. Wilfrid Laurier University Press took on this manuscript when it was seeking refuge, and the Press has been for us the model of what a publisher should be. Harold Remus, the Director of the Press, and the Press's Editorial Committee accepted willingly what was a difficult project. Heather Blain is responsible for the book's layout, and she accomplished this difficult task in record time. Doreen Armbruster, the Press's Production Co-ordinator, was responsible for almost everything else. She even gave door-to-door service with proofs; she merits special thanks. Lisa Cheeseman has sorted out the difficult problems of our index.

The *Kitchener-Waterloo Record* has been most generous in allowing us access to its fine collection of photographs. Sandy Baird, the publisher, was especially helpful. He encouraged us in our work and offered us full use of the *Record*'s fine facilities. We owe the *Record* and its staff, especially Jon Fear, a great debt. Others who have provided photographs include the Kitchener Public Library, the Public Archives of Canada, the Public Archives of Ontario, the Waterloo Historical Society, Peter and Betty Sims, Ross and Yvonne Weichel, Michael and Irene Knell, Dr. Louis and Roxy Lang. Dr. Lang has also given us hours of his time and has cleared up

many problems for us. Harry Huehnergard of the *Record* not only identified many of the individuals in the photographs but also made available
the photographs for us. They have made this a much richer book.

The distinguished artist, Peter Etril Snyder, kindly granted us permission to reproduce his painting of the Joseph Schneider House for our
cover. All will agree that it has made the book more attractive.

We would also like to thank our wives, Hilde and Elizabeth, for their
encouragement and their patience. They have lived with the manuscript for a long time, and they are probably even more pleased than we are
that it has appeared.

Finally, we thank Lorne Ste. Croix of the Ontario Heritage Foundation and the Ministry of Citizenship and Culture for the generous financial
support which has made publication possible.

THE EARLY YEARS

1

On April 16, 1833 young James Potter had gone toward Berlin. In hunting for the "Town" he walked through bush and swamp . . . and found his way to Bishop Eby's when he was told that he had missed the "Town" which consisted then of a few straggling houses around the corner of King and Queen Streets. All west of Gaukel's tavern was a dense and impassable swamp.

— Galt *Reporter*, June 7, 1883

The site on which the village had begun to develop was most unlikely. Far removed from navigable water, it was not even at the crossroads of a highway or thoroughfare, and it was without a major river to provide water power for the needs of future inhabitants. Adjacent to a dense cedar and tamarack swamp, the settlement was located where the Great Road from Dundas cut across the farm of Joseph Schneider, a Mennonite pioneer who had arrived in Upper Canada in 1807. The few houses and shops were strung along the road which was bounded by sandhills over which loaded wagons could hardly be drawn and on a windy day the sand would form ridges almost obliterating the roadway. The Great Road was something of a misnomer; it was virtually impassable during the wet season, and for years boardwalks would have to be raised on cedar posts to keep wary pedestrians out of the mud.[1]

Prior to 1833 this area near the first Mennonite meeting house was simply called "Ben Eby's—a mark of respect and affection for the Mennonite bishop, Benjamin Eby, who had settled there in 1807. It was also known as Ebytown and, appropriately enough, Sandhills. It was certainly not known for its natural beauty or for its convenience for travellers. The site was part of what had once been a tract of more than six hundred thousand acres set aside by the British Crown in 1784 as a reserve for the Six Nation Indians. It was both a reward for their loyalty to the Crown during the Revolutionary War and a compensation for part of their traditional homelands and hunting grounds lost to the newly independent United States.[2]

The Indians, led by Joseph Brant, concluded that it would be to their benefit to sell a large part of these vast holdings so as to provide an annuity for themselves. Brant's plans were first blocked by the Lieutenant-Governor of Upper Canada, John Graves Simcoe, and then delayed by Peter Russell, who succeeded Simcoe as administrator of the province.[3] Russell's concerns were twofold: that the Indians did not have the right to dispose of these lands; and that if they were given that right Brant was prepared to sell "to subjects of the United States," some of whom were officers in the American revolutionary army. It was finally agreed in 1797 that the land would be surveyed and sold by the government on behalf of the Indians. On February 5, 1798, the Executive Council of Upper Canada signed deeds for the conveyance of 352,710 acres, more than half of the Indian reservation. The land designated as Block 2 of the Six Nation Reserve—94,012 acres—was sold for the sum of £8,887, provincial currency.[4]

Colonel Richard Beasley, who acquired the major interest in the new purchase, would have satisfied even the scruples of John Graves Simcoe, for Beasley evinced an unquestioned loyalty to the British Crown. A United Empire Loyalist, he had already received a grant of twelve hundred acres of land, the maximum fixed for Loyalist grants. As a cousin of the Cartwrights of Kingston, he was well connected in the small society of Upper Canada, and indeed he had entertained the Simcoes at Barton, his home near Burlington at the head of Lake Ontario. He was also a member of the Legislative Assembly at York and represented the electoral district of West York, which included the greater part of the Indian reserve. Beasley immediately began offering land from his Indian purchase for sale. Although land some thirty miles inland from the centres of commerce along the lakefront might not have been especially appealing, it did attract one group of settlers—Mennonite farmers from Pennsylvania for whom such isolation was an advantage.

The Mennonites in Pennsylvania, like other American colonists, had been caught up in the excitement and ferment of the revolutionary era. The war itself had directly affected them, as the fighting had reached far into Pennsylvania. Although the Mennonites had been indifferent to the American revolutionary movement, they were somewhat less than sanguine when the Quakers' hold on the state government was ended and political control of the state shifted to the more radical western section.[5] Some of their fears were quelled by the Continental Congresses of 1775 and 1776 which determined that Quakers, Mennonites, and other such sects could continue to practise freedom of worship and be exempt from bearing arms—the same guarantees they had enjoyed under the British Crown. Nonetheless, the unhappy experience of some Mennonites during the war had made them sceptical about Congress's ability to guarantee these rights.

By the end of the Revolutionary War, land prices in Pennsylvania were prohibitively expensive. Cleared land was selling for more than $100 an acre and farms in Pennsylvania had already been divided several times during the previous century of occupancy. The Mennonites, like so many other colonists, began to seek out new areas for settlement.[6]

A number of Pennsylvania Mennonites joined the trek in search of inexpensive land in Ohio and in Upper Canada. The earliest settlers from Pennsylvania had arrived in Upper Canada in 1786. Although not

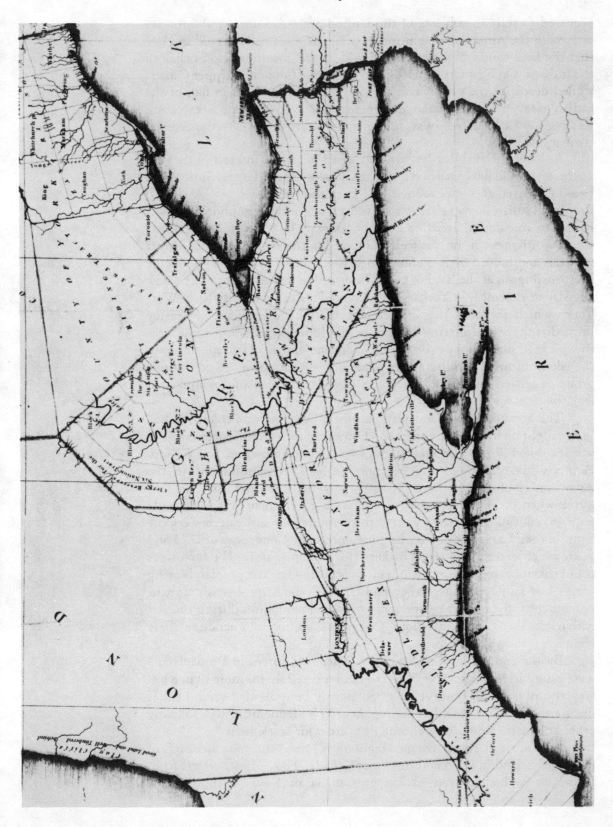

Loyalists, they found it easy to live under British rule and by 1802 more than thirty Pennsylvania Mennonite families had settled along the shore of Lake Ontario in a community known as "the Twenty"—being twenty miles from the Niagara River. The Twenty had become something of a stopping-off place for their co-religionists journeying from Pennsylvania. Hence, in 1799 when Joseph Schoerg and Samuel Betzner came to Upper Canada in search of land, they stayed there and probably first learned of the new inland area purchased by Richard Beasley the previous year. In the spring of 1800 Betzner and Schoerg travelled to Beasley's Tract where each chose a homestead site and acquired a deed for their property from Beasley.

Despite the arduous trip from Pennsylvania, which took up to five weeks, the Betzners and Schoergs were soon joined by others from Pennsylvania. Within two years some twenty-five families had settled on Block 2 of the former Indian lands. It came as a painful shock to them when one of the Pennsylvania farmers, Samuel Bricker, learned that some of Beasley's creditors had called his land dealings into question and that the Pennsylvania Germans did not hold a clear title to their land. Beasley, it appeared, had not been empowered to provide legal title to his land until the entire amount of the mortgage had been discharged.[7]

Popular accounts have impugned the motives and character of Richard Beasley for selling some of the lands on Block 2 before he had retired the mortgage, and this interpretation has become enshrined in local legend.[8] But Beasley was the victim of a continuing dispute between Joseph Brant and the Executive Council over the disposition and control of the Indian lands. While Beasley had made only one interest payment on his purchase to the government trustees, he had paid considerable sums of money to Joseph Brant as the duly accredited agent of the Five Nations. In the end, at Joseph Brant's urging, the Executive Council extended Beasley's title for a year, which enabled him to raise enough money to pay off the entire mortgage. In November 1803 he entered into an agreement for the sale of a large part of his lands to representatives of the Mennonite immigrants.[9]

The financing of the purchase of the Beasley Tract has become a part of Mennonite lore.[10] The Mennonite settlers whose land titles had been threatened were at first anxious and despairing. Two of them, Samuel and John Bricker, sought to take advantage of the situation which now confronted them. They offered to purchase all of the unsettled portion of Beasley's lands—more than sixty thousand acres—hoping to arrange for the financing within their own families in Pennsylvania. In November 1803 their agreement with Beasley was duly filed with the Executive Council and an initial payment of £4,692.10 was made to Colonel Claus, the Chairman of the Trustees for the Six Nation Indians. A bond was given for the balance of the purchase—£6,102.10—to be paid on May 23, 1805.[11]

Like Richard Beasley, the Brickers, too, could not make full payment on the stipulated date. According to one author, the reason for this was

Opposite page—
Chewitt's map of Upper
Canada, 1813

obvious: "This small group of men [Samuel Bricker and his in-laws, John, Jacob, and Daniel Erb] hoped to be able to secure title to the Tract in their own names. . . . It is believed that they hoped to secure an extension of the time limit to enable them gradually to dispose of the property to incoming settlers and to pay off the balance with the proceeds, with resultant profit to themselves.[12] Certainly this was the opinion of Colonel Claus, who insisted that the terms for the final payment would be extended for not longer than one year plus one week.

Having invested so heavily in Upper Canadian lands, the Brickers and the Erbs had to return to Pennsylvania and convince their families and co-religionists to raise enough money to complete the purchase or all would be lost, including the lands of the other Mennonite settlers. Eventually, the remainder of the money was raised through an appeal to religious sentiment as well as economic advantage. This was a unique opportunity to create a new Mennonite colony where religious ideals could be put into practice. A group of twenty-six individuals, most of whom had no intention of ever going to Upper Canada, contributed the requisite funds. In order to divide the land in an equitable basis, they formed a company, variously known as the Lancaster Company, the Swiss Company, and, most commonly, the German Company. This name was used officially to describe their portion of the Indian land, now called the German Company Tract. Augustus Jones, the government surveyor, was commissioned to survey the entire tract, and simply to divide it into even-sized farm lots of 448 acres each. The farms were then numbered and lots cast so that the division of the property would be fair to each member.[13]

The German Company's sixty-thousand-acre purchase established a Pennsylvania Mennonite colony in Upper Canada which contrasted markedly with the rest of the province. Not only was it isolated from the normal commerce and development along the lakefront, but in its religious and spiritual ethos it seemed also to eschew many of the Anglo-Saxon, Protestant values. The colony was entirely non-Anglo-Saxon. There were no Crown reserves, no clergy reserves, and no large Loyalist land grants through which to establish an Anglo-Saxon elite or presence in the community. Even the land survey had not been done in lots and concessions, but rather divided into equal-sized farmsteads without the customary road allowance. Furthermore, the German Company Tract was seen as a closed community. Lands were purchased not in York, but in Pennsylvania. The settlers were often related by family ties, and they shared a common religion and a common language. The trek from Pennsylvania over the Allegheny Mountains, the terrifying ferry ride across the Niagara River above the falls, and then along the lake to Dundas, where they had to penetrate the tortuous Beverly Swamp, created a shared experience and a common folklore which further united the colony. Loyalties and family ties as well as religious and social leadership remained oriented toward Pennsylvania and not toward the provincial capital at

Opposite page— German Company Tract, 1805

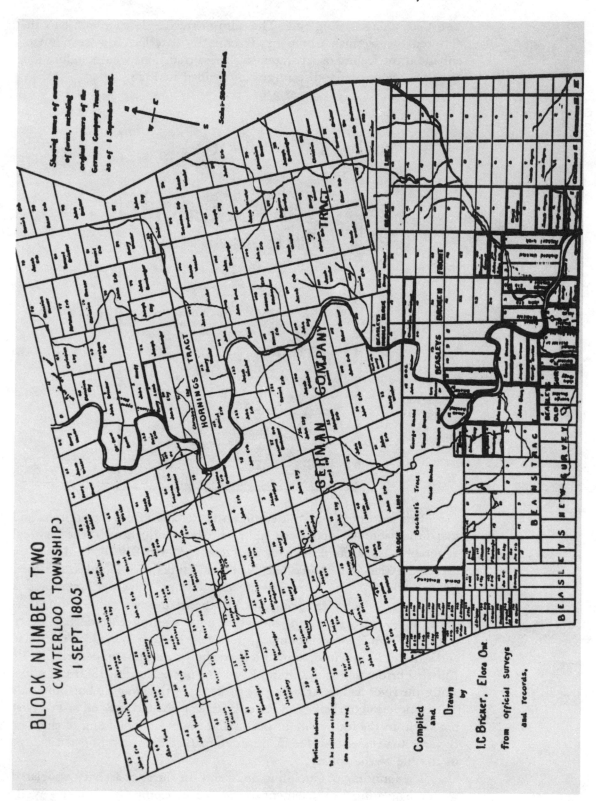

York, let along to England. The administrative decision in 1816 that elevated the German Company Tract into Waterloo Township merely enhanced the feeling of separateness. These traditions would endure long after the major Mennonite migrations ended in 1828.

German Bible, Title Page

This sense of a Germanic community, set apart from the political and social traditions of Upper Canada, had also been influenced by the very real geographic isolation of many of the settlers. Until 1819 the trail used by the first settlers represented one of the main links with Dundas, the chief grain market for the area. The Beverly Swamp, however, presented a formidable obstacle: "In spring and fall, the swamps were almost impassable to the deftest horsemen, the weary horse sinking knee-deep at every step. In summer, swarms of mosquitoes were enough to madden the horse and rider, and in winter snow blocked the way almost impenetrably."[14] The first bridge across the Grand River was not built until 1820 and travel along the river had never been practical due to the swampy bottom land. The completion of the Grand River bridge on the Great Road at Freeport not far from the future site of Berlin and the belated opening of the new Beverly Road eased travel to Dundas and marked the beginning of a change in the life of the colony.

The founding of Guelph in 1826 and the flurry of activity associated with the opening for settlement of the Canada Company's lands in Wellington County to the east and in the Huron Tract to the west thrust the Mennonite settlers more fully into Upper Canadian life.[15] More significantly, the 1820s also marked the end of the dominant Mennonite migration and the arrival in Waterloo Township of a large number of German-speaking immigrants from Europe. Arriving at New York from Hamburg or Le Havre, these immigrants were attracted to Upper Canada by the idea of a German-speaking community where good land was available and where there was a market for their skills.[16] These German immigrants caused a dramatic change in the lifestyle of the township.

> Whilst the Pennsylvania Germans and Mennonites were mainly interested in agriculture with only a few trained as millers, blacksmiths, weavers, shoe-makers, tailors, carpenters, and the like, the European Germans, who began to arrive in the 1820s, were only incidentally interested in farming. The majority of them were tradesmen, artisans and craftsmen, and industrialists, eager to make use of the opportunities that seemed to lie in Waterloo township, and apparently very much encouraged in finding an area already well-settled by people who spoke a form of German that they could understand.[17]

The period between 1825 and 1835 was an era of tremendous growth throughout the township encompassed by the German Company Tract. The urban expansion during this decade was in marked contrast to the previous period of Pennsylvania German settlement. Yet it was the very lack of village development so characteristic of Mennonite societies that provided the German craftsmen with the opportunity for rapid economic expansion. They were able to supply not only the needs of a well-established local market but also, via the Beverly Road, the more distant markets of Dundas and York.

As a result of the continuing arrival in the township of these new immigrants it was decided in 1833 that the hamlet near Bishop Eby's meeting house should be named Berlin. A blacksmith shop and roadhouse had been located on the site since the early 1820s. There was also a saddlery and carpenter shop. In 1830 Bishop Eby had sold a store site to David and William Miller and in 1832 Jacob Hailer, from Wilferdingen, Baden, had purchased an acre of land and established a chair and spinning-wheel shop. Shortly after, Frederick Gaukel, a native of Württemberg, purchased the original blacksmith shop site on which to establish an hotel. Standing there, in the summer of 1833, amidst the densely forested terrain, bounded by sandhills and swamps of willow, cedar, and tamarack and surveying the "few workshops, the two stores and the twenty-five dwellings—mostly log buildings,"[18] it is doubtful if either Bishop Eby or Joseph Schneider, the two Mennonite pioneers who are thought to have been responsible for the choice of the name Berlin, could have foreseen the remarkable growth of their village.[19] Within little more than two decades Berlin would become the county seat of the newly created Waterloo County, with prestigious county buildings, a branch of the Bank of Upper Canada, two doctors, a host of commercial trades, steam-powered manufacturing industries, and more than one hundred artisans and craftsmen representing a remarkable variety of skills and trades.

The Mennonite farmers who ultimately were persuaded to provide lots for these newcomers were not land speculators, nor were they hoping to profit from the urban development that ensued. When Bishop Benjamin Eby and Joseph Schneider sold part of their holdings—lots 2 and 17 of the German Company Tract—they were moved in part by compassion for the immigrant German artisans. Berlin's growth was largely conditioned by factors outside Upper Canada. It was a direct result of the political upheaval and the social and economic uncertainties in Germany after the Napoleonic Wars. New economic policies and major changes in landholding practices in the German states forced many small farmers off their traditional lands. Others were simply weary of wars not of their making. Skilled craftsmen and artisans found their status threatened by mechanization and industrialization. Both handicraftsmen and agriculturalists were no longer secure in their homeland.[20] The result in Germany and elsewhere in Europe was an unprecedented migration to North America, which has been described as "the western world's greatest folk movement of modern times."[21] In 1833, the year of the naming of Berlin, over twenty thousand are said to have emigrated and in the decade of the 1840s it is estimated that between sixty and one hundred thousand people left Germany annually.[22]

British North America, of course, received very few of these immigrants. The direct steamship lines were from Bremen and Hamburg to New York, not to the British colonies. As late as 1883 when Sir Charles Tupper visited Europe to promote emigration to Canada he discovered that "Canada was practically unknown to European steamship agents, and that no agent of a foreign country was allowed to solicit immigrants."[23] The Americans had subsidized ocean steamers since the 1840s, but it was not until 1857 that the privileges of British subjects were extended to German immigrants and that vessels flying flags of Northern European nations were granted permission to pass through British North American waters. Nonetheless, many German immigrants did find their way to Upper Canada, often by way of Pennsylvania. There they learned of the German settlements in Waterloo Township and of the newly opened townships of Wilmot, Woolwich, and Wellesley where the Mennonites and the Amish, also from Germany, had begun to take out land.

Typical of these immigrants was Philipp Lautenschlager who reached Upper Canada in 1831. He had arrived in New York, intending to settle in Pennsylvania or Ohio. Several of his companions, however, had heard of a German-speaking settlement in Waterloo Township where there were said to be greater opportunities than in Ohio. His letter to his father in Germany provides an interesting illustration of the experience of these early-nineteenth-century immigrants as well as of the lifestyle in the German settlements in Upper Canada. "I am with a cooper . . . [and] I earn nine dollars a month during the winter; in summer I'll earn more . . . a carpenter earns a dollar every day which is two and a half guilders, a blacksmith fifteen to sixteen dollars a month—and each handworker earns much money . . . also wagon makers and shoemakers are well paid. A hired man earns 110 to 120 dollars a year. A female worker earns four to five dollars a month."[24] Lautenschlager was greatly impressed by a number of the features of Upper Canadian life. "The women folk," he said, "do not dress as you do at home; they all dress as the fashionable people of Germany," and he also noted that "the women have it good; they do not have to go out into the fields. Nor do they have to prepare food for the cattle; they cook only for people. In this land the fare is good; three times a day there is meat, butter and apple butter. The bread is as white as your loveliest cakes at home." Land was plentiful in Waterloo Township, and "not expensive; one may buy an acre for two to three dollars. There is forest and more forest." He urged his father and the others in his family to follow him to Canada. "If you would like to come, take your wagon and your horses; drive to Bremen, there you can take some things from your home on board ship." Rumours abounded that Germany would again be involved in war. "Here one does not have to fear war. Everyone is free. There is money to earn like making hay, if one is willing to work."

The characteristics of the German immigrants do much to explain the subsequent development of village life in Berlin. They came from all parts of Germany—from Baden and Bavaria, from the province of Hesse-Darmstadt, the kingdom of Prussia, the principality of Waldeck, the kingdom of Württemberg, and from Alsace and Lorraine. Others came from the Baltic states, the kingdom of Saxony, and the Grand Duchy of Mecklenburg and the Duchy of Holstein. There was no predominant geographical area, nor did the immigrants represent any single religious, social, or economic group. It was a movement of individuals, often with their families, but not of social groups. They would maintain this sense of individuality and initiative in their attitudes toward commercial and industrial development. At the same time their common language and pride in their various crafts provided them with a corporate identity.

Those who settled in Berlin were weavers, wagonmakers, shoemakers, and coopers. They were builders, masons, carpenters, and mechanics, as well as chairmakers, pumpmakers, potters, blacksmiths, metalworkers, and general merchants. Day labourers, too, took up residence in the village. In the following influx of settlers, the village took on what were to be its unique characteristics. The Germans built their houses close to the street line after the old country fashion and cultivated gardens in the rear where they raised large quantities of potatoes and other vegetables and kept pigs and a cow to furnish meat and milk for their families.[25] As German immigrants continued to arrive and spread into the surrounding townships a large Germanic hinterland was created for which Berlin soon became a religious and cultural centre.

With a printing press brought from Pennsylvania by oxen and supported by subscriptions from leading Mennonite and German settlers, Henry William Peterson began the publication of the *Canada Museum und Allgemeine Zeitung* in Berlin in 1833.[26] The establishment of Upper Canada's first German newspaper did much to reinforce Berlin's primacy as the culture centre for the new immigrants, just as Bishop Eby's presence and the opening of his new meeting house or "Versammlungshaus" in 1833 had confirmed its importance as a religious centre for the Mennonites. In 1835 a Lutheran congregation was organized in Berlin and other German congregations quickly followed. An Evangelical Sunday School was held in Jacob Hailer's furniture shop by 1837 and, following a particularly successful "camp meeting" conducted by Bishop Seybert in 1839, Canada's first German Evangelical congregation was formed and a church opened in 1841. The German Baptists had been meeting in the township hall in Berlin since 1837 and the Swedenborgians, another German sect, had been meeting regularly in Berlin since 1833 under the leadership of Christian Enslin, a bookbinder from Germany who had also produced a collection of German songs and hymns "for the Christian people of Berlin and district." By 1840 Berlin was clearly seen as the social and religious centre for the German-speaking area which would be a powerful magnet as the community developed.[27]

The rapid increase in population throughout Upper Canada had made a reorganization of the form of government at the township or district level inevitable. What was equally inevitable was that any change in local boundaries would generate a great deal of excitement and interest in Berlin. The area encompassing Waterloo Township was originally part of York District and after 1798 part of the Home District. In 1816 the government created Halton County in the District of Gore which included the new townships of Dumfries, Waterloo (Block 2 of the Six Nation lands), Woolwich, and Nichol. Beginning in the 1830s, however, there were proposals to create a new district, the District of Wellington.[28] As early as 1836 the *Canada Museum and Allgemeine Zeitung* began to call for township meetings to establish Berlin's rightful place as the new "district town" and to emphasize Berlin's position as the centre of German population. In 1837 the *Canada Museum* again pressed Berlin's claim to be "the district town when a new district town becomes necessary." To attest to Berlin's suitability, the editor pointed out that nine new houses had been built that spring and five more were underway:

> In only a few years more Berlin will be one of the most flourishing of inland towns in the Province of Upper Canada. Here in the nicest locality in Canada are gathered all manner of workers, but we need 1 tinsmith, 1 butcher and other artisans. There are now here; [a] potter, chair and spinning wheel maker, bookbinder, printer, windmill maker, saddler, shoemaker, smith, carpenters, pumpmaker, beer brewer, hotelman, dry goods and grocery stores, weaver, tailor, mason, wagonmaker, clockmaker and some day laborers.[29]

When Berlin's claims were overlooked in 1841 and the village was included in the new District of Wellington, with Guelph as the district town, strong objection was raised by the *Canada Museum*, which complained that the "German settlement" had been overlooked.

When the Baldwin government, in keeping with its policy of establishing greater local autonomy, proposed to create smaller counties in 1849, Berlin's leading citizens were quick to put forward the claim of their village as a future county town. A host of private member's bills and numerous petitions poured into Toronto advocating the merits of a variety of territorial divisions. In Berlin, the reeve, Dr. John Scott, had long emphasized the need for representation of his village, especially since the meetings of the township council were held in Berlin. Furthermore, Berlin seemed an appropriate choice for a new county seat because of its central location within Waterloo Township which, with the single exception of York, was "the most thickly settled township in the province."[30] When it was learned that the village of Galt, which had been part of Dumfries Township, would be included within the boundaries for the new county, Berlin was faced with a strong rival for the county seat.

Galt was nearing incorporation as a town and was "the foremost place between Hamilton and London."[31] By comparison neither Brantford nor Guelph were at all prominent, and Berlin was "only a small straggling village." Galt also seemed to have the support of Francis Hincks, whose government introduced a new bill into the Assembly in 1850. In the expectation of their victory the citizens of Galt gave a large celebration ball, attended by the premier. In the meantime, Berlin sent its leading citizens to Toronto to press their claims. Dr. John Scott, Charles Ahrens, Christian Enslin, George and William Davidson, D. S. Shoemaker, Elias Snyder, and Jonathan B. Bowman, the former reeve of Waterloo Township, pleaded Berlin's case. In Parliament Dr. Rolph and especially David Christie, "a power in the Hinck's [sic] government . . . [whose] will was almost law in this section," strongly supported them.[32]

Christie's motives in pressing for Berlin as the new county seat appear to have had little regard to its central location in the new county or to its traditional role among the many German settlers, but had rather more to do with his determination to have his own town, Brantford, as one of the new county towns. For this reason he insisted on Dumfries being divided into two townships. He was actively opposed in this by the citizens of Galt, for their town had been the natural commercial centre for Dumfries and their relationship with the German settlers was only tangential. Hincks certainly would have preferred Galt as the new county seat but as the residents of Galt "with stubborn misjudgment" persisted in opposing Christie's scheme to divide Dumfries, Hincks "finally decided to pass over Galt and make its then rival [Berlin] the county seat." The decision was telegraphed to Brantford and carried thence by Dr. John Scott and others who rode all night to do so. A holiday was proclaimed in Berlin with bell

The original Waterloo County Court House

ringing and a procession. Within less than one year, in January 1853, handsome new county buildings had been built and occupied.

The following year the inhabitants of Berlin petitioned Queen Victoria to raise the status of Berlin to an incorporated village under the terms of the Upper Canada Municipal Corporations Act. In the first election, Dr. John Scott, in addition to his position as the first reeve of Waterloo County, was elected reeve of Berlin. The new village now set about to pass the necessary laws and ordinances to create a proper environment for the new seat of government. The social concerns of the new village were also immediately attended to. Inns, temperance houses, taverns, and public houses would now have to be licensed and inspected. The rural nature of the village, however, was still very evident in the fifth by-law of the village, designed to "restrain and regulate the running at large of certain kinds of stock or cattle"; horses, sheep, and cattle were not allowed to go as "free commoners." Milk cows, however, were allowed to run at large and pasture throughout the village from March until December provided that they were "confined on the premises of the owner during the night."

A much publicized view of Berlin shortly after the Court House had been completed, looking down King Street, shows a sweeping vista down an unpaved roadway, including fifty or so houses, several churches, and, of course, sitting majestically on a rise of land to the north, the new county buildings. At the time of its selection as the county town, W. H. Smith had described Berlin as "a considerable village, containing about seven hundred inhabitants, who are principally German or of German descent." There were a number of features which differentiated Berlin from other villages in the township. It was not merely a trading or service centre but it also contained two factories manufacturing cabinets and chairs whose machinery was driven by steam.

View of Berlin, 1854, expressing artistic license

Surplus agricultural produce and the availability of hides and wool as well as local resources of white pine and such hardwoods as cherry, maple, and beech attracted artisans who began a series of small industries. Similarly, clay deposits for brick and pottery encouraged craftsmen to establish trade shops. The introduction of steam power in 1846 led other craftsmen to diversify and to establish or expand into more effective production: a chair factory, several pump factories, a foundry, two breweries, a fanning-mill shop, and a tannery were all in operation by the 1850s. There were two schools, a post office, and the newly constructed County Court House.

But for all of this, Berlin was still very much a small, almost encapsulated community.[33] Artisans and craftsmen lived above or beside their places of work. Only a few establishments employed other artisans or apprentices. There was no distinction or differentiation of land uses. Most of the commercial, industrial, and residential establishments were built along the Great Road. Little had been done either to level out the high sandhills or to fill in the swamps. Until 1850 the entire block from Foundry to Queen Streets, at the very centre of the "business district," remained vacant. Almost the whole of this block was a "spongy swamp with willow trees along the edge." Cattle were in danger of becoming mired in the swamp should they wander off the road. Human traffic was somewhat improved. Along the streetfront there was an elevated sidewalk

Berlin landscape

erected on cedar posts with stringers. The sidewalk was about six feet wide and high enough to enable boys to explore underneath. The technique of raising the sidewalk on cedar posts was resorted to whenever the terrain proved too wet. In most other places, however, the sturdy residents of Berlin did without the benefit of a boardwalk.

Jacob Hailer

Conveniently located on the other side of the Foundry Street corner was Reinhold Lang's tannery, with his house, a one-and-one-half storey frame building alongside. The tannery, of course, could make good use of the fresh spring water which created the swamp, and Lang, like most German craftsmen, felt it entirely appropriate to live next to his business. Similarly, Jacob Hailer, one of the most prominent Berlin businessmen, resided in an attractive one-and-one-half storey building with a large porch partly enclosed by lattice work. Although Hailer's barn was some distance back from the street, "next along the streetfront was his shop where he manufactured spinning wheels, etc., and chairs. He had two foot-powered lathes and a number of German assistants." It was also not uncommon for artisans to reside above their shops. Mr. Hoffman, a wood turner, who made small household items, did so, as did Mr. Bosenberger, a shoemaker, and Mr. Fuchs, a tailor, whose wife was an expert in repairing clocks.

Almost all of the houses and buildings were of frame construction. There were only three brick houses in the village and one log cabin—that occupied by "a negro, Levi Carroll, a one legged ex-slave from the Southern States." Carroll was obviously the object of some wonderment to the inhabitants of Berlin. He owned several acres near his house which he "cultivated with a longhandled hoe only, planted with corn from year to year and which looked something like a plantation field in the south."

Levi Carroll's log house in a later photograph

Probably the most impressive building and certainly the most prominent was Gaukel's hotel situated where Schneider's Road intersected the Great Road. The hotel, built in 1835, was the first major building in

Berlin and its owner, Frederick Gaukel, was one of Berlin's most prominent citizens. Gaukel's hotel was a two-storey building with a wide colonial-style verandah, used for years as a rostrum for political orators coming to Berlin.

There is a pleasant simplicity to the early Berlin buildings. Usually painted white or a red ochre mixture, they seemed more a reflection of the 1830s and not much in keeping with the exalted image of Berlin as a county town. There were no elaborate frills or vergeboard for these German craftsmen and artisans. Nor did there appear to be any clearly perceived social distinction represented by the style of residence of the village's inhabitants. There had also been very little land speculation. Although lots had been bought and sold since the 1830s, the original Mennonite farmers were still the only large landowners. Jacob Hoffman, one of the earliest and most successful entrepreneurs, had acquired a number of town lots, but the time had not yet come for the businessmen to own large areas of land for speculation. Nonetheless, it is significant that many of Berlin's artisans and craftsmen were renters and did not own their own homes.

Frederick Gaukel

By the 1850s Frederick Gaukel's custom of sending a young lad out to forage nearby for speckled trout or partridge to serve something special before distinguished guests at his hotel would soon seem as much a part of the past as when he first came to Berlin in 1833 and Indians in government blankets still stopped by for something to eat. In his own life, Gaukel had symbolized many of the forces which had shaped Berlin. The name Berlin was chosen at the site of his tavern and most major events in the history of the settlement, in one way or another, were debated in the tavern or were influenced by Frederick Gaukel. When he died in 1853 the signal of the train whistle and the smoke of the factory had not been heard or seen in Berlin, but they were on the horizon. The sandhills which had been so characteristic a feature of Berlin would soon be levelled and the swamps drained. Bankers, insurance men, lawyers, and clerks would all come to Gaukel's tavern looking for rooms, creating a new Berlin that Frederick Gaukel would not know.

COUNTY TOWN, 1852-1880 2

Economic Growth

The Honourable James Young's description of Berlin as a straggling village at the time of its selection as the county town was perhaps not a great exaggeration. In 1852 there were only some seven hundred inhabitants; Young's own village, Galt, thirteen miles away, had more than twice the population. It also had the advantage of extensive water power and, unlike Berlin, had developed from the beginning as a commercial centre. By the 1850s Galt was describing itself as the "Manchester of Canada":

> Not only was the village the best grain market for twenty or thirty miles west, but in consequence of its flouring mills, foundries, woollen mills, axe and edge tool works, paper mill and numerous mercantile establishments, it had already become sufficiently prominent, more particularly for the excellence of its manufacturers. . . .[1]

The contrast with Berlin was striking in other ways. In 1854 the Great Western Railway opened a branch line to Galt, assuring the town's economic growth. Ironically, Galt's businessmen had never seen Berlin as an economic threat; the German community which comprised so much of the new Waterloo County still seemed remote. Within this context, however, there began a dramatic shift of population growth and economic influence from the town of Preston to the new county seat at Berlin. Preston had also been settled by Mennonites from Pennsylvania as part of the original migration to Upper Canada, and had attracted large numbers of German artisans in the 1830s and 1840s—in fact, many more had settled there than in Berlin. Preston had the economic advantage of an abundant water supply. Even before Bishop Eby and Joseph Schneider had begun to clear their land near Berlin, John Erb had built grist and sawmills at Preston. As the road system developed throughout the township, Preston became the focal point. Indeed, prior to the 1850s Preston could fairly be described as "a dominant urban centre in comparative isolation from the other settlement frontiers."[2] By 1855, however, Preston had reached the high point of its expansion; it was in fact the turning point marking the beginning of Berlin's economic dominance in the township.

Why the village of Berlin should have attracted so many of the new arrivals after 1850 is explained by many factors. As the county seat, Berlin was clearly established in a position of political influence as well as being the centre of German culture and religion in the township. This was given credence by the decision of the German Catholics in the area not to build two smaller churches outside of Berlin, but rather to erect one main Roman Catholic church in the centre of Berlin. Berlin's prestige as the seat of government, the central registry, and the general expenditure of public funds at the county seat also drew new immigrants to the village. Berlin's newspaper, *Der Deutsche Canadier*, published by Bishop Eby's son Henry, was the most successful and widely read German newspaper in the country, publishing both Canadian and European news as well as maintaining a high literary tone.[3]

Berlin's rise to political and economic prominence in the 1850s was clearly at the expense of Preston. By contrast, Galt continued to grow, but its development was almost entirely unrelated to the Germanic community in the northern part of the county. Instead Galt's merchants vied with Guelph and Brantford. As the county seat, however, Berlin became not merely the judicial and administrative centre, but it also benefitted from the opening of a branch of the Bank of Upper Canada in 1853, which was followed shortly by the agencies of two insurance companies, as well as the establishment of a wide variety of trades, two lawyers, and several doctors. Most important for Berlin's economic dominance within the German settlements, however, was the decision to extend the Grand Trunk from Toronto to include Waterloo's new county town.

The arrival of the Grand Trunk Railway in 1856 added a striking new dimension to the economic and social life of Berlin; it seemed to signify that the village had come of age. "How near the Railway brings Toronto," the editor of the weekly Berlin *Chronicle* excitedly proclaimed. "We leave Berlin in the morning at 40 minutes past seven—stay there three or four hours—and get back to tea here!"[4] Toronto daily newspapers were now on the streets of Berlin on the morning of publication, bringing all the news and an aura of sophistication to the village which would not have its own daily newspaper for another twenty years. Berlin's citizens were clearly captivated by the novelty of the railway. When the Grand Trunk brought a special excursion train to Berlin with seats for one thousand passengers to see Toronto, "the great capital city of Canada West," over seven hundred eager passengers, led by Berlin's reeve and his fellow councillors, set out on their great adventure to see the world. The world, of course, had also come to Berlin. On August 23, 1856, the Spalding and Rogers circus made its

GRAND
EXCURSION!!
ON THE
Grand Trunk Railway
FROM
BERLIN TO TORONTO
AND FROM
TORONTO TO BERLIN!
ON THE SAME DAY!
ON
Thursday, July 24, 1856.
FARE REDUCED TO HALF PRICE.

IN ORDER to give the inhabitants of Berlin and surrounding country an opportunity of seeing Toronto and the country through which the Railway passes, the Grand Trunk Railway Company have agreed to furnish Car accommodation for

1000 PASSENGERS,

for a trip from Toronto to Berlin and back the same day, for TWO DOLLARS, being half the usual fare.

It is confidently anticipated that the public will turn out well on this occasion, as it will be a grand opportunity to see

The Capital of Canada West!
and the magnificent
Bridges, Works and Country
along the line.

☞ The Cars will leave Berlin at 7 40 a. m., arrive at Toronto at 11. Leave Toronto at 4 p. m. and arrive at Berlin at 7 15.

TICKETS can be obtained from the following Gentlemen, who have been appointed a Committee of Management :—Messrs. John Scott, David S. Shoemaker, John Klein, F. D. Tims, H. S. Huber, T. G. S. Nevills, Geo. Thomson, P. N. Tagge, David Chalmers, Charles Hendry, M. P. Empey, C. Dœring, John Ernst, Jacob Beck, and Moses Springer.

Berlin, July 15, 1856.   28-j2

☞ The German Canadian, Waterloo Bauernfreund and Hamburger Neutrale to insert once and send their accts. to Mr. F. D. Tims.

Anzeige.

Grand = Trunk = Eisenbahn.

Die Züge fahren wie folgt:

Der Passagierzug fährt von Berlin um 7 20 Morg.
    do.   do.   do.   3 00 Nachm
und die Frachtzüge drei Mal in der Woche :
Dienstags, Donnerstags, u. Samstags
jedesmal des Morgens um 9 Uhr 20 Minuten.

Berlin, den 1sten Juli, 1856.   26-4

GRAND TRUNK RAILWAY.

TORONTO AND BERLIN

ON and after TUESDAY the 1st JULY, Passenger Trains will leave Toronto Station, Queen's Wharf, every day for Guelph and Berlin, at 8 A. M., and 4 P. M.

Returning, will leave Berlin at 7. 40 A. M. and 3 P. M.

Passengers for Kingston, Brockville and intermediate ports arriving by Morning Train can proceed by Royal Mail Line of Steamers from QUEEN'S WHARF, immediately on their arrival.

An arrangement to that effect having been completed with the Proprietors.

Until further notice, Freight Trains will leave Toronto Station at 9 A. M., on Mondays, Wednesdays and Fridays—and will return alternate days, arriving at 2. 55 P. M.

N. B.—Goods by this line must invariably be accompanied with proper bills of lading, and delivered at the Stations before 5.00 P. M.

C. R. CHRISTIE,
Traffic Agent.

first appearance in the village, the troupe arriving, horses and all, by railway. It drew immense crowds—between three and four thousand people were present at each exhibition and as one observer put it—"the 'quarters' of the whole country West appeared to flow into the coffers of the troupe."

Grand Trunk Railway advertisements, 1856

The local newspaper confidently predicted that the "general business" of the town would be doubled as the merchants and businessmen were "paving the way for a permanent connection with the commercial establishments of Toronto."[5] New businessmen and commercial travellers were arriving daily and Mr. Butchart of the Queen's Arms Hotel procured a "large and handsome Omnibus" for his daily trips to the railway depot. Newspaper editors from across Western Ontario travelled to Berlin to describe the wonders of the Grand Trunk to their readers. The editor of the Stratford *Herald* reported that the railway had brought tremendous prosperity to Berlin, and that "six buildings were going up in Berlin for every one in Stratford."

The real boon to Berlin in the 1850s came to the merchants and commercial interests, who profited greatly from the trans-shipment of agricultural produce through Berlin. For example, in the past scarcely a bushel of grain had been purchased in Berlin. Producers had carried their grain to Preston or to Galt and, of course, they had also made the majority of their retail purchases there. Berlin's merchants had served primarily a local clientele, coming to the village to market. In anticipation of the Grand Trunk's service to Berlin wheat buyers began to locate their businesses in the village, and less than two weeks after the line opened for traffic, Messrs. Abraham and Waddel, who had moved their business from Hamilton to Berlin, shipped a large quantity of prime wheat to the Toronto market. "There can be little question that during the ensuing season Toronto will receive almost every bushel of wheat grown between Berlin and Lake Huron," the editor of the Berlin *Chronicle* observed. "The sale of so much produce at our doors will inevitably augment the business of the place, and we shall see in the future a happy time for the tradesmen of the town."[6] By 1857 two large grain warehouses had been located in the village.

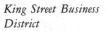

King Street Business District

The railway had also brought a marked change in the style of business operations in Berlin. There was an overall increase in the number of merchants and professional people conducting business. There was also increasing specialization in the trades, offering more varied and sophisticated goods. Mr. Susand started a coffee house in Berlin in 1857 and Mr. Nickolaus' saloon and "oyster rooms" opened later that year. Two new three-storey commercial blocks were built in 1857, illustrating the rising confidence of Berlin's merchants as well as their role as the dominant commercial and financial centre for the German and Mennonite communities.

Berlin's experience with railway construction differs markedly from that of many Ontario towns. Unlike both Galt and Guelph, Berlin's leading merchants had not been involved with the financing of the railway. Nor had the municipality had to raise funds or purchase shares in the Grand Trunk. As the county seat, Berlin was automatically included as a main stop on the Grand Trunk when the railway extended its original Toronto-Guelph line to Sarnia. At one and the same time this decision ended Guelph's vision of grandeur of controlling all of the trade to Lake Huron, and recognized Berlin's potential as the trading centre for a prospering and well-developed agricultural area. It is significant to note, however, that all of this had been accomplished without much effort or direction on the part of Berlin's citizens. Equally, of course, without such local visions of expansion, often promoted along with the coming of the railway, Berlin also avoided the flurry of intensive land speculation near the proposed route of the railway. In fact all of the lands had been bought up by Sheriff George Grange of Guelph who had received "advanced information concerning the route of the rail line and the location of stations."[7]

The sense of excitement engendered by railway construction and the possibility of apparently unlimited commercial expansion did belatedly infect even the stolid citizens of Berlin, but it was with the Preston and Berlin line, not the Grand Trunk. The Grand Trunk had ensured that Berlin's trade would now be directed to Toronto rather than to Hamilton or Dundas. The Berlin *Chronicle* pointedly described the impact of this new commercial alignment with Toronto:

> There our merchants and manufacturers will buy and sell. Every yard of calico will in a short time be purchased there, and every ounce of grain sent there for shipment. It will take a few months to sever the business connexion we now have with Hamilton; but though the separation be slow it will not be the less sure.[8]

In a move to retain Berlin's trade the Hamilton Board of Trade tentatively supported the building of a northern railway through Berlin to Lake Huron. In a more practical vein, it was suggested that an extension of the railway from Guelph to Galt joining there the Great Western could easily be connected to Berlin through a separate line from Preston to Berlin.[9]

The ratepayers of Berlin, led by their reeve, Dr. John Scott, met in the Court House to recommend that the municipality support the projected rail connection to Hamilton. On September 26, 1856, the stockbook for subscriptions in the future Preston and Berlin branch of the Galt and Guelph Railway was opened. Along with a number of private investors, including some from Berlin, the City of Hamilton purchased two thousand shares for $50,000, while the village of Berlin purchased four hundred shares for $10,000. The Preston and Berlin Railway Company was duly incorporated on June 10, 1857.[10]

Berlin's experience in railway construction, however, was to leave a bitter memory. The railway was underfinanced; Berlin's original debentures, which failed to include provision for a sinking fund, were deemed illegal and the municipality ultimately withdrew them, refusing to issue new bonds. "When a new by-law was submitted to the electorate [regarding these bonds] they recalled that the issue was only to be used as collateral security; that on account of the short curves trains could not be operated at more than ten miles an hour; and that the company had broken a promise when they placed their station in West King Street, near the G.T.R. tracks, instead of near the G.T.R. station on Weber Street."[11] The voters refused to tax themselves for a railroad which was so obviously not in keeping with the promises originally held out to them. In turn, the company sued the village over the original debentures and attempted to blackmail Berlin's council into granting another $20,000 debenture with the threat that the terminus would be moved to Waterloo. The final disaster occurred on January 27, 1858, less than three months after the railway had commenced operation. An early spring freshet severely damaged the company's bridge across the Grand River. The railway, which had been operating through an arrangement with the Great Western, ceased to function and engaged the village of Berlin in a lengthy legal battle to re-issue the bonds which Berlin's citizens were unwilling to sanction and which would now be used to pay for a non-existent rail service.

This would be a heavy burden for a village whose total taxable assessment was only $37,785 and whose annual income from taxation was less than $8,500 per year. A majority of council, however, were willing to buy the second $20,000 worth of stock to avoid a lawsuit. A petition was circulated in Berlin urging an independent slate of councillors to run for municipal election in opposition to this scheme. This new group of anti-railway candidates, H. S. Huber, Reinhold Lang, Henry Stroh, Dr. D. S. Bowlby, and Dr. T. H. Legler, was easily elected. Furthermore, the court ruled that "the company had no grounds either in law or in equity for entering the action" against the village. Berlin, however, was forced to re-issue the original debentures and the village paid the interest on them until 1873. In that year the Mowat government distributed a provincial surplus among the municipalities of Ontario. A special grant to Berlin retired the debentures amidst a great public celebration. Other municipalities had not escaped so easily from their financial entanglements with early railway promoters, and it was commonly said in this regard: "In Berlin only did the man not fall on his head."[12]

Berlin's economy developed at a steady, even rate throughout the 1850s. The first edition of the *Grand Trunk Railway Gazeteer, Commercial Advertiser and Business Directory*, issued in May 1862, described Berlin thus:

> Berlin, C.W.
> The chief town of the county of Waterloo and an incorporated village. It is a station of the Grand Trunk at which all the trains stop. It is a very good wheat market and is doing a brisk local trade in the dry goods and grocery line. Population 1,500.

What the Grand Trunk directory overlooked, however, was that Berlin's great economic weakness, a lack of water power, had now been overcome by the effective use of steam power. If the German immigrants brought a spirit of commercial and industrial enterprise to Berlin, it was the combination of their energy and talent when added to the use of steam power for manufacturing that now made possible the rapid growth of the village.

In 1846 John Hoffman, a furniture manufacturer who had recently returned from the United States, bought a steam engine and boiler in Buffalo, New York, and had them hauled to Berlin by Isaac Shantz with three span of horses.[13] Berlin's steam power attracted the attention of its rivals in Galt and Guelph where businessmen had prospered because of their access to water power. What is striking is the detailed, almost adulatory description in the Galt *Reporter* of the new steam engines in Berlin, "which for neatness, strength and finish of workmanship and smoothness in efficiency in working we have never seen surpassed":

> The engine of 7-horsepower in the newly erected establishment of Mr. Noah Ziegler was only put up and started last week and really it was pleasing to witness the regularity and smoothness with which the complicated machine commenced its first movements—not a jar or vibration could be perceived, but off it went like a thing of life as if impelled by instinct rather than steam to make the fortune of its enterprising master.[14]

By the 1860s extensive steam power had become commonplace in Berlin's furniture industry, which by this time employed more than sixty men in the process of turning chairs and bedsteads, in operating planing and flooring machines, and in sash, blind, and door factories. Steam power was also used to run Simpson and Aldous' sawmill, which in 1867 had a manufacturing capacity of two million feet per annum, and it would soon be applied to a number of other industries.[15]

The inland location of Berlin could now be compensated for by steam power, which was especially appropriate for the small, diversified manufacturing establishments in Berlin. Unlike those communities on the lakefront or on major river systems, where businessmen had invested heavily in the extremely expensive although picturesque operation of a grist or sawmill, the steam engine could easily be accommodated in Berlin's existing buildings, or in the new brick buildings springing up throughout the village. Nor did the manufacturers of Berlin incur expensive shipping or transportation costs, for the village was at the centre of a large and expanding local market for which it was the only supplier. By contrast, merchants and manufacturers in Guelph faced stiff competition for their markets and staggering costs in attempting to make use of the water-power potential of the Speed River.

From the tiny hamlet of 1852, Berlin had expanded by the 1870s to include twenty-seven industrial firms employing approximately seven hundred hands. Almost all of this work force and most of the new industrialists were German immigrants attracted to the community because of its Germanic character. These immigrants also brought with them new skills and new technology to add to the economic diversity of the community. A good illustration of this may be seen in the career of Emil Vogelsang.[16] Arriving from Germany in 1866 with the somewhat unusual trade of a buttonmaker, Vogelsang mentioned this to H. S. Huber, a prominent local merchant. With Huber's backing a button lathe was manufactured locally, and Huber ordered a shipment of ivory nuts from South America from which buttons could be turned. Vogelsang was able to lease a room and access to power for his lathe from one of the furniture factories. Within a few months he was producing an excellent grade of ivory buttons—the only such manufacturer in Canada—with extensive markets awaiting in Canada, the United States, and the British Dominions. Vogelsang subsequently entered into partnership with Huber and before long he had built a $20,000 factory at King and College Streets. As a direct result of this success of the button works, two other local merchants, who had recently immigrated to Berlin, August and Charles Boehmer, began the Boehmer Box Company in 1872 to supply boxes in which to ship the buttons.[17] Vogelsang's success can no doubt be attributed to the unique skill which he brought with him from Germany and to the initiative of H. S. Huber, as well as to the access to power with which to begin production.

Another immigrant, Louis Breithaupt, described later by the Berlin *Daily News* as the "Prince of Businessmen,"[18] was the fifth generation of his family to be a leather tanner. Breithaupt had emigrated from Germany as a child and established a tanning business with his father in the United States. Through a friendship with Jacob Wagner, a German Evangelical minister who had served the congregation in Berlin, Breithaupt began coming to Berlin to purchase hides for his tannery in the United States. He also became acquainted with and married Catherine Hailer, a daughter of Jacob Hailer. When Louis Breithaupt decided to establish his own tanning business he quite naturally turned to Berlin, acquiring the necessary property for his tannery from his father-in-law. By 1875 Breithaupt had

H. S. Huber

Louis Breithaupt

succeeded Hailer as one of Berlin's most prominent landowners and he had diversified from the tanning business, owning an hotel and a large commercial block.

These German businessmen, supported by numerous skilled craftsmen and artisans who had also emigrated from Germany, dramatically changed the economic lifestyle of the town. With their common ethnic background, they shared a clear determination to succeed.

What is significant is not just the rise to prominence of so many German businessmen, but that from the beginning Berlin's political leaders evinced a positive attitude toward economic growth; and this was clearly seen in the village and more especially after 1870 in the town council's policies. Berlin's council was made up almost entirely of businessmen. H. S. Huber, whose timely intercession had aided Emil Vogelsang, served seven terms as reeve of the village. With the exception of Dr. John Scott and Dr. D. S. Bowlby, almost all of the councillors from the time of Berlin's incorporation as a village in 1854 to the 1880s were German businessmen or merchants—from silversmiths to brewers, general merchants to leather tanners; and with one or two exceptions, all were of Germanic origin and supported at the polls by a solid phalanx of German workers.

It is hardly surprising that this council encouraged and promoted new businesses by tax concessions and municipal assistance—especially when the businesses coming before council were almost always inaugurated by Berlin's own citizens. As early as 1868 the municipality had begun to grant tax exemptions to encourage local citizens to expand or develop new industries: exemptions were granted, for example, to James Maude, to Vogelsang's button factory, and to Breithaupt's tannery, which had been

destroyed by fire, as well as to the Berlin Pioneer Tobacco manufactory and
to C. E. Moyer's woollen mill. This municipal support for industrial
enterprise culminated in 1874 in an official "factory policy," as a result of a
motion by two prominent businessmen on council, Reinhold Lang and
Conrad Stuebing, who requested:

> That this council, with the view of fostering and encouraging of Manufactur-
> ing Establishments in this Town, offer as an inducement that all new manufac-
> tories be exempted from taxation for the term of five years and that an annual
> bonus, equal to the rental of the buildings required, be granted, provided the
> continuous employment of not less than 75 hands in each such establishment
> during the said five years is guaranteed.[19]

Berlin's council used its factory policy to great advantage. From 1874
onward an increasing number of tax exemptions were conceded to local
industrialists. Initially for five years, later for eight, and eventually for ten
years, exemptions were granted not only for existing establishments, but
for any additions that might be made, thus permitting owners to expand
production without any increase in taxation. This system was seen to be
related to the firm's capacity to generate employment for Berlin's citizens
and many of Berlin's most prominent and prosperous firms were aided by
this policy.

By 1879 Berlin's economic base had been clearly established and
although the Berlin *Daily News* continued to lament the high freight rates
as compared with those in Guelph, its manufacturers had more than
seventy commercial agents leaving Berlin every week on the Grand Trunk
to promote the business of the town.[20] The industrialists and merchants
like Breithaupt, Vogelsang, Lang and Boehmer, Stuebing, Kranz,
Anthes, and Shantz were lauded as the community's leaders, "as those who
add to the beauty and wealth" of Berlin.[21]

Population Growth and Ethnicity

The growth of Berlin in the 1850s must have seemed phenomenal to those
immigrants who had erected the log cabins that comprised the village only
twenty years earlier. It would seem all the more remarkable in 1857 when
the Grand Trunk Railway brought ninety immigrants to the village in a
single day—quite a dramatic experience for the residents of Berlin whose
village had barely reached one thousand inhabitants, the statutory limits
for incorporation, three years earlier. Within the next decade the population had reached nearly three thousand and the village council prepared to
petition the Lieutenant-Governor of Ontario for incorporation as the Town
of Berlin.

It was the Grand Trunk Railway that had transformed Berlin from an
isolated inland settlement into an "inland port" able to receive immigrants
directly from Europe. As a result of the daily train service to Berlin,

Dominion immigration agents at Quebec regarded Berlin as a centre for non-Anglo-Saxon immigrants. Germans arriving at Quebec were redirected to Berlin as a matter of course. In the summer of 1857, for instance, the local newspapers announced in almost every edition that new immigrants had arrived: "The people thus thrown among us are chiefly Germans, and we can safely say that a finer, healthier or more stalwart set of men never came to improve and enrich our country."[22] The result, according to the reminiscences of Isaac Moyer, was the beginning of urban expansion:

> About that time [1857] Berlin started to grow more rapidly. The Mecklenberg people came to this country and many of them bought lots south of Church Street (when it was yet full of stumps) from William Moyer, my uncle. They bought the lumber to build small frame houses from Jacob Y. Shantz also on time.[23]

Although Berlin's population growth did not keep pace with the larger centres along the lakefront—in 1854 Kingston had 11,697 residents, Toronto, 30,775, and Hamilton's population had increased from 10,300 in 1851 to 27,500 by 1856—nonetheless Berlin continued to grow steadily.[24] An important consequence of the already obvious Germanic character of Berlin was that the impoverished Irish immigrants who swelled the urban population of Ontario during this decade rarely settled in Berlin. The political tensions of Toronto which reflected the vigour of the Orange Lodge's crusade against Catholic schools as well as unsettled social conditions engendered by the railway construction gangs were seen as a source of amazement and ridicule in Berlin where the Roman Catholic population was German, not Irish, and where the sectarian tensions of the 1850s expressed by the Loyal Orange Order seemed strangely out of character. The Germanic nature of Berlin's population was clearly illustrated when the Dominion Census was taken in 1871; 73 per cent were German by ethnic origin and nearly 30 per cent of its citizens had been born in Germany.

This high percentage was a result of political and social unrest in the old country which would only abate with the unification of Germany in the 1870s and the end of the Franco-Prussian War. The farmers and craftsmen who had fled Germany settled not only in Waterloo County, but also in Bruce and Grey Counties. Berlin's Germanic hinterland was thereby significantly increased. It has been estimated that as many as 47,829 German immigrants came through Quebec between 1846 and 1860, with more than 15,000 deciding to remain in Canada. During these years the Bremen-to-Quebec route had become increasingly popular for emigrants.[25]

The immigration to Berlin was of a very special kind. There was none of the "polyglot" feeling which arose at a later date in western Canada as a result of the mixed nature of European immigration, nor was there in

Berlin a sense of Anglo-Saxon superiority as one might find in Toronto or London. There also appears to be little evidence of a floating population of day labourers or of the unemployed moving through Berlin as was later so common in both Winnipeg and Calgary.[26] The problem in Berlin was not one of assimilating large numbers of foreigners, but of demonstrating that this German community could also be a Canadian community while retaining its Germanic heritage. The intent of the German groups in Berlin to enforce their cultural norms contrasts markedly with other urban centres in western Canada where Germans often settled but where the cultural norm was Anglo-Saxon.

Berlin lacked an Anglo-Saxon charter group to establish British cultural values and traditions. Most of the original Mennonite families had resettled in the rural areas of the township, selling their land as the village encroached or moving into the new townships of Wilmot, Wellesley, and Woolwich. Those who did stay in Berlin such as Henry Eby, who published *Der Deutsche Canadier*, became the spokesmen for the new immigrants and for German culture rather than for the specific Mennonite way of life which was not easily reconciled with urban values. Some Mennonites who remained in Berlin often joined the other German Protestant churches or new sects such as the Evangelical United Brethren, whose teachings were more in keeping with a modern secular age. The charter group in Berlin, if there could be said to be one, consisted of those early German immigrants who had established flourishing businesses. It was a German-Canadian culture and German-Canadian values appropriately enough expressed by the name of Berlin's newspaper, the *Deutsche Canadier* that had come to dominate in Berlin.

The predominance of German culture and traditions in Berlin and the accommodation to it that the Anglo-Saxons in the community had to make is perhaps best illustrated by the elaborate celebration staged in 1871 to mark the victory of Germany over France in the Franco-Prussian War. A peace festival or *Friedensfest* was held in Berlin on May 2, 1871.[27] More than ten thousand people, mainly of German origin, came to celebrate Germany's victory and the ensuing peace settlement. Speeches emphasizing German history, special concerts, and German choirs "singing the music of the people" were staged, culminating in a great *Friedensfest* ball. What is especially significant is the response of the English-speaking citizens, such as John King and Sheriff George Davidson, who felt obliged to make an official presentation to their fellow citizens, while at the same time admitting that they could not "feel the peculiar interest" which the Germans of Berlin felt "in the events of this day's commemoration." Nonetheless, they praised the rise to power of Germany, concluding with

... heartfelt expression of the genuine esteem in which we hold you, not only as friends, neighbours and citizens, but also as fellow workers with ourselves in the erection, on this continent, of a great Canadian nationality... [and] laying for our common country a foundation similar to that upon which now stands the powerful and united empire of Germany.[28]

Friedensfest *celebration, 1871*

The celebration of the *Friedensfest* illustrates the strength and vitality of Berlin's German citizens while demonstrating that German immigration to Berlin had created a community that remained very emotionally involved in European affairs.

In this context the incoming German immigrants were easily absorbed into the dominant social and cultural ethos of the community and within a short time they could rise to a position of prominence. The example of Hugo Kranz clearly illustrates this phenomenon.[29] Born in Lehrburg, Hesse-Darmstadt, in 1834, Kranz emigrated with his parents in 1851, living in Milwaukee and Buffalo before coming to Berlin in 1855 where he and his father opened a general store. In the municipal elections of 1858, the slate of candidates led by H. S. Huber was victorious— according to the Berlin *Telegraph* primarily because of Huber's control of the German vote. When the new council proceeded to replace the English-speaking town clerk, Charles Stanton, with the young Hugo Kranz, the editor of the *Telegraph* was incensed: not only did Kranz lack municipal experience, but he was not even "sufficiently acquainted with the English language to qualify him for the responsible position of clerk."[30] Within ten years, however, and despite his German accent, Hugo Kranz would be one of Berlin's most prominent citizens, as well as its mayor. His pre-eminence in Berlin's politics led to his election in 1878 as the first "German" Member of Parliament, defeating the incumbent M.P., Isaac Erb Bowman, scion of two prominent Mennonite families. Kranz's election to Parliament signified the first time that "the formidable Mennonist [Mennonite] vote in North Waterloo had been beaten."[31] It was also a clear indication of the political strength of the new German immigrants in Berlin and the growing predominance of Berlin in what had once been thought of as a rural riding.

If the Germans in Berlin had any reason to suspect that the emphasis on their unique German culture might at some time come into conflict with a pan-Britannic vision of Canada's future, this was clearly not present in the 1860s and 1870s. Nor was it the view in government circles in Canada. Quite the opposite was true. German virtues and the German presence in Canada were openly praised, encouraging the local elite to retain its cultural separateness from the dominant Anglo-Saxon values of the rest of the province. In two separate vice-regal visits to Berlin—one in 1874 by the Governor General, the Earl of Dufferin, and another in 1879 by the Marquis of Lorne and his wife, the Princess Louise—lavish praise for the German tradition and character of Berlin was the keynote of both addresses. Both governors general seemed only to speak to the "German" character, entirely overlooking the Mennonite and the Anglo-Saxon elements in the population. There was considerable resentment in 1879 that those greeting their excellencies seemed to be only German. The Waterloo *Chronicle* described the Mennonites and the English as "being like a certain class down South, known among the darkies as 'no count white trash.' "[32]

In 1874, the greetings brought to the Earl of Dufferin by Mayor Hugo Kranz had been on behalf of the municipality of Berlin and only in his conclusion had Kranz noted that the town was "inhabited principally by Germans who loyally contribute their share to building up our Canadian nationality, and who glory to live, labour and prosper under the British Law and constitution."[33] By 1879 two addresses of welcome were deemed necessary: one in English by Mayor Breithaupt on behalf of Berlin, and another in German on behalf of the German citizens by Hugo Kranz, now the federal Member of Parliament.[34] Kranz's address, prepared by a committee of leading German citizens, described at length the virtues of their Germanic character: "We strive to live like British subjects without abandoning our German peculiarities, to make indigenous German labour, German thrift and heartiness, the German language and even German song in Canada without separating ourselves in affairs that concern public life, from our fellow citizens of British descent, or, without even making a distinction."

Lorne's response to Breithaupt's greeting illustrates the predominant impression held about Berlin in Canada's official circles in the 1870s: "Here where the virtues of the Anglo-Saxon and German races meet to hasten your prosperity by their friendly rivalry, we who descend from both English and German parents gratefully accept the tokens of affection given by you here, on behalf of the people of Berlin, and thank you in the name of our sovereign." He replied to the German delegation, speaking entirely in German, in an even more lavish manner. The Princess and himself, he said, were .

> all the more happy from the fact that we are welcomed in the beloved German language, and the assurance of German faith and friendship given from German lips. . . . Though you have received us so heartily and shown your esteem for the Queen, you will still remain good Germans, and you may therefore be proud that you can instruct your children and grandchildren in their forcible mother tongue. The love for the old German Fatherland should never die. It will not interfere in the least with the use of the English language, so much of which comes from the German.

Both Lorne and Dufferin remarked on the great pleasure that it would give to them to inform the Imperial family of Germany of the prosperity and happiness of the Germans living in Canada. Dufferin further declared,

> It is needless for me to assure you gentlemen that I, in common with all your fellow British fellow subjects, am prepared to recognize you as fellow citizens with the utmost cordiality and affection. I believe that in saying this I am accurately expressing the general feeling of the British section and of every other section of the Canadian people, who all recognize in the German element a contribution of strength to our national constitution.[35]

Hugo Kranz's election to Parliament in 1878 had ended his dominance in municipal politics where he had been mayor for five consecutive terms. John Fennell and John A. Mackie, two of Berlin's most prominent Anglo-Saxon merchants, were anxious to run for the vacant mayoralty. So, too, were Louis Breithaupt and John Motz, the publisher of the town's German newspaper, the *Berliner Journal*. As the editor of the Berlin *Daily News* wryly observed: "Of course it remains entirely with our German friends to say, whether an English-speaking Mayor should be elected, for it is well known they have a large majority of the votes, and if the national cry were raised it would be almost hopeless to put forward a gentleman not belonging to the majority nationality." In the end neither Fennell nor Mackie were candidates and Louis Breithaupt was easily elected, continuing a trend in which the predominant German business class also served at the head of municipal affairs in Berlin. The dominance of business leaders in local politics was not unusual. What was unusual was that these men had few professional or social contacts in other communities in the province. They had either come directly from Germany where they had acquired an apprenticeship in business or, like the Breithaupts and the Kranzes, had come through the United States. In neither case did they have any education or experience within Canada outside of Berlin.

A number of other factors, however, served to temper the German influence in Berlin. As the county seat, Berlin had acquired an English-speaking professional class. The first crown attorney, Aemelius Irving, had been a prominent member of the old Upper Canada Club. His successors, Thomas Miller and especially W. H. Bowlby, played an active role in the social life of the community. The Bowlbys, Ward Hamilton, and his brother David Sovereign, were of United Empire ancestry, graduates of Upper Canada College and the University of Toronto. The Bowlbys took an active interest in municipal affairs. David served on the village council for five terms and Ward was reeve of the village for four terms, from 1865 until 1869. The Bowlby properties of "Geneva Lodge" and "Bow Hill" were the most elaborate estates within the village. Judges William Miller and Anthony La Course as well as Sheriff George Davidson were also prominent in the life of Berlin. All of these men were of Anglo-Saxon, non-Germanic background. They represented a tradition that contrasted markedly with the original Mennonite settlers, and they came from a social background at variance with the German mechanics and artisans who formed the majority of Berlin's population.

"Bow Hill," the residence of W. H. Bowlby

The choice of Berlin as the county seat also led to the establishment of two new English-language newspapers, the *Telegraph* and the *Chronicle and Waterloo County Reformers Gazette*. The German newspaper, the *Deutsche Canadier*, continued to publish in German. In fact, the *Deutsche Canadier* and the *Telegraph* were both published in the same building by Benjamin Eby's son, Peter. Within a few years of becoming the county seat the village of Berlin had three weekly newspapers, two in English and one in German. In a sense this became Berlin's form of bilingualism. Canadian political news and the official life of the municipality were reported in the English papers. The *Deutsche Canadier* and, after 1859, the *Berliner Journal* related directly to the German community and promoted the separate ethnic identity of Germans in Canada. German news and German happenings were prominently featured. C. Kranz & Son, for instance, frequently advertised that cash remittances could be sent to Germany for passengers coming to Canada, and the *Berliner Journal* advertised inexpensive fares between Hamburg and Quebec as well as Le Havre and New York.

In contrast to the exclusivity of the original Mennonite settlement, and the traditions represented by the German churches and newspapers, "a very powerful provincial agency for the assimilation of ethnic groups, the public school system, began in 1851 to combat the trend toward cultural segregation."[36] The German schools, established by the early settlers and managed by the local citizens, became part of the centralized provincial system created under the leadership of Egerton Ryerson in which the primary language of instruction was to be English. Despite the fact that Berlin's teachers, although German, were highly qualified, the local superintendent of Waterloo County, the Reverend J. McMechan, recommended that the certificates of such teachers should be abolished and that "all teachers in the western province should be capable of writing, teaching and speaking English."[37] His opinion was "that any other course of action retarded progress in education and amalgamation of the different nationalities into 'a homogenous people.'" The German teachers in the schools survived McMechan without great hindrance, but the new School Act of 1871 had far more dire consequences.

The 1871 Act established stricter linguistic standards for teachers and created the position of county inspector. The new inspector, Thomas Pearce, was unsympathetic to the German language and to German schools. In his first report in 1872 he claimed that ". . . three-fourths of the children spoke a 'foreign language,' and could not understand the teacher's explanations and instructions [if given in English]. . . .The learning of both German and English lowered the standards of the schools."[38] As a result, Pearce adopted a system which obliged German-speaking children to learn English immediately on beginning school, with German available only in the higher grades.

The gradual erosion of the teaching of German in the schools did not, of course, predetermine the demise of German culture. The social customs, the religion, the music, and the literature maintained and preserved their German inheritance. In Berlin, these ethnic sensitivities remained very close to the surface, especially as the prosperity of the German manufacturers and merchants became more pronounced. Within the community there

were occasional grumblings of discontent. Dougall McDougall, the editor
of the Berlin *Telegraph*, fulminated against the bloc political support of
German immigrants for political leaders such as H. S. Huber, who served
seven terms as reeve of the village. In another instance, P. E. W. Moyer,
the editor of the Berlin *Daily News* criticized John Motz, the editor of the
German weekly, the *Berliner Journal*, for his references to the Germanic
origins of the original Mennonite settlers:

> The genuine Pennsylvania Dutchman would not be insulted worse to be called
> an Irishman than a German. He claims no affinity whatever for the latter and
> looks down upon all such immigrants as the editor of the *Journal* [John Motz]
> as foreigners in his native Waterloo—only to be tolerated, not loved or
> venerated however pretentious they may be.[39]

Many Mennonites undoubtedly had an aversion to the apparently overwhelming German presence. They may have resented the changes in the
community that had resulted from the increasing numbers of German
immigrants, as evidenced by the German plays and *Turnvereins*, German
choirs and *Sängerfests*, German folksongs, German styles of dress, and
German imported goods in the stores of Berlin's merchants.

Within the community, however, there was a definite closing of
ranks against the outside, Anglo-Saxon world. Moyer might well criticize
a rival editor whose political views he also opposed, but he applauded Louis
Breithaupt in his quest for the mayoralty and suggested that Breithaupt
ought to be knighted when the Governor General visited Berlin in 1879.
"It would be honoring a representative and worthy man of the same race
and blood as our excellent Queen."[40] Good Queen Victoria's German
ancestry was never lost sight of in Berlin, for it was a wonderful justification for their role as German-Canadians within a British Dominion.

The Urban Landscape

Berlin's urban development in the nineteenth century was much simpler
than that of many Canadian cities and if its urban landscape was less scenic
and less grand, it was also accomplished without the creation of an
especially impoverished district such as that located in Quebec's lower
town, the slums of Halifax's waterfront or Montreal's celebrated "city
below the hill."

The primary characteristics of Berlin's urban pattern were established
in the 1850s. Commercial development was located along the Great Road.
This was not a crossroads village in the usual sense. The central intersection
was at the point where the road from Joseph Schneider's farm met the Great
Road—soon to be given symbolic importance in the tradition of many
Ontario towns by being renamed King and Queen Streets.[41]

The Court House and county buildings, located on a ridge running
parallel to King Street at the corner of Frederick and Weber Streets, would

ultimately lead to the beginning of a residential area. Even the arrival of the Grand Trunk had little immediate effect on the streetscape of the village, although Sheriff Grange's survey provided the first major urban plan with industrial, town, and park lots.[42] It covered nearly five hundred acres destined to create a discordant street system running parallel to the railway while the original street system had developed parallel to the Great Road. Berlin's industrial development did not immediately relocate along the railway, but continued for some years along King and Queen Streets and the first effect of the railway was not to create a rush of land sales. Commercial and industrial growth remained in the traditional area for, ironically, the rail line had crossed King Street at the high sandy ridge which had always marked the natural westerly limits of the village and the town's development did not expand beyond the rail line for another one-quarter of a century.[43]

King Street was located in a valley, surrounded on three sides by sand ridges and open only to the south where the terrain was swampy and unsuitable for development. The natural advantage of Queen Street was that it intersected King Street near a high point in the valley. From here the commercial and residential districts began to grow. A series of cross roads developed both east and west of Queen Street, Benton, and Frederick to the east and Ontario (Foundry), Gaukel, Young, and College Streets to the west. As Berlin's population grew, development also continued along King Street, eventually cutting across the sandhills to the north and filling in the swamp to the south. None of the streets parallel to King, however, ran the entire length of the commercial area, thereby reinforcing the natural tendency to retain King Street as the focal point for development.

The railway boom left little in the way of an architectural legacy. Nor was land speculation rampant as it had been in Guelph or as it would be in Winnipeg at a later date. That is not to suggest that Berlin in 1856 was an unattractive target for land speculators. George Grange, from Guelph, had purchased two large blocks of land along the proposed railway line in Berlin. His major purchase was from Abraham Weber for his farm which comprised most of Lot 16 of the original German Company Tract as well as forty acres from Samuel Moxley.[44]

When Grange put this land up for sale it was widely advertised in Toronto and in "all the principal Hotels and Public Offices in Western Canada." He described his Berlin properties as

> . . . the most desirable opportunity for investment that has yet been submitted to the public connected with railway enterprise. Berlin is situated on what is deservedly acknowledged to be the richest agricultural district of Western Canada, backed up by a tract of land extending to the shores of Lake Huron, that is daily becoming second to none for agricultural purposes in the Province.[45]

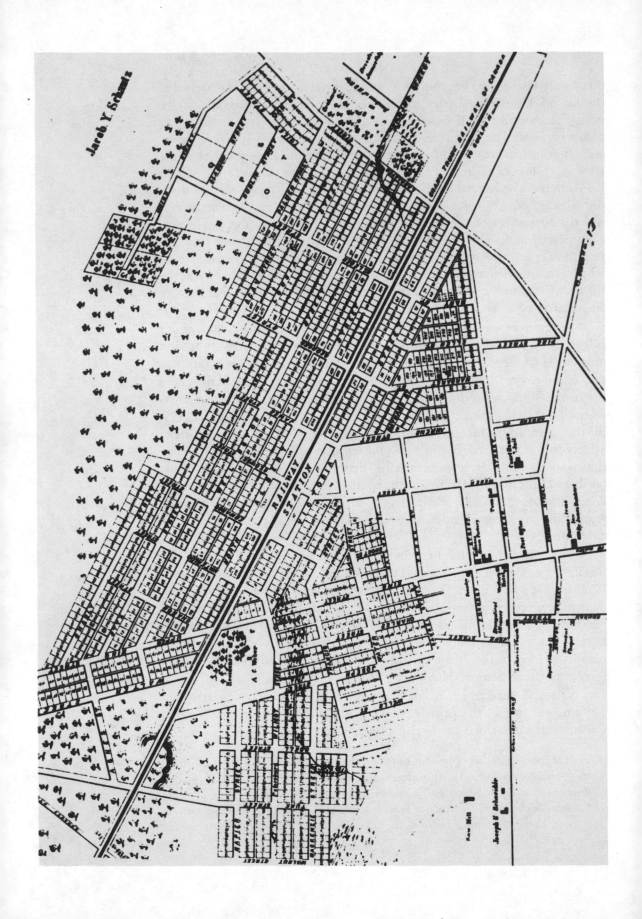

On the first day of the sale Grange was said to have realized two-thirds of his original purchase price. The lots near the Grand Trunk sold well, for this was the area which some people believed would soon "become the centre of our business [district], so that our handsome County Buildings, instead of being at the side of the town, will soon be in the middle of it."[46] This prediction, however, proved unfounded. For a long time a large block of land between Ahrens and St. Leger Streets, extending from the line of Young Street to the railway, remained an empty field known locally as "The Commons" where a large herd of village cows freely grazed and where visiting circuses could be accommodated.

Much of Grange's survey was purchased by speculators from outside Berlin. The local residents felt a perverse satisfaction in the failure of the survey to develop, especially when incoming settlers were still able to buy land from Mennonite farmers such as William Moyer and establish their residences away from the railway line. This created a diversified form of urban development quite different from many other towns where a river or other major topographical feature forced urban development into a more restrictive pattern. As for Grange's own holdings, a large number remained unsold. Finally, in 1859 a sheriff's sale was threatened for his non-payment of municipal taxes on nearly four hundred town and park lots.[47]

There was no compelling reason for Berlin's businessmen to purchase lots along the railway line in the Grange survey, for there were still many lots available on King Street. For instance, when Frederick Gaukel's properties were put up for sale in 1853, they were quickly acquired for commercial expansion. Gaukel's estate included a one-quarter-acre lot on the corner of King and Queen Streets, a building lot on the corner of King and Foundry, six building lots of twenty-four-foot frontage on King Street, ten lots on Queen and Glasgow Streets, two building lots on the south side of King Street and several others. The King Street lots sold for from $250 to $500 and the quarter-acre at the corner of King and Queen was sold for $1,600.[48] Thus, there was still a great deal of underdeveloped land in the central district at very reasonable prices.

Berlin's residential growth remained steady to meet the demands of incoming immigrants. Homes continued to be mainly of frame construction although the presence of local brickyards since 1846 had also resulted in many new brick homes being built. Whether of brick or frame, the style was the same: a decidedly unattractive and unadorned one-and-one-half or two-storey house with gable ends without vergeboard, gingerbread, or even patterned brickwork. There was no leavening as provided by the small stone-crofter's cottages in Galt or London's more elegant Regency-style cottages, although some very plain examples of the "Ontario Gothic" with its high central gable were interspersed. The arrival of three brickmakers in the late 1850s—John Bramm, Henry Schwenn, and Joseph Dauberger— as well as the ever-present danger of fire, and the inadequacies of fire protection in the village, soon resulted in a predominance of brick. From

Opposite page—
The Grange Survey,
1853-54

that period on, Berlin's ubiquitous pressed white brick made its presence felt everywhere. By 1872 a municipal by-law forbade new buildings constructed of wood or even major renovations to existing wooden buildings, in an attempt to reduce the risk of major conflagration in the village. As a result, Berlin's buildings began to take on a monotonous regularity with little diversity of style, colour, or building materials and the older clapboard houses were inevitably replaced by new and often larger brick homes.

First brick house in Berlin

King Street continued to be the centre for development, benefitting greatly from the new mercantile prosperity associated with the railway. In 1858 Henry Bowman built a three-storeyed brick mercantile block, the first major commercial building of its kind in the village. Other merchants soon followed his example, often also living above their stores. In fact, one of Berlin's most prominent citizens, Mayor Hugo Kranz, found it entirely appropriate to live on King Street, above his general store, and it was there that the Governor General and his wife were entertained in 1874. King Street retained its varied uses; breweries, furniture factories, commercial and mercantile blocks, and private residences, as well as the Town Hall, were located along its route.

Although King Street was the major business thoroughfare, its character in the 1870s still had something of the appearance of a rural village. After describing the stores and the new business blocks, one prominent observer remarked that in order to complete the picture,

the reader must figure to himself a goodly number of frame homes, here and there, many with pumps at their front doors, and nearly all with well-kept gardens. These were commonly fenced for cows, tho' not pigs, were free commoners. . . . It was not till 1882 that the cows' rights were abridged. Nothing had been done to make the streets neat till in preparation for the

"Saengerfest" of '75 King Street was "ausgeputzt" and a few lamp posts erected, on which coal oil lamps were lit on moonless nights.[49]

In the growing business district along King Street the merchants petitioned annually after 1875 for a special rate to provide for the road to be watered in order to keep down the dust. But the limits of the village's expansion had not changed greatly, and in 1877 when Ratz and Kaufman established their new planing mill on King Street just beyond the railway tracks they were ridiculed for locating "so far out in the country."[50]

The most dramatic change to the urban landscape occurred in 1877 when the sandhills in front of the Town Hall were levelled and the soil used to fill in the swamp at the corner of King and Foundry Streets. The impact of these changes was rather startling as the street level was altered in some instances by as much as nine feet, and many merchants found their stores dramatically above or below the road level. Some storekeepers sought compensation from town council, while other citizens were sufficiently indignant to elect an "anti-improvement" slate of candidates to council the next year, thereby thwarting any further levelling of King Street.

The improvements along King Street, however, were an indication of the continued prosperity of Berlin and the expansion of her industries at a time when an economic depression had severely hampered trade and commercial growth in central Canada, and when the streets elsewhere were often filled with the jobless and the unemployed. In Berlin, however, new houses continued to be built and in 1878 the assessor reported that there was only "one unoccupied residence in the whole of Berlin."[51] Berlin's steady rate of growth is also evident in the range of commercial, industrial, and residential buildings under construction throughout the 1870s.

Part of the petition to the Lieutenant-Governor of Ontario praying for the erection of the village of Berlin into a town in 1870 had called for the necessary division of the town into wards for electoral purposes. Often the division into various wards either accommodates existing social and economic distinctions in the residential areas or allows for urban expansion. In Berlin neither was the case. There was to be no increase in land size and the village was simply divided into four units with the boundaries of King and Queen Streets and the existing village limits serving as the focal points. There were no clearly perceived economic or social distinctions in any of the wards when the town was incorporated in 1870.

By the end of this decade, however, the area along Queen Street North, in Berlin's North Ward, on a ridge above King Street, was becoming very fashionable, although it was by no means a restricted or exclusive area. Not only did the North Ward have its share of smaller homes, but many of Berlin's leading citizens also located elsewhere. The new Italianate residence of Charles Boehmer, on the opposite side of town, in the South Ward, was one of the finest homes in Berlin. Nearby, J. M. Staebler was constructing another Italianate villa, "Buena Vista," on Queen Street South. Referring in 1878 to this area around Queen Street South, the *Daily News* noted that "There is no portion of the town that

King Street, looking west from Young Street

presents so striking an appearance of growing prosperity as that in the vicinity of the Baptist Church. Almost within a stone's throw of each other are five palatial residences approaching completion. All are of white pressed brick and built on commanding sites.''

Berlin's merchants and industrialists were part of what was still a very small community. They lived close to their place of work, not segregated off in a single district, but often taking advantage of the rise provided by the sandhills which could offer a view of the growing town as well as a pleasant breeze on a sultry summer's day. Not far from Charles Boehmer's fine home on Benton Street, George Underwood was constructing a one-and-one-half-storey brick home, and nearby Emil Vogelsang had built a large Georgian home close to his Queen Street factory which was less than two blocks from Staebler's house. Louis Breithaupt, too, had built "Waldeck," the first of the Italianate villas in Berlin, near his tannery. With its high tower, deep bracketed eves and rounded windows, it was the model house for the rising industrial and mercantile class in Berlin. The next generation of Berlin's industrial elite would no longer build near their factories and the commercial and municipal leaders would no longer find it appropriate to live above their stores on King Street. The style and fine detail of Breithaupt's "Waldeck" and Staebler's "Buena Vista" clearly

"Waldeck," the Breithaupt residence

illustrated an awareness of new social distinctions, as represented in the latest architectural style, but Breithaupt's location near his tannery equally indicated the tradition and the experience of many of Berlin's leading citizens. By the end of the 1870s Berlin's urban landscape had entered into a transitional phase, represented in more elaborate homes of a more cosmopolitan and sophisticated style, but the sense of community in Berlin seemed to outweigh the obvious social distinctions evident in the new styles of architecture.

The Hailer residence

Social and Political Life

Berlin's urban growth did not create the dramatic social dislocations of some of Canada's larger urban areas where the maintenance of social order and the protection of the public welfare seemed to require endless attention. The common background of the employers and their workers in Berlin softened the social distinctions and racial animosities that might have been caused by an Anglo-Saxon elite ruling over a predominantly German working class. Labour unrest and labour organizations were not in evidence in Berlin, where unemployment was rarely a serious problem. Berlin's workers had also been spared the wild boom in land prices which had occurred in so many other Ontario towns as the shift from artisanal to industrial production took place across the province.[52] The result was that in Berlin a strong sense of community endured.

This is not to suggest that social change and rapid growth of population throughout Ontario had no impact on Berlin's citizens. The arrival of the Grand Trunk in 1856 had clearly ended the social isolation of the earlier years and had brought a sense of sophistication to the village. This was evident in some of the new brick houses, built in the latest style, three-storey brick stores, designed by Toronto architects, and especially in the wide range of goods and services available. As early as 1856 prime oysters could be purchased for as little as $1.50 per keg and a "capital assortment of liquors" and delicacies such as "lobsters, sardines, etc., etc." were offered by John Koch, "which he flatters himself he can serve up in such style as to suit even the most fastidious appetite."[53] In addition to books in English and German, stationery, musical instruments, and Meerschaum pipes, the firm of Baedecker and Steubing had an elaborate collection of over eighty samples of the most stylish wallpapers—"all of which will be found handsome patterns and enduring material"—which they offered for sale to Berlin's residents in 1857.[54]

In the Berlin Medical Hall, Groff and Bell sold a full range of medicines, including many questionable products and such supposed abortifacients as Dr. Clarke's "Female Pills." The primary aim of these and a host of other abortifacients advertised openly in the Berlin *Telegraph* was clearly stated—the "female pills" would "remove all obstructions, and bring on the monthly period with regularity." For those who might feel too embarrassed to call in at Groff and Bell's, Dr. H. Heneburger's "Golden Female Pills" could be purchased by mail. Berlin's citizens were also free to travel to Hamilton where Dr. Davis carried on an extensive practice in "private diseases." Of course, he would also mail his "celebrated Monthly Female Pills" directly to Berlin. But, he warned, "Married ladies who have reason to think themselves pregnant, should not use them, as miscarriage will be the consequence."

The widespread availability of these products in Berlin in 1857 would have been unthinkable only a few years earlier. The village, however, was moving from the isolated pioneer era and in its morals as in its politics the residents of Berlin would be drawn into vortex in Canadian society at mid-century.

Family morals, too, were no longer always the closely guarded secret of the small, country village. In 1857 convictions were brought against two women in Berlin who had failed to register the birth of their "illegitimate" children. The discovery of a case of infanticide in the village also shocked Berlin's citizens. Although it was not uncommon in a city the size of Toronto on occasion to find an abandoned baby at the railway station, it came as a considerable surprise to the foreman of the railway work gang in Berlin who found the dead body of a newly born infant under the platform of the railway station. The mother had been a domestic servant from Germany travelling through Berlin to Preston. The child had come "before its time," born in an hotel room near the station. The mother believed the baby to have been stillborn and she had been told by "her betrothed" that he had taken the child and buried it. Unfortunately, in disposing of the child the "betrothed" had also given it a sufficient blow to the head to have ensured its death. The coroner immediately issued a warrant for the arrest of the "suspected parties."[55] The age of innocence was a thing of the past.

Prostitution was also known to have existed from time to time in most Canadian cities. It became something of a *cause célèbre* in Berlin when the town constable was thought to have assisted an "offending" party and her male consort in their departure from Berlin so that the case would not be tried in court and the names of those local citizens who had frequented the "house of ill repute" would not have to be mentioned in court. The editor of the Berlin *Daily News* was filled with moral indignation and printed this allegation in great detail. The Waterloo *Chronicle* observed, with obvious delight: "The Berlin *News* is going for 'Con' Gerbig the Berlin Town Constable and High Constable Klippert on the charge of favoring the keepers of a house of ill repute in the County Town. It has a promise of a libel suit from the parties who are accused of keeping the said house."[56] A successful libel suit on behalf of the "offended" party was initiated by John King, the father of the future prime minister, and provided entertaining reading for Berlin's citizens throughout the month of December 1879.[57]

These events, however, were all related to influences from outside of Berlin and did not accurately reflect the nature of Berlin's social mores. Crime, criminality, and social unrest were rarely evident. Fisticuffs and failure to turn out for the local militia muster were the most common misdemeanours. Taverns were closely regulated and after 1875 limited to fourteen in number. Indeed the licensing of inns, temperance houses, and taverns was among the first by-laws passed by the village in 1854. It was followed in importance by a tax on the owners of dogs, a by-law to regulate and restrain stock and cattle running at large in the village, and, of course, the appointment of a "fence viewer" so as to ensure that fences were in good order, capable of restraining livestock. By 1878 it was frequently suggested that the danger to citizens walking alone on the streets of Berlin came not from criminals, but from stray cattle roaming freely throughout the town, creating a hazard for unwary pedestrians, and also known to attack the gaily-dressed wives of some of Berlin's leading citizens. The police constable's job was to keep the streets "clean" as much as to keep them safe. In 1874 when the town council reorganized the local police in order to create the office of chief constable, the duties of the constables were detailed. Conrad Gerbig, the town's constable, was also acting "sanitary inspector" and responsible for the shovelling and removal of all snow, ice, and dirt from the sidewalks leading along any property belonging to the corporation.

The town had also legislated for public morals, forbidding the sale of liquor to minors without the consent of parents, and outlawing drunkenness and the uttering of "any profane oath, or obscene, indecent, blasphemous or grossly insulting language"—or, indeed, any other immorality or indecency. Lewd and indecent books were also proscribed. In this omnibus bill of public morals it was also illegal ". . . to keep, maintain or support or be an inmate of or habitual frequenter of, or in any way connected with, or in any way contribute to the support of any disorderly house, or house of ill-fame or other place for the practice of prostitution . . . ." Next among the social evils was horse racing on the public streets, followed by the ills of gambling houses, indecent exposure, and vagrancy:

> . . . all vagrants and mendicants, every common prostitute or night walker, every person winning or losing money or other valuable things . . . and every person pretending or professing to tell fortunes or using any subtle craft, means or device, by palmistry or otherwise to deceive or impose upon any person; each and every person wandering about and endeavoring by the exposure of words and deformities, to obtain and gather alms within the said Town, shall be subject to the penalties of this By Law.[58]

The evils inveighed against were mainly those brought to the community by outsiders. There is no evidence of a moral crusade against social ills within the town by Berlin's religious leaders. The attitude in the community was that these evils were not endemic to Berlin and that the wrongdoers should be encouraged to leave Berlin.

The town's attitude toward the problem of "tramps" or vagrants illustrates this point of view. The poor and the indigent were always thought of as merely "passing through" Berlin. Because of Berlin's relatively isolated location, its strong Germanic character, and the lack of unemployment within its own community, the citizens were perplexed by the arrival in their midst of wandering, unemployed men. Sometimes these "destitute immigrants" were summarily dismissed; most often, however, they were given a night's lodging and a free ticket to the next stop on the Grand Trunk. The municipality had no provision for the "over night confinement" of vagrants other than to house them in the main room of the engine house where, as the standing committee on fire and water reported in 1878, "they had ready access to the fire apparatus, which is thus liable to be tampered with by not overscrupulous hands."[59] At the last council meeting before the Christmas of 1879, a special committee of council dealing with "the tramp nuisance" prepared a report in an attempt "to devise means whereby the number of tramps visiting this town may in some degree be lessened." The answer was to procure a quantity of firewood to be kept near the engine house, and "tramps kept over night at the lock up be made to cut about twenty sticks before breakfast."

With a strong sense of community and few evident social divisions, set amidst a prosperous rural, agricultural setting, Berlin's politics lacked the fractiousness of many municipalities and its municipal leaders were without the flamboyance of some first magistrates in other towns. Berlin's political evolution had been both easy and inevitable. There was no opposition from large landowners such as the Hudson's Bay Company whose properties would now be taxed by a municipal levy, nor were there prominent land speculators seeking to encourage municipal growth in one direction or holding land off the market in the hope of future gains. Berlin's councils did not pursue an elaborate "growth ethic," but proceeded with cautious optimism to create and extend roads and to provide boardwalks throughout the village as they were needed.

It was not surprising that from the beginning municipal politics in Berlin showed a consistently high degree of involvement of merchants and businessmen. Their participation in municipal government seemed quite natural in Berlin, especially in light of the aversion of many of the Mennonite farmers to such activity and the inclination of so many of the German immigrants to settle in an urban environment. This situation differs markedly from some North American cities where "businessmen gained control of the local government only by pushing aside an old and established social elite."[60] The businessmen of Berlin were its first and natural leaders. Almost always of Germanic origin or background, they were supported at the polls by the workers and tradesmen who had chosen to settle in Berlin, drawn to the community because of its strong identity as a place where thrift and enterprise would be rewarded and where business was flourishing.

The lack of organized social amenities or diverse clubs that might have linked Berlin's leading citizens to interest groups outside of the Germanic community merely served to reinforce the position of the merchants and businessmen as the community's leaders. Other than by success in business or politics there were few if any other means to achieve a position of social status. In this sense, Berlin clearly lacked the distinguishing characteristics of many other urban centres in Ontario and its prominent citizens were rarely known outside of their own community.

Municipal politics certainly reflected this sense of a united community. The four wards which constituted the electoral districts remained evenly divided in terms of class and ethnicity. Committees of council were obliged to have representatives from each ward, thereby maintaining a strong sense of community in all of council's affairs. The social life of Berlin largely sustained the sense of a separate community life from the rest of Ontario by emphasizing traditional German pastimes, German theatre, *Turnvereins* or German gymnastic societies. Choirs and traditional German musical societies, encouraged by municipal grants and assistance, had flourished from the first days of Berlin's incorporation as a village.[61]

Opposite page—
Sängerfest, 1886. John King is wearing hat in the front row; Sheriff George Davidson is seated at far right.

As early as 1845 a small band along with a choral group had been organized. By 1853 there was also a Men's Singing Association. In 1856 a German tailor, Heinrich Glebe, along with George Hess, formed the first Berlin band. Shortly after, Wilhelm Kaiser formed a rival musical group, ultimately coming together with the band as the famous Berlin Musical Society which performed regularly and which represented the esprit de corps of the village. The band accompanied the first great excursion train to Toronto in 1856, setting a lively, festive tone. Music was a part of every ceremony and every official function in the village. Dominion Day and Victoria Day were always an occasion for musical displays in which German songs and German lager beer were both much in evidence. German song festivals and singing associations were the hallmark of Berlin's social calendar. In 1862 the first song festival was held, with two hundred singers, bringing together all of the smaller choirs from nearby villages. By 1880 the great singing master Theodor Zoellner, an extremely talented musician, had organized the Berlin Philharmonic and Orchestra Society. Under his direction the Berlin Philharmonic performed the works of European composers: Rossini's *Stabat Mater*, Mendelssohn's *Hymn of Praise* and his *St. Paul*, as well as Handel's *Messiah*. The Concordia Club, founded in 1873, also developed a strong choral tradition, organizing festivals in which as many as eight hundred people took part, bringing together German traditions and providing friendship, familiarity, and a place for young German couples to meet. Music was an important bond in Berlin, drawing together young and old, merchant, industrialist, artisan, and labourer, dissolving pangs of homesickness and providing relief from the toil and ennui of work. It became the common meeting ground for the town. Its symbolic value was recognized in 1875 when the town council decided to build a permanent exhibition building at Woodside, the town park. The building, which would be used to display the town's diverse industrial products, would also be used as a concert hall for the *Sängerfest* of 1875, as well as other music festivals, combining the two great strengths of the German tradition in Berlin.

THE COMING OF AGE, 1880-1912

3

Economic Growth and Urban Development

Augustus Bridle, an Ottawa journalist, stepped down from the train onto the platform of the new Grand Trunk station at Berlin in 1904 and looked around him. Across the street, Hartman Krug's furniture factory extended two blocks. Bridle soon heard Berlin's boosters describe it, in the imperial currency of the day, as the biggest in the British Empire. Perhaps it was, for the impossibility of measuring it merely assured the repetition of the claim. In any case, its bulk alerted Bridle to the dominant impression Berlin left on all visitors. Berlin, Bridle justly remarked, was "a town of smokestacks" which contained "more brick factories than any town or city of its size in Canada." There were other physical distinctions too. "In most big towns and cities factories congest in the extremities, usually the east end. Berlin's are everywhere." The smoke from Berlin's industries, as Bridle observed, floated over the houses "no matter where the wind is."[1] By 1912, as Berlin approached cityhood, it was said that people throughout Canada talked "with amazement" about Berlin.[2] Across the major cities of the west, Berlin "had everywhere a reputation as one of the busiest and most prosperous manufacturing cities of the east."[3] This impression was doubtless spurred on by the more than two hundred commercial travellers, criss-crossing the country, proudly boasting of their community's German character, thrift, and enterprise.

    Quite the opposite had been Berlin's reputation in 1879 when Canada's new minister of finance, Sir Leonard Tilley, toured the manufacturing centres of Ontario to inaugurate the Conservative party's National Policy. Sir Leonard had scheduled visits to London, Brantford, Galt, and Guelph. To the consternation of Berlin's businessmen, Tilley had entirely overlooked their town. After considerable pleading and frantic negotiations,

they persuaded Tilley to come over from Guelph on the Grand Trunk for a brief two-hour visit before proceeding to London.

In Berlin the finance minister toured the town's leading industries: two button factories, two furniture factories, two tanneries, a foundry, a marble works, and a slipper factory. Although Tilley has left no record of his impression of Berlin, one would doubt whether it was particularly favourable. Although the Berlin *Daily News* reported that he was "surprised" and "delighted" by the town's prospects, it would only be under the stimulus of the National Policy that Berlin would be transformed by 1912 to a prosperous, diversified manufacturing centre.

The town would be able to take advantage of growth of the Dominion in the last two decades of the nineteenth century as the west was opened for settlement and as other areas shifted from a rural to a more urban complex. Breithaupt's tannery would continue to be lauded as the largest in the Dominion; before long George Rumpel, who presided over one of the few felt works in Canada, would be described as the "Felt King of the Dominion"; Berlin's button works, unique in Canada, expanded dramatically; while the two furniture companies operating in 1879 were the nucleus of an industry that by 1912 would result in the accolade, the "Furniture Centre of Canada," with more than fifteen furniture companies located in Berlin.[4]

By the time of Berlin's incorporation as a city the number of manufacturing establishments had grown from twenty-two in 1879 to seventy-six, and the number of employees had risen from 896 to nearly 4,000. The economic transformation of Berlin is equally evident as property assessment rose from $650,065 in 1879 to $2,726,396 in 1895, $4,949,384 in 1905, and $10,159,000 in 1915.[5]

Berlin's economic growth, however, did not result in the creation of a new "metropolitan" status for the town; it was rather that Berlin's manufacturers, standing somewhat aloof, saw themselves as competing for a national market with goods and services to be sold across the Dominion. This sense of separateness or distinctiveness was clearly recognized by those who visited Berlin. The Toronto *Mail* in 1886 described Berlin as "A Patch of Old Germany Set Down in the Garden of Ontario,"[6] noting that Berlin's population was overwhelmingly German and that its merchants and industrialists as well as its labourers were almost all of German origin. Berlin's role was that of a dominant German centre where the townspeople in 1886 were busily planning a *Sängerfest* for their exhibition centre and music hall. "It is not surprising to find therefore," noted the Toronto *Mail* "in so important a centre as Berlin, the townspeople are as celebrated for their love of music as for their enterprise in manufacturing and other industries." Nor was it surprising to find that the newly established Board of Trade avidly supported the German *Sängerfests* as being especially good for business, with excursion trains "from all parts of Canada" bringing thousands of visitors to the town.

Sketch of the Berlin skyline, 1883, by W. H. Schmalz

Berlin's continued economic expansion throughout the 1880s caught the attention of the Toronto *Globe* which sought to explain Berlin's "phenomenal growth . . . at a time when Toronto is draining the population of many Ontario towns." The *Globe*'s report set the tone for almost all of the subsequent accounts of Berlin for the next decades:

In these fierce days of competition for the location of factories how is it that Berlin has so many more than her share? The situation of the town is not more favourable for manufacturing than dozens of others in Ontario. There is no water power in the town and the factories are operated with steam. There is no convenient lake, no harbour. Low freight rates come from the proximity of navigable water to a railway line. Berlin has not even the advantage of competing railways. And yet with it all the town is, to use the expression of the commercial who vouched for the truth of his words, "Berlin is the most rapidly growing and liveliest town west of Toronto."[7]

German industriousness, skill, perseverance, and frugality were the factors cited in Berlin's success in establishing a market for its goods in Canada and in retaining its identity as a thriving centre of manufacturing and commerce. The *Globe*'s reporter put it quite explicitly when he observed that as other Ontario towns began to lose population and people swelled the ranks of the unemployed in Toronto and Canada's larger urban centres, "the people of Berlin instead of moving themselves have set themselves the task of moving a city into their midst."

The Berlin Furniture Company

Indeed, the feeling of economic prosperity and a strong sense of community seemed to have made an overwhelming impression on outsiders in 1889. The people of Berlin had "all the conveniences of a city now, water, light, fire protection, street cars, factories, plenty of work for the factories to busy themselves with. The factories are large, built for the expansion of trade, and almost on every street may be heard the rattle of the workman's hammer or the hum of machinery." The *Globe*'s reporter, as were other visitors, was struck by the "large, airy, square-shaped white brick houses—where the workers live" which were being built "everywhere, on all sides." That is the "advantage" of such a town as Berlin, "factories are not too large and the individual has not become a 'hand.'" It also explained the observation of Augustus Bridle. The factories were everywhere and there was no single, dominant industry which overwhelmed the community, dictating both its economic terms and its urban growth which in so many cases resulted in little more than urban squalour. In Berlin, for instance, the two largest industries, the tanneries, in 1886 together employed only one hundred "hands"; the four furniture factories employed only two hundred, and the felt factory employed eighty. The two button factories employed only three hundred. In fact, the largest single employer was the Williams, Greene, and Rome shirt factory which employed two hundred and fifty of Berlin's residents.[8] Significantly, it had recently moved to Berlin from outside of the community and it was generally agreed that, including the employees who did piecework in their own homes, the firm had very quickly reached the maximum number that it could expect to employ from within Berlin.

The presence of a bank in Berlin since its selection as a county seat had given Berlin an advantage over other towns and villages in the county. Prosperous local farmers had deposited their money in Berlin's banks, as well as in its new, but very successful, insurance company, the Economical Fire Insurance Company, which closely identified itself with the fortunes of the town. The Bank of Commerce, located in Berlin since 1879, was said in 1893 to have more than $1 million in savings accounts. In their quest for expansion and development capital, Berlin's manufacturers were especially well served by the local branches of some of Canada's largest banks. The requests for loans inevitably exceeded the local supply of funds and money had to be brought in through the banking system. As one example, the Merchant's Bank in Berlin loaned out $42 million to local industrialists between 1886 and 1900.[9] Berlin's development as a manufacturing centre also led to the establishment in rapid succession of branches of many of Canada's other major banking firms: Bank of Hamilton (1893), Bank of Nova Scotia (1900), Bank of Toronto (1906), and the Dominion Bank (1907).

Berlin's economic growth in this period differed markedly from many other Ontario communities. It had been based largely on an evolution of small local businesses, expanding to take advantage of a growing Canadian market; it had often involved entire families and it was financed primarily by local investment with only the Williams, Greene, and Rome Company and one or two other companies coming to Berlin from outside.

The increase in Berlin's growth—seen here as elsewhere in North America as a sign of progress—had been the result of a number of factors, not least of which was the organization in 1886 of a dynamic, energetic, and shrewd Board of Trade which by 1902 had more than two hundred members. Made up of Berlin's manufacturers and commercial leaders, it vetted new industries, persuaded the town council to grant generous tax exemptions for new buildings as well as additions to existing plants, and sought out local capital necessary for investment in Berlin's industries.

Indeed, the Board of Trade was so assiduous in its scrutiny of firms seeking to locate in Berlin that it frequently turned down more applicants than it recommended to council. With very few exceptions, all of the firms located in Berlin and supported by municipal tax assistance flourished and prospered.

During the 1880s and the 1890s the Board of Trade was especially successful in its promotion of industrial expansion in harmony with Berlin's town council which, as well as tax exemptions, granted municipal bonuses for new companies locating in Berlin. Tax exemptions were routinely given, for instance, to Simpson's and to Hartman Krug's furniture factories, as well as to the Kaufman, Hibner, and Anthes factories. A bonus was issued to the Williams, Greene, and Rome Company, to the J. E. McGarvin Company, and to the Berlin Piano Company. D. Hibner and Company was given a $5,000 bonus to rebuild their furniture factory which had been destroyed by fire. Other prominent and long-established Berlin companies also continued to benefit from the town's generous policy of tax exemptions for existing companies which wished to expand: Rumpel Felt, the Breithaupt and Lang tanneries, the Williams, Green, and Rome Shirt and Collar Company, the Ahrens, Hall, and Simpson furniture companies, C. H. Doerr confectionaries, and Von Neubron's Cigars were among those exempted from municipal taxation in order to assist their companies' industrial expansions. Even when the tax exemptions had expired, industries continued to benefit from the peculiar vision of the town's assessor. In a tax appeal case in 1901, town assessor Janzen testified that he was assessing manufacturers at 50-60 cents per $1.00, fine homes like those of the Kaufmans, Langs, and Breithaupts at 60-65 cents, and others at 80-90 cents.[10] Although this admission undoubtedly caused some stir, it was vigorously defended by the Board of Trade, who argued that without the Breithaupts, Langs, and Kaufmans, workers would have no homes. In their view, Janzen's treatment merely worked to correct the natural advantages and economic incentives which surrounding communities had. It was a case of loyalty to Berlin and a recognition of Berlin's struggle against her competitors in other Ontario towns; it was certainly not thought of as being purchased at the workers' expense.

This close relationship between the Board of Trade and council illustrates a shared belief in the importance of industrial growth for the progress of the community. No conflict of interest was seen to exist between manufacturers and community leaders, for they were often one and the same person. The mayor's chair and the presidency of the Board of Trade were almost interchangeable and the Board of Trade would often add the mayor to one or the other of its committees. In fact council relied heavily on the Board of Trade for advice; rarely were the two in opposition prior to the twentieth century.[11] Nor was it uncommon for the Board to strike its own "ward committees" to assist in getting legislation passed and the names of the town's manufacturing families are ever prominent on such committees. In 1886 Messrs. Breithaupt, Lang, Krug, Staebler, Mueller, and Ahrens were among the Board's members serving on such committees. The fact that these men and their families lived in the wards which they canvassed and were not segregated in discrete residential districts enhanced this sense of community involvement. That they all also spoke German, the language of their employees and of 70 per cent of Berlin's voters made their task all the easier.

Left: Daniel Hibner

Right—
J. C. Breithaupt

The Board of Trade's interests went beyond the industrial expansion of the town: it also proudly sponsored the *Sängerfests* and German cultural events of the 1880s and 1890s. In 1905, the first "Made In Berlin" exhibition, consisting entirely of articles manufactured in the town, was held in the exhibition hall and organized by the Berlin Musical Society.[12] Even the new passenger station from which Mr. Augustus Bridle had surveyed Berlin's industrial growth was a result of the Board of Trade's successful lobbying with the Grand Trunk Railway.

The Board, of course, was concerned with more than just the physical appearance of the station. From the beginning it was obvious that the railway was crucial to Berlin's growth and progress as a manufacturing centre. All of the new industries established in Berlin were dependent on the railway as their presence along both sides of the rail line so graphically illustrated. Even those factories not physically present along the tracks, such as the Williams, Greene, and Rome or the Dominion button works, relied extensively on the railway. The Board of Trade, therefore, took a particular interest in railways, achieving a reduction in shipping rates and parity with neighbouring manufacturing centres. Of all the Board's committees, the railway committee was the most vigorous and the most active.

*The "new" Grand
Trunk Station*

A significant result of the orientation of Berlin's society was that the working conditions in the factories seem to have been relatively less onerous as well as less dangerous than in other industrialized areas. In the beginning employers and employees had worked side by side. The Breithaupts, the Langs, the Rumpels, and the Vogelsangs had certainly shared this experience. Mrs. Rumpel had assisted in the plant; both the Langs and the Breithaupts had taken in boarders from their tanneries and continued to concern themselves with the welfare of their employees. Although wages in Berlin were generally less than those in Guelph or Toronto, the nature of Berlin's diversified industry meant that unemployment was never a serious problem.[13] Nor did Berlin ever experience a wild boom in prices such as Winnipeg did in the 1880s or a major depression as occurred in Hamilton after 1857. Furthermore, the work force in Berlin was limited in number so that Berlin's employers, unlike their counterparts in Toronto and Winnipeg, could not count on an ever-increasing labour supply with workers desperately in need of employment regardless of the conditions of labour or the terms of employment.[14] One Toronto observer, reporting on the industrial development of Berlin in 1889, painted a rosy picture of the conditions of employment and the relations between the workers and their employers:

It is in the evening, however, after the bells have tolled the summons to cease work, that the extent of the industry of Berlin is made evident. Along King Street and down Queen come throngs of work people from the factories, laughing, joking, cheerful and contented. There are many women workers too, not the pale, undeveloped girls of city workshops, but bright, plump, ruddy-faced lasses, who do not feel life a burden and work an unending weariness. But it is not all of history to say, pointing to her prosperous factories, Berlin must be growing rich. There are two sides to the making of wealth. Men do not say, looking at Pittsburg, "Pittsburg is becoming rich," they say "Carnegie is making millions." There is nothing of that in Berlin.[15]

Elsewhere in Canada the 1890s was a decade of economic uncertainty. The movement of population from the countryside into the cities had caused a tremendous sense of insecurity and the transition of the economy from production for a local market to industrial production for a national level had generated a great deal of unrest, especially when in many cases the number of small manufacturing establishments steadily declined as the process of industrialization was matched by the centralization of capital. These changes in the system of production altered forever the lives of the workers and their families. A great deal of these anxieties were vented in the racial and religious antagonisms that came to dominate Canadian politics—in the frustrations of the Orange Lodge and the rhetoric of the Ultra-Protestant, anti-Catholic crusade which existed in many urban areas.[16] Led by the Protestant Protective Association this movement had hoped to unite Protestantism with jobs as a guarantee of economic security.

In the midst of this unrest, the residents of Berlin seemed strangely isolated. Never was this more evident than when the prime minister, Sir Charles Tupper, visited the town in June 1896. Tupper was leading the Conservative party in what was clearly the most difficult election campaign of his career, travelling throughout the urban centres of Ontario urging support for his government's policy of protective tariffs and vainly endeavouring to hold his ultra-Protestant supporters in check over the government's recognition of the rights of the French Roman Catholic schools in Manitoba. His reception in Berlin during that campaign was in marked contrast to the rest of Ontario. Not only was the Manitoba school question deemed insignificant, but Berlin's employers and their employees turned out to welcome him and the Catholic-Protestant antagonism so evident elsewhere in urban ridings was entirely absent.[17] In an amazing display of community spirit a number of "sturdy mechanics" fastened a rope to Sir Charles's carriage and hauled it to the rink along with a procession of seventy-two employees from Williams, Greene, and Rome, seventy men from the Krug Furniture Company, forty from J. Kreiner's furniture plant, one hundred and ten from Daniel Hibner's, eighty from Rumpel's Berlin Felt, fifty from the Berlin Piano and Organ Company, and a number of other smaller firms. It was not without significance that every one of these firms had received a major tax concession or a financial grant as a result of Berlin's factory policy; nor was it at all out of character that the

man greeting Sir Charles on behalf of the community was one of the town's leading industrialists, Mayor J. C. Breithaupt.

Berlin's commitment to industrial growth is also illustrated in the determined way that the community wooed and supported the establishment of Canada's first sugar beet industry in 1901. Early that year the Ontario Agricultural Department had made Berlin a sample district for sugar beet cultivation tests. Before the results were in, several of Berlin's businessmen decided to try to attract Canada's first sugar beet factory to the town. They learned that Bay City, Michigan, was a centre for the sugar beet industry, so S. J. Williams, the president of the Board of Trade, organized a tour to Bay City for politicians, businessmen, and members of the Trades and Labour Council. The trip was successful; all returned lauding the sugar they had tasted and the balance sheets they had read. Williams reported that an American sugar beet company would consider Berlin, but $25,000 and a ten-year tax exemption were necessary inducements. Thus a by-law referendum had to be held. In the campaign, the Board of Trade organized a thorough canvass. The three newspapers and the Trades and Labour Council offered equally enthusiastic endorsements, so it is not surprising that the by-law carried by a remarkable 857 to 196 margin. But the Americans were not yet seduced: Dunnville had also become a suitor. Berlin's charms therefore had to be enhanced. To this end, Williams agreed that Berlin residents would take $100,000 stock in the company. Within a month, the stock was taken, and as Christmas arrived, Berliners had visions of sugar factories dancing in their heads. On December 23, 1901, the managing director of the Ontario Sugar Refinery Company was named: S. J. Williams.[18]

Williams' triumph was widely hailed. A joint labour-business committee called on him with a 475-name petition beseeching him to run for mayor. The Trades and Labour Council declared that no one had done so much so well for the city. But Williams pleaded overwork and refused to run. The petitioners contented themselves with a major banquet which they organized to surprise Williams on his return from a visit to Bay City. Speakers seemed to know only the superlative case; Williams, though, took it well.

The major organizer for the sale of the sugar beet stock issue had been Daniel B. Detweiler, a Mennonite by background and an agent, in the true sense of the word, for leading Berlin businessmen. Detweiler has often been described as a manufacturer, but that term considerably exaggerates his role. What he did was act for others whose crowded schedules did not permit them to organize business ventures or who did not choose to be identified. His pay usually took the form of stock. Thus, in the case of the sugar beet factory, Detweiler got options on stock whose purchase was carried out through loans. In another case, Pollock and Welker simply offered him in stock 5 per cent of the value of the stock he sold. Detweiler was used to commissions and promotions, for he had been a travelling

Opposite page—
Sir Charles Tupper,
Prime Minister of
Canada, 1896
(Notman photograph)

salesman for the J. Y. Shantz button factory and some other Berlin firms in the 1890s. A splendid promoter but a poor financial analyst, Detweiler continually teetered on the fringes of impecuniosity. Respectability was maintained through credit and through the Micawberish belief that something eventually really would turn up.[19]

In 1902 something did. Fresh from the success of the sugar beet company, Detweiler turned to the problem of transmission of power derived from water—what came to be called hydro-electricity. In 1900 Detweiler, E. W. B. Snider, and Jonas Bingeman had organized the Michipicoten Falls Power Company which was intended to produce water power for mining purposes north of Lake Superior. Detweiler had used his government connections to obtain a lease. Writing to C. M. Bowman, M.P.P., on December 14, 1899, Detweiler advised:

> If the government treated as liberally in the matter, . . . I would see to doing quite a bit towards the results of a favorable return in the coming [North Waterloo] by-election. I could interest Martin H. Bowman and one or two other representative Mennonites to get out a full vote as well as a few others in other parts. Without any connection whatever with any association or the parties being able to scent any object of mine. I am sure quite a favorable result would be obtained without any of the machine or any other flavor it. What say you?

Bowman apparently said yes, and Snider, a former M.P.P. himself and a Waterloo manufacturer and miller, became president of the Michipicoten Falls Power Company.

This early experience with power and politics may have been in Snider's mind when in February 1902 he urged the Waterloo Board of Trade to invite neighbouring towns to discuss the acquisition of Niagara power. Technological improvements had made transmission of electricity possible over longer distances, and water power, it was well known, was much cheaper than steam power. This naturally had serious implications for Berlin's factories so dependent on competitive energy rates. Would not factories move to Niagara or elsewhere where they could get this cheap power? The answer might be, bring Niagara here! Berlin or Waterloo could not act alone, unlike Toronto, which might well do so, with disastrous results for the inland communities. To justify and distribute more widely the costs of transmission the inland communities might join together "to secure some special privileges that might not be secured later on." To Detweiler, Snider expressed his belief that "it would have a tendency to greatly facilitate locating new industries in the midst of our several towns if electric power were secured on a satisfactory basis—the sooner the better."[20]

Haste did become necessary when the Toronto syndicate of Pellatt, Mackenzie, and Nicholls gained a power franchise at Niagara that threatened to raise power costs and to assure Toronto control over Niagara power. Moreover, the Pennsylvania coal strike of 1902 affected Waterloo

County industries, warning them of the dangers of foreign supply and of the likelihood of a continuing rise in the price of coal. Even before these events, Detweiler and Snider had organized a meeting in Berlin to which boards of trade, manufacturers, and "leading citizens" from surrounding communities were invited. The gathering drew mainly Berliners, who heard Snider lament the difficulties the inland towns faced. Lacking the shipping facilities of a Hamilton or Toronto, their coal, and thus their energy, cost more. Hydro-electricity might offer a marvellous solution. The Conservative M.P. and manufacturer, George Clare of Preston, was blunter: "Shall we bring the Falls here or shall we move to the Falls?" The rhetorical question was answered by the striking of a committee to consider a co-operative venture to bring hydro inland.[21]

With Snider as chairman and Detweiler as publicist and researcher, this committee organized support throughout 1902. They found much need for energy, but no solution to their problem. The provincial and municipal governments were reluctant to assume the costs of ownership of either production or transmission. It seemed that it would be necessary to work through the private power companies, and this the committee did, negotiating for a guaranteed rate through the offer of a large guaranteed market. Detweiler travelled indefatigably around the countryside in 1902 trying to get the commitment to take power from villages, towns, and industries. By early 1903 he had them, and another meeting was called for February 17, 1903.

This time Berliners were outnumbered by representatives from other major urban centres of Ontario. Mayor Thomas Urquhart from Toronto, and especially Mayor Adam Beck from London, took a dominant role. A resolution was passed urging the Ontario government to build lines for the transmission of electricity to the various towns and cities of Ontario. From this point on Berlin's key role diminished and leadership passed to others. In July 1906 the new provincial government of Sir James Whitney passed an act to facilitate the transmission of power to municipalities such as Berlin. At the same time the government created the Ontario Hydro-Electric Power Commission, soon led by Adam Beck, which established the framework for the distribution of Niagara power through a co-operative, municipally owned, electrical distribution system.

It was fitting that it was in Berlin on October 11, 1910, that the switch was thrown to inaugurate the new hydro-electric system. The benefits to Berlin's citizens and its industries were obvious. Not only had the inception for Niagara power had its origin in Berlin, but of all Ontario's towns and urban areas Berlin had proudly overcome the most obstacles to success in its inland location. Now its industrialists stood poised to take advantage of a new secure and apparently inexpensive source of hydro power.

The growth of Berlin as a manufacturing centre had resulted in a series of boosterish publications extolling the town's attributes and chronicling Berlin's dramatic growth and progress in spite of the lack of

"Power to the People,"
1910

any natural advantages.[22] How to explain Berlin's success was the perennial question as Berliners themselves became avid boosters of their community. Berlin's success was based firmly in the character of its people! In those trying years during the 1880s and 1890s, so the version goes, "the predominating traits of the German character stood them well: Industry without measure; a thoroughness that led them to exhaust every subject necessary to be mastered; and the sheet anchor of thrift. . . . A town full of hustlers is bound to make things move." In H. M. Bowman's eyes it was "the superior quality of the labour to be had in Berlin" that attracted manufacturers to the town "at a time when the town as yet had little else to offer in the way of inducements."[23]

The "Made In Berlin" label affixed to the town's manufactured goods became a symbol of tremendous pride, of triumph over adversity, and indirectly of the superiority of the German character. To this label was added the new epithet of "Busy Berlin"—depicting not just the rush of the many factories but, even more, the workmen of Berlin who, "being German are intelligent, industrious, frugal, . . . living in trim, neat houses and well kept lawns. . . . It follows that the man who loves his home, loves his town. Here is the secret of Berlin's prosperity and steady growth."[24] It was also customary in these publications to note that 70 per cent of Berlin's residents owned their own homes, a further indication of the prosperity of the town and the frugality of its workers.[25]

As a result the citizens "all pull together for the good of Berlin, doing yeoman service and 'spreading the gospel of Busy Berlin.'" This intense loyalty to Berlin created a sense of mystique about the town and about its economic success. It was true, of course, that the habits of community life seemed stronger in Berlin than in many urban centres. It was also true that the town's growth, which was steady but not overwhelming, meant that many of the ills befalling larger cities in Canada were less likely to develop. This gave a continuity and stability that surrounding communities often admired.

It would be wrong, however, to exaggerate the continuity. Berlin's traditional nineteenth-century industries were furniture, shoes and felt, leather goods, buttons, and shirts. During the first part of the twentieth century, the first three expanded moderately, the last two remained fairly stable and, in relative terms, actually declined. Just before the new century began, Berlin's leading industry, rubber, made its first appearance when two local businessmen, George Schlee and Jacob Kaufman, created the Berlin Rubber Company (1899). Four years later, Berlin Rubber's book-keeper, T. H. Rieder led in the formation of another company (Merchants) and in 1907 A. R. Kaufman, Jacob's son, organized his own Kaufman Rubber Company. By 1912 there were three large rubber factories, Dominion Tire, Kaufman, and Merchants; they had become the city's largest employers.[26] Although all had begun through local initiatives, both Dominion and Merchants were part of the consolidation movement in Canada after 1906. In 1907 Rieder left Berlin—with bad feelings—and became vice-president of the Canadian Consolidated Rubber Company of Montreal which incorporated the Merchants and Berlin Rubber Company. Here, for the first time, a significant Berlin industry became externally dominated. The change was noticed and sometimes resented locally.

The rubber industries' location in Berlin derived partly from the entrepreneurial shrewdness of Schlee and Kaufman and the former's visit to Akron, Ohio. But like other Berlin industries, it was a logical offspring of previously established manufacturing activities. What George Schlee saw (and tried on) in Akron were rubber-soled shoes. What Berlin had, of course, was leather, Breithaupt and Lang Tanneries being long-established and thriving industries. For the inside of these leather shoes with rubber soles and heels, Berlin's long-established felt industry could supply soft, warm felt for Canadian winter nights. Thus Rieder, not long after his establishment of Consolidated Rubber, created Consolidated Felt in the fashion of American trust-builders of the age. Later came tires for the automobile and the hundreds of other uses that extraordinary natural material has. Berlin's lower wages for unskilled workers and its transportation links combined to keep rubber in Berlin and Kitchener long after George Schlee's first pair of shoes wore out.[27]

The bulk of the rubber factories came to dominate the industrial area near the Grand Trunk tracks. The owners, however, did not dislodge Berlin's traditional business leaders from their leading community roles. Indeed, although the rubber factories employed the most workers, the leather, button, and felt factories had higher capitalization and financial resources.[28] Their workers regarded themselves as the aristocrats among Berlin workers, because they tended to be skilled and because they were generally better paid. They were the first to organize in trade unions and sometimes, as in the case of furniture, workers like A. G. Schreiter, George Lippert, John Anthes, and Jacob Baetz, became leading businessmen, using the skills their first employer, William Simpson, had taught them. This would not happen with rubber!

To many, the rubber industries' location in Berlin was itself merely the exception that proved the rule and its location in Berlin was the result of Berlin's entrepreneurs rather than the town's location. In most other cases, Berlin had been unable to attract American investment. The Board of Trade had advertised extensively in leading American trade journals in 1910, but had had discouragingly few replies and the terms sought— usually either a substantial bonus or a major stock subscription by Berlin's residents—were so unreasonable that the Board rejected them. As a result, the Board of Trade returned to its original belief that "while every effort should be made to secure outside industries, Berlin's future industrial development must be largely from within."[29] The Board's philosophy had come to reflect the view of its own boosterish publications, that Berlin's greatest resource and its future success lay in its people. In 1911 the Board of Trade's influence was felt as one of its most prominent members, W. H. Schmalz, was persuaded to contest the mayoralty, clearly representing the business interests of the town. Schmalz's overwhelming victory seemed to illustrate the commitment of most of Berlin's citizens to the idea of economic growth. It was with a sense of great pride that the Berlin *Telegraph* lauded the new town council with the observation that "Berlin will have a decidedly representative Council this year."[30] What this meant was not that the new council represented Berlin's class structure, but that it was indicative of the support of the citizens for Berlin's business leaders: "eleven of the fourteen councillors being located during business hours on King Street." Nor would the citizens of Berlin be disappointed in their new mayor and his council. During the next year eight new factories were added and thirteen new additions were completed to existing enterprises, all either owned or controlled "by Berlin's own citizens." As the town fathers prepared their plans for a mammoth celebration in 1912 to mark the attainment of cityhood, the Board of Trade proudly recommended that a "Made In Berlin" exhibition be held at the auditorium in preference to an old boys' reunion, and they were right! Few of Berlin's citizens had gone afar to return to a "homecoming." Berlin's remarkable growth was based on the diversity of its manufacturing industries and the stability of its work force. Its growth had been from within and the pride of its citizens was expressed in the phrase, MADE IN BERLIN.

W. H. Schmalz

Population Growth and Ethnic Relations

In 1902 Prince Heinrich of Prussia, like most tourists visiting the United States, wanted to see the Niagara Falls. He was undoubtedly impressed by the grandeur of the falls and equally surprised by the enthusiastic reception that he received from a delegation of German-speaking Canadians. The prince had momentarily crossed to Canada for a better view of the falls when a group of prominent citizens from Berlin, Ontario, presented him with a leather case containing a photograph of the monument to Kaiser Wilhelm I erected in their town five years earlier. Not able to be present at Niagara Falls, L. J. Breithaupt, the member of the Legislative Assembly for North Waterloo, used the occasion of Prince Heinrich's visit for an earnest statement in the Ontario Legislature of Berlin's Germanic sentiment, evoking the pride of German Canadians in their heritage:

... as a grandson of the late and much beloved Queen Victoria, as a nephew of the reigning King Edward and as a cousin of the popular Crown Prince who recently visited our land, Prince Heinrich is very close to us. He is the representative of a truly great nation, one of the first empires of modern times; and his brother, His Majesty, the German Emperor, is one of the most diligent and progressive of today's rulers. . . . German Canadians are loyal to the British Crown, but no one should begrudge them a few fond memories of their mother country.[31]

Berliners, nearly 80 per cent of whom in 1902 were of German ethnic origin, had in fact become accustomed to celebrate their German inheritance. Both Bismarck's and the emperor's birthdays were occasions for rejoicing and the statue to Kaiser Wilhelm in the town's newly created Victoria Park was a visible focus of these memories of the greatness of the fatherland.

The fourteen-foot memorial was a bronze head-and-shoulders bust, mounted on a granite pedestal. Made in Germany from a model by the sculptor Reinhold Begas, it also featured two reliefs, one of Bismarck, the other of Moltke, attached to the column. The bust was said to have "warmed the heart of many an honest German," especially as it stood resplendent beneath its huge German flag ordered by Kurt Mueller, president of Berlin's German social club, the Concordia Club. The erection of the monument reflected an increased sense of German pride. This Pan-Germanic movement, much like the British imperialism which swept throughout most of Ontario, was a world-wide phenomenon in the 1890s.

The symbolic importance of the monument was strongly supported by Berlin's leading citizens. John Motz, editor of the *Berliner Journal*, and George Rumpel had headed the Kaiser's committee. The mayor, John Christian Breithaupt, and his brother, Louis J. Breithaupt, both made strong speeches at the unveiling of the bust evoking the greatness of the German character and its heritage. To all who heard them the clear impression was that Berlin, not thirty miles from Brantford which Sara Jeannette Duncan was using as the fictional setting for a vivid description of the strength of the "British Imperial idea" in small-town Ontario, was a town with a strikingly different ethnic identity.

The early arrival in Berlin of large numbers of German-speaking artisans, craftsmen, and skilled workers, sustained until the 1870s by continuing immigration from Germany, had resulted in the establishment of an essentially German-speaking urban charter group. From the beginning of Berlin's urban settlement the Anglo-Saxons—including those in the professions—had found it necessary to become bilingual. A young Scottish Presbyterian minister, on arriving in Berlin in 1871, soon discovered that "you heard scarcely anything spoken in the streets but German. It was necessary for anyone living there [in Berlin] to speak both languages." One result of having to learn German, however, he said, was that it "did much to draw the German and the English speaking people together."[32]

The predominance of an established German economic and social elite in Berlin shaped the character of its ethnic relations in a way that was different from other Canadian or North American cities. For one thing, there was none of the sense of the "English getting the best jobs" as was commonly expressed in Winnipeg. In Berlin the Breithaupts, the Langs, the Rumpels, and the Kaufmans, all of German ancestry, were the wealthiest families. Furthermore, the meagre immigration from Germany after 1870 meant that Berlin's rate of urban growth increased slowly, mainly drawing on the rural areas of the nearby counties. As a result, the ethnic balance remained virtually unchanged during the period of industrialization between 1880 and 1912. Just as in the 1850s Berlin had not attracted the unskilled Irish navvies, so in the 1890s it did not get the poverty-stricken peasants who poured into the west with neither training nor skills to start anew in Canada. New arrivals in Berlin from the predominantly German-speaking townships shared the language, religion, and background of the earlier German immigrants. As an urban community Berlin escaped from the racial and ethnic antagonisms when foreign immigrants, changing the ethnic balance of a community, often became the scapegoat for ridicule or were blamed for unhappy economic circumstances not of their making.

Berlin's urban population grew at a rate which allowed civic leaders to provide for the orderly development of municipal services. In 1871 the population had been barely 3,000; by 1881 it had reached 4,000; ten years later it had increased to 7,425 and at the beginning of the twentieth century it stood at 9,696. Such increases, numbering sometimes only one or two hundred inhabitants per year, also tended to reduce strains caused by assimilation. Problems with health or building codes were rarely matters of concern. This was in marked contrast to a city like Winnipeg where, as Artibise has pointed out, working men's budgets were unable to reach even a minimum standard of living and where, in fact, "thousands of families had an inadequate standard of living in an apparently prosperous city," or, more dramatically, in the North End of Winnipeg which was described as "a howling chaos, . . . an endless grey expanse of mouldering ruin, a heap, seething with unwashed children, sick men in grey underwear, vast sweating women in vaster petticoats."[33] Berlin's situation, at least as described by the president of the Board of Trade, was less dramatic. In 1905 Berlin's population was 11,715 and had increased by 1,065 over the previous year, but this was clearly less than the Board had hoped for, and as C. H. Mills explained:

> There is one condition at present existing in Berlin that makes it very difficult for us to attract any very large industry that proposes to bring in with them experienced labour. I refer to the scarcity of homes. Notwithstanding the rapidity with which these have been erected during the past years, from one to two hundred per year having been built, it is today almost impossible to secure a house of any kind to rent.[34]

The demand for homes was clearly exceeding supply by 1907, and the housing shortage became a persistent concern of local councils. There were 275 new houses built in 1907, but the town's population grew by 932. By 1912 land values in the city had risen 50 per cent over their 1907 level. Speculators, contractors, and realty companies now began to compete to open up new areas of the city. Traditionally, Berliners had directed the building of their own houses, usually bartering skills or goods with friends or neighbours in exchange for other skills or material. By 1910, however, contractors were building homes in bunches into which families could move. The newspapers abounded with advertisements which stressed the ease with which a family could acquire a home. Modest six- or seven-room homes on the fringes of the old city in the East or West Wards sold for from $1,400 to $1,800. This was already too much for some Berliners who lived in conditions city assessor William Cairnes described as "scandalous," "unsanitary," and "repulsive." As many as six families inhabited a single home, and yet there was much vacant land held for speculative purposes. Because of favourable taxation treatment, there was not much incentive to develop these lands quickly. Hold out for more next year was familiar and unfortunate advice.

It was only in 1911 that the population rose to more than 15,000 the number necessary for city status. On July 17, 1912, when Berlin finally celebrated its position as Ontario's newest city, it was said to be the only town in Ontario that had waited until the statutory limit of 15,000 had been achieved. It was thus entirely appropriate that Berliners should take pride in the fact that they alone had achieved incorporation as a city on their own merits and not by virtue of special legislation.[35]

In this, as in the use of German throughout the town, Berlin continued to see itself as different from other Canadian urban centres. The maintenance of the German language had not been sustained by large numbers of immigrants from the fatherland as it had been in earlier decades. Nor was it encouraged by the presence in Berlin of distinguished German visitors, none of whom seemed even aware of the existence of this proud German colony within the midst of Canada. Those German tourists, like Prince Heinrich of Prussia, were primarily interested in seeing the United States, although some went on to visit Montreal and Quebec City, attracted by the European-like atmosphere of rural Quebec. Alas, Berlin seems not to have been mentioned or noticed in nineteenth-century German travel literature.[36] Berliners, however, were not daunted by this; in a sense, like so many other Canadians, they were seeking an identity which, although Canadian, would link them second-hand to the glories and to the adventure of empire, and this was only heightened by their sense of isolation.[37]

If there was one single force that accounted for the continued pre-dominance of the German language in Berlin, it was Berlin's role as a religious centre for the German community. "The retired German farmers

Opposite page—
Urban growth, King
and Water Streets

came to Berlin, as a father with a fortune and boys to educate takes up residence in Kingston or Toronto," wrote one commentator. "A very large number of the residents of Berlin are retired merchants and farmers, attracted by the fact that it [Berlin] is the [religious] headquarters" for the Lutheran, Mennonite, and Evangelical congregations for whom the use of German was very nearly an "article of faith."[38]

For the Lutheran Church, which in 1891 claimed 40 per cent of Berlin's residents as its adherents, the language question was at the very heart of belief. The German ethnic identity and the church were complementary parts; and "by continuing to speak German to their God, they [the churches] preserved the German language for their children long after they had begun to communicate with each other in English."[39]

St. Jerome's College with Mayor Aaron Bricker and the Reverend Theobald Spetz at the laying of the cornerstone of the new college buildings, 1907

Interestingly, Berlin's Roman Catholics, who made up the second largest religious group (nearly 20 per cent of Berlin's population in 1891), while not sharing Luther's theology, nonetheless contributed greatly to the maintenance of Berlin's ethnic identity. Roman Catholic missionaries had returned to Germany to raise money for the "German orphans" in nearby St. Agatha, and Catholic Church organizations in Munich and Vienna had supported local congregations. But it was the location of St. Jerome's College there in 1865 which established Berlin as the centre for German Catholic education in Canada that settled the matter. Under the direction of priests of the Congregation of the Resurrection, St. Jerome's College became the centre for the training of young German-speaking Catholics for the priesthood. Indeed, under the leadership of Father Louis Funcken, by 1879 the seminary was producing sufficient numbers of strong candidates for the priesthood to have been considered a success by Archbishop Lynch of Toronto who left the education of the German priests to the direction of Funcken in Berlin.[40] As a result, even within the Catholic Church, the German community remained very much enclosed and set apart from the main currents of the English-Canadian experience. The Roman Catholics, however, did not view the use of German as a cultural tradition to be preserved but rather as a means of communicating with their parishioners. By 1911, as the use of the German language became less common, sermons in the Roman Catholic churches were regularly preached only in English. Baptists and Methodists, too, had originally conducted their services in German. Even in 1901, nearly 80 per cent of the town's population still worshipped in the German language. It was only in the first decade of the twentieth century that German as a language of worship began gradually to be replaced by English.[41]

Elsewhere in Ontario the 1890s marked the outpouring of a British imperialistic spirit or *Zeitgeist*, which saw Canadians revelling in Rudyard Kipling's tales of empire or glorying in the adventures of British missionaries in far-off Africa. This cult of Empire was also reflected in Berlin, but with a notable difference. Under the leadership of Pastor von Pirch, the Prussian-born son of a nobleman who served as the minister of St. Peter's Lutheran Church, an attempt was made to instill a proper German nationalistic spirit within Berlin instead of a sense of the glory of the British Empire. In 1886 von Pirch became involved in the publication of a strident and aggressively German newspaper, the *Freie Presse*. Concerned about the growing international dislike of Germany, the paper suggested that the only way to counter such hostility was for Germany to become a strong, united nation. Significantly, the *Freie Presse* was not well received in Berlin and was forced to discontinue publication after two years. Its militant attitude was too extreme for many of the older settlers as well as for many others who were now second- and third-generation Canadians and who did not wish to remain a race-conscious minority.[42]

In 1891 a group of prominent German Berlin businessmen began the publication of the *Deutsche Zeitung*. The *Zeitung* intended to set a high literary standard to combat the decline of the German language as well as to present information on German events and personalities in the fatherland. German festivals and celebrations were extensively reported; the birthdays of Emperor Wilhelm II and Bismarck were treated as special events. Like the *Freie Presse*, its editorials recognized a growing dislike of Germany in some parts of the world and resented the "English nativism" which existed in Canada and which it countered "with all the vigor it could muster."

But the *Zeitung*, too, despite the backing of von Pirch and such leading businessmen as George Rumpel, Casper Heller, Henry Gildner, and Joseph Emm Seagram, was doomed. Its exaggerated emphasis on the maintenance of the German cultural atmosphere in the face of a younger generation who had not known Germany, who could no longer read German easily, and whose only experience of life had been in Canada made its failure inevitable. Other German newspapers in the surrounding hinterland of Waterloo and Bruce Counties also found their subscriptions waning and circulation faltering. Only the *Berliner Journal* would survive this period and even then only by amalgamation with other German papers such as the *Ontario Glocke* of Walkerton. Unlike the *Freie Presse* and the *Deutsche Zeitung*, the *Berliner Journal* eschewed all forms of intense German nationalism and instead developed a tradition of concern for the German Canadians. It was a German paper with a pronounced local flavour reflecting what was the reality of the Canadian experience.

By 1912 only 8.3 per cent of Berlin's population had been born in Germany although some 70 per cent were German by ethnic origin. German immigration had slowed to a mere trickle in the later decades of the nineteenth century, and Berlin had never attracted those intellectuals or professionals who represented the rising wave of German nationalism elsewhere. The German immigrants coming to Berlin had been mainly farmers, craftsmen, labourers, and artisans. As a result, one author has suggested that, "although a semblance of spiritual contact with Germany was maintained by newspapers [singing festivals and German choirs], a predominantly Canadian character also manifest itself early in their development. This early preoccupation on the part of the German newspapers with the Canadian scene was a prelude to the process of fusion and assimilation of the German minority."[43] This was conditioned by the composition of German settlements such as Berlin "in which it was difficult to maintain the element of racial solidarity because of a lack of intellectual leadership." Heinz Lehman put the matter quite explicitly when he declared: "The stream of educated individuals from Germany which migrated to the United States after 1848, and there became the leaders of the German community, found no counterpart in Canada, so that there was here always a complete lack of intellectual leaders from their own circles."[44]

The other problem, of course, had been that the Ontario school system, particularly under the administration of George W. Ross, had made it increasingly difficult for German instruction to be available in the public schools. As Minister of Education and an enthusiastic British imperialist, George Ross had made certain that English would be the predominant language of instruction. Legal changes to the Ontario Education Act in 1885 and 1889 had made English obligatory in all schools and by the 1890s English was the language of instruction throughout Ontario, including Berlin.

Ross's legislative changes came at a time when most students in Berlin were second-generation German Canadians and when the common language in the streets of Berlin was a form of German known colloquially as Pennsylvania Deutsch or Pennsylvania German.[45] In addition, English was the language of commerce, of law, and of the town's daily newspaper. It was, therefore, not the obvious strength of the German linguistic tradition, but instead its near demise by 1900 that led a commission headed by three of Berlin's German clergymen—Pastor von Pirch, The Reverend F. Friedrich (Baptist), and The Reverend C. H. Tafel (Swedenborgian)—to attempt to stem the further erosion of the German language. A protest rally was held in the Berlin Town Hall in June 1900 and a German School Association was founded "to safeguard the rights and privileges of the Germans in regard to the retention of their mother tongue."[46] Speakers such as L. J. Breithaupt emphasized the advantages of being multilingual in a cosmopolitan business world; von Pirch "repeatedly emphasized the rights of German Canadians to be taught in the language of their choice as one of the fundamental human freedoms of the new world"; others pointed out "that more children of English parents were attending German classes than those of German descent" and that it was "not necessary to forget German to learn English." The German School Association, in concert with the Berlin school board, developed a programme of special language classes. Attendance rose dramatically: in 1900, 166 students had been taking German-language instruction; by 1904 this number had increased to 550, and in 1911 it was reported that 1,300 out of 1,600 students attending Berlin's public schools were now enrolled in German-language classes. Two features of this phenomenon are of special significance: the German School Association had the visible, active support of Berlin's business leaders; and many students who participated in the German-language programme were of Anglo-Saxon descent, for the German tradition in Berlin was by no means racially exclusive.

Victoria Park, 1898

Berlin's Germans had always been proud of the consanguinity of the German and the British empires and this had legitimatized their emphasis on German ethnicity. When Queen Victoria died in 1901, Berliners mourned their monarch, and leading citizens organized a fund to build a statue to honour that most remarkable queen. Nothing seemed more distant than a conflict between the British and German empires. Naturally the statue of Victoria would stand in the new Victoria Park; and there it would look upon the bust of one of her favourite relatives, Kaiser Wilhelm I. Berliners could see no difficulty in dual loyalties, as was clear in the speech of L. J. Breithaupt, on Victoria's death:

> Teuton and Saxon have clasped hands over the bier of her we mourn. Well also may old North Waterloo, the most German constituency not only in Ontario but in Canada, and, by the way, I think it is safe to say the most German constituency under the British flag and whose county seat is called after Germany's capital feel proud with the old Fatherland itself at the reception and welcome accorded the German Emperor [at the queen's funeral in London].[47]

Breithaupt's dual loyalty seemed particularly appropriate and reflected the reality of ethnic relations in Berlin, where there had never been any doubt that to be German in a British Empire reigned over by Victoria was also to be a good Canadian. Berlin's publicity, like that of Canada itself, pointed to the advantages of two cultures, and there is every indication that most Berliners believed it.

Anglo-Saxon and German alike had thrived as Berlin grew in numbers. Perhaps the Toronto *Mail* best expressed this sentiment in 1886: "There is not in the Province of Ontario a name that more fully conveys the idea of energy, push and business tenacity than that of Louis Breithaupt—[who] was born in Allendorf, Kurhessen Germany."[48]

It is clear that as Berlin approached incorporation as a city a complex relationship had developed between ethnicity, wealth, and power. Unlike most of its southwestern Ontario neighbours, Berlin was not dominated economically, socially, and politically by a British elite. And yet Berlin, like its neighbours, revealed a greater influence of the British than sheer

"Forest Heights," built by Sheriff George Davidson; later the residence of the Rumpel family

numbers would justify. This was especially true in the professional life of the community and in the social notes of the newspaper. It was also true that most of the British in Berlin spoke German and quite willingly encouraged their children to do so. Germans in Berlin took pride in the fact that their countrymen held the highest offices, lived in lavish houses, and led in the economic transformation of their town. One doubts that they sensed that their part in the community was defined within a narrower compass than their Anglo-Saxon neighbours in other Ontario towns. As one author has observed, "What is chiefly interesting . . . is how such a typically 'Canadian' community could evolve from a settlement so completely 'foreign' in its people—their customs, speech, religion—in almost every respect."[49] Berlin was very much a part of the Ontario environment that surrounded it, its architecture, its capitalism, its labour unions, its reformers, and its optimism; yet in each case, Berlin's expression of these qualities was subtly altered by its peculiar ethnic structure. In the halcyon days of Berlin's imminent rise to become one of Canada's newest cities these deviations seemed merely eccentric. In wartime, they could become the catalyst for confrontation.

King Street looking east from the railway tracks

The Urban Landscape

The decade of the 1880s brought significant changes in Berlin's urban landscape. In 1887 the only vacant lot in the original settlement along King Street was filled when the Economical Fire Insurance Company—which numbered Berlin's most prominent citizens among its directors—built its new office at the corner of King and Foundry Streets. The streetscape was now a continuous row of shops, factories, institutional and commercial buildings. By 1890, the old buildings from Berlin's early years had all but disappeared. There was now little tangible evidence of the pioneer era.

The handsome clapboard home on King Street of Bishop Benjamin Eby, who had been responsible for so much of the early growth of Berlin, had been demolished in 1879. In 1885 C. A. Ahrens tore down the Stroh property on Queen Street—built in 1835 and once considered to be one of the finest homes in the village—to make way for a shoe factory. In the same year the Breithaupt Leather Company purchased the Klippert estate on

Some Directors of Berlin's Economical Mutual Insurance Company

Queen Street North in order to build a three-storey shoe factory near the original intersection at King and Queen Streets. Then, in 1889 J. C. Breithaupt bought the home of Jacob Hailer at King and Scott Streets. It was in 1834 in this house that Catherine Hailer, the first child of the new German immigrants, had been born in Berlin. She had witnessed the remarkable growth of the village and it was Catherine Hailer as the executrix of the estate of her late husband, Louis Breithaupt, who had become the wealthiest landowner in Berlin. With the purchase of the original Hailer property by her son, J. C. Breithaupt, the forces that had influenced the changes in Berlin had come full circle.

King Street, turn of the century

Material comforts, too, came to be part of life in the new, modern Berlin. Local improvements such as street lighting and sidewalks, paved roads, water and sewage systems were integral parts of Berlin's urban growth. The hallmark of Berlin's streets for the next three decades was mud, mud everywhere as streets were dug up to install the waterworks system (1898), gas and electric services (1903), the street railway (1888), and sewers (1891). By 1900 both Queen and King Streets had been macadamized, but the residents of Berlin's fashionable centre ward still had to make do with muddy roads and gravel streets. By the time of the attainment of cityhood in 1912, macadamized streets and cement sidewalks had been built in the residential areas near the centre of the town, and the business district along King Street was paved with bitulithic asphalt, a far cry from 1880 when merchants petitioned to have the dust controlled by watering the street. By 1912, too, more than 75 per cent of Berlin's residents had been connected to the sewage system, "town water" was available to all, and the latest tungsten electric lights were planned for every street as a result of Berlin's inexpensive supply of Niagara power. Transportation had also improved dramatically. The town's own street railway now ran on a double track along King Street to neighbouring Waterloo, with a spur line to the Grand Trunk station. And the automobile was already making its presence felt as Berlin's progressive citizens had begun to replace their carriage sheds by "adding small garages for automobiles" to their houses.[50]

The City Beautiful movement had come to Berlin in 1896 with the creation of Victoria Park. Berlin's citizens could now while away their afternoons sitting on the "shores" of its artificial lake on the site of the farm of Joseph Schneider, the Mennonite pioneer who had settled on this land in 1807. There, according to the descriptive phrases of a 1912 publication, lovers pledged their troths beside old bridges (built only a few years before), and "old memories" lingered "where the shades and foliage pleases."[51]

However delightful Victoria Park may have been in a town with so few other natural amenities, it was Berlin's factories which would come to dominate the urban setting of the town. It would not be the beauty of the park, but a vast panoramic view of factories that would be chosen to illustrate the frontispiece of the town's special publication, *Berlin 1912: A Celebration of Cityhood*. This photograph, covering two full pages, looks down the track of the Grand Trunk Railway, over factory rooftops in all directions, stretching as far as the eye could see. Along Berlin's streets were rows of large, white brick homes, of a distinctive vernacular style, each home standing on its own property with shade trees in front and fruit trees in the rear garden. Such was the picture of urban life in Berlin taken on Dominion Day, 1912.

Perhaps because Berlin lacked outstanding natural landmarks, visitors to the town were struck by the predominance of the factories. A reporter for the Toronto *Globe* who arrived in Berlin in August 1889 took his readers on a tour, factory by factory, along the route of the Grand Trunk to King Street from Breithaupt's tannery, to Brown and Witting's slipper factory, to George Rumpel's Berlin Felt Company, to Hartman Krug's furniture factory, and as the reporter traversed the tracks came the following description of Daniel Hibner's furniture factory: ". . . farther up the track is located the commodious three story and basement, 100 × 100 feet, white brick premises of D. Hibner & Co. . . . A visit to this establishment, fitted up as it is with new and improved machinery, is a real treat to all interested in the progress of advancing mechanical ingenuity."[52] Many Berliners seemed to share this fascination with the growth of factories as a symbol of their town's urban progress.

The increase in Berlin's factories—whether one accepts the number of 76 as listed in the Dominion Census for 1911, or 120 as Berlin's boosters chose to record in their publication describing Berlin's achievement of cityhood—had left an irrefutable imprint on the urban landscape. Most of the factories followed close to the Grand Trunk's tracks through the town, but there were many exceptions, including Berlin's largest employer, Williams, Greene, and Rome, a shirt manufacturer. Other firms maintained their locations along King Street and on the Queen-Courtland intersection which they had taken up many years before.

Industrial Berlin, from the Margaret Street Bridge

Although there were fewer factories in 1901 than there had been a decade earlier, the decrease reflects consolidation rather than economic decline. The factories that remained had swollen to embrace expanded activity, and this was reflected in their architecture. The characteristic factory building was a three- or four-storey brick structure with two or three distinct segments; its clean bricks beside grimy older ones reflected the enlargement of the original plant. Adaptations to new technology—for example, steam—often created protuberances which denied the buildings a regular configuration. Although many of the Berlin manufacturers were Germans, they expressed little of the distinct and rather formalistic industrial architecture of the fatherland; as in their houses, they followed the general North American pattern. One observer has noted some continental European influence upon brickwork, but one should not make much of this.

The expansion of industrial growth between 1880 and 1912 changed Berlin's urban landscape in other, more subtle ways. Most obvious was the creation of a new exclusive residential district in the Centre Ward and equally a working-class district in the North Ward. The new Centre Ward became the showplace for the homes of the industrialists, professionals, and mercantile leaders whose wealth had been largely created by the growth of commerce and industry. Queen Street North, framed by the Court House and the spires of the newly completed (1906) St. Andrew's Presbyterian Church, provided an attractive entrance to the area where the busy atmosphere of commerce and industry could be replaced by the dignified splendour of Ontario's High Victorian architecture.[53] Within the confines of a district bounded by Weber, Lancaster, Frederick, and Victoria Streets lived merchants and managers, doctors and lawyers. Members of the town's most prominent families—Breithaupt and Lang, Anthes and Ahrens, Boehmer, Hibner, Bowlby, and Clement—all resided there. So, too, did A. R. Kaufman, T. H. Rieder, Harvey Sims, Peter Hymmen, and John Motz. By and large it was generally only the older generation of industrialists such as Jacob Kaufman, George Rumpel, Charles A. Ahrens, George C. Lang, S. J. Williams, and Hartman Krug who continued to reside outside of this district in the prominent homes they had built before the Centre Ward had become so fashionable. Still others chose to reside in the area near Victoria Park.

E. Vogelsang and Company, Button Factory

Centre Ward, turn of the century

The August Boehmer residence, Queen Street North

The whimsy and eclecticism of High Victorian residences overflowed the newer streets of the Centre Ward. In Berlin, as elsewhere, High Victorian architecture, with its lavish ornament, soaring turrets, and free-spirited pattern, spoke "loudly of an age of buoyant personalities, fabulous enthusiasm, prosperity, and plenty."[54] These were, of course, the homes of the mason become contractor, the storekeeper become merchant, the "men of substance" of the town. There was little of the vernacular left; even the German contractor-mason Caspar Braun built a home whose façade would have fitted indistinguishably into the riot of High Victorian on any Ontario street. Occasionally there would be lingering traces of a local vernacular which the acute observer could find, but, generally, Berlin's architecture was distinguished from other Ontario towns by what it did not have rather than in any striking cultural adaptation of Ontario's style. The British influence, which left a legacy of "regency" or "Ontario" cottages throughout other urban centres in Ontario, was generally missing. So, too, was the Ontario Gothic style with its high-pitched gable and delightful vergeboard. Such a style, of course, requiring a sense of space, may have seemed out of keeping with the industrial growth of Berlin. Similarly, the Second-Empire style, with its mansard roof and dormer windows so prevalent elsewhere in the province, was conspicuously absent except in one or two isolated examples.

The A. J. Kimmel residence, Ahrens Street East

It is in the less affluent, working-class districts such as the North Ward that Berlin's vernacular or indigenous style developed. "The proportion of wooden homes is very small comparatively," wrote an early commentator; "in a very few years the town will be built almost entirely of white brick, and the white brick buildings are in most cases owned by the inhabitants."[55] On street after street these homes appeared—one-and-three-quarter, two, and sometimes three storeys in height. Perhaps in keeping with the styles in Germany, where land was scarce and urban houses frequently two and three storeys high, the dimensions of these homes seemed to emphasize their height. They were solid, practical homes, with a large kitchen added at the rear and either a verandah or a "stoop" at the front entrance. There was none of the "aspiring, imaginative feeling" often associated with the Gothic, pointed styles of architecture. Nor did they have the solid, rustic appeal of contemporary communities such as Galt or Guelph which had been settled by Scots. The homes of Berlin's workers were plain, unadorned, and generally often lacking even such modest detailing as return eaves to balance the main gable or façade facing the street. But airy and spacious they were, on lots with sixty-foot frontage and still with adequate depth for large vegetable gardens in the rear. Row housing, which had become a common feature of many Ontario towns, had little appeal in Berlin.

King Street's architecture, concealed behind a cluster of wires, awnings, and false façades, also remained uninspiring. The monotony was only occasionally broken by an interesting remnant of a less hurried time such as the fine late Victorian Walper Hotel (1892-93). Berlin's main street was seldom, in this period, a familiar subject for the photographer's lenses or the booster's rhetoric.

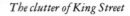

The clutter of King Street

Despite the obvious residential character of the Centre Ward, where so many of the industrial and commercial elite now resided, Berliners continued to proclaim that "strictly speaking there is no residential district as accepted in other cities."[56] And certainly the lack of natural boundaries between Berlin's wards and the fact that the wards had not been designed to reflect economic or social distinctions meant that economic or class divisions in Berlin were less apparent than in many other urban centres. The boundaries of the Centre Ward went far beyond the "exclusive" central residential district, which made up only a part of the ward. Furthermore, despite the wealth of many of its residents, both Queen Street North and Frederick Street remained natural routes from the commercial centre on King Street to the working-class residences in the North and East Wards. Even within the Centre Ward there were anomalies which juxtaposed very inexpensive housing side by side with the homes of some of Berlin's most prominent industrialists. For example, on Ahrens Street, less than a block away from Charles Boehmer's fine High Victorian residence was a very modest brick home selling in 1912 for $1,800, less than the price of many working-class homes in the North Ward. Similarly, on Queen Street North, across the street from "Sonneck," L. J. Breithaupt's prestigious estate, was John Dauberger's small frame cottage. Dauberger, a brick mason by trade, had subsequently built a larger, neo-classical home on the same side of the street as "Sonneck," but the continued existence of such housing did not seem entirely out of place in Berlin.[57]

The location of Berlin's factories, dispersed throughout the town, also influenced the pattern of working-class housing. Lacking any single, dominant industry, Berlin had not developed an overwhelmingly working-class district. Nor does there appear to have been any serious discrimination in the provision of social services to the various wards. The small size of Berlin was also a factor: in 1912 more than 90 per cent of the population lived within a one-mile radius of the centre of town and their place of work. Similarly, the central location of Berlin's churches drew residents to the centre of town, rather than segregating them into particular wards. There was no decay of entire sections of the town, no clear segregation on the grounds of class or ethnicity. Instead, a sense of place, even of homogeneity, was maintained.

Few of Berlin's workers would have been so awe-inspired by the magnificence of the industrialists' homes as to feel that similar homes would not be within their own grasp in the future. The leading merchants and industrialists were, after all, not unlike themselves. Instead of jealousy or envy, "Boys in humble homes," as one early author stated it, "[could] draw inspiration from the lives of the early manufacturers."[58] They worshipped at the same churches, be they Lutheran, Roman Catholic, Swedenborgian, Evangelical, Presbyterian, or Anglican, and many of the older industrialists lived near their places of work, albeit in the more lavish architectural styles of the period. A. L. Breithaupt still resided at "Waldeck," the great Italianate villa on Adam Street in the North Ward near the tannery, while J. M. Schneider had moved to Queen Street South in "Buena Vista," the Italianate villa built by J. M. Staebler not far from Courtland Avenue where Schneider had first begun making sausages in the basement of his home. These businessmen were conspicuous examples of what initiative, perseverance, and energy could accomplish and they kept alive a sense of community in Berlin long after the economic and social results of industrialization had created deep divisions in many other urban communities. For as Berliners themselves proudly boasted, there were no sections in the town where grand homes might not be found.

Society and Politics

With sleighbells silenced, at 1:00 A.M. on Saturday, February 11, 1905, the Berlin police raided a house of ill-repute on Lancaster Street near the

Bridgeport hill. The house was said to have been frequented by large numbers of men—"some of whom are well known in Berlin and Waterloo, while men from outside towns would come to Berlin with a view to 'paying a call.' "[59] When Berlin's crown attorney, W. H. Bowlby, refused bail to the "keepers and inmates" of the house and determined to press charges, "the frequenters of the place became alarmed. It was said that there was a hurrying and scurrying around among many of those known to have been seen at this house of ill fame, in order to get the prisoners to plead guilty and prevent these frequenters from being summoned as witnesses." Needless to say, when the case came before Police Magistrate Weir the "prisoners" quickly pleaded guilty; the fine for Mr. and Mrs. Joseph Crout (alias Phillips) as "keepers" of the house was $25 and costs and the four inmates $10 and costs. Local onlookers at court that day left "asking one another— 'where did the money come from?' " and the *Telegraph* announced that the keepers and inmates of the house—all of whom were said to be Americans—"Must Leave Town."

Berlin's civic officials

The "Lancaster Street episode" as it came to be known provides a clear insight into the Victorian morality of Berlin's society. Unlike frontier cities such as Vancouver or even Winnipeg, where a transient population and a predominance of males created a social environment in which the liquor trade and prostitution flourished, no such licentiousness was permitted in Berlin. But the drama of the late-night raid on Lancaster Street heightened the awareness of Berlin's citizens that their town in many respects still saw itself as a country village. The "bell-less" sleigh which allowed the police to nab the wrongdoers had had to be rented at a local livery, for the town had no patrol wagon and no means to transfer "a number of men and women under arrest to the town lock-up." Despite this flurry of activity, Chief O'Neill and his four constables felt that they could continue to maintain law and order without any difficulty, and the chief reported annually thereafter that "The town is free from houses of ill fame so far as I know."[60]

The Bar, Grand Central Hotel, owned by Joseph Zuber

Law and order seemed little affected by Berlin's urban growth and increased population.[61] Burglaries and thefts were few and usually quite trifling. Murder and suicide were almost unheard of. Even liquor-related offences were remarkably rare in staid Berlin. In 1911 six people were convicted of being drunk and disorderly on the town's streets, one for being drunk "on the Indian list," and forty convicted of vagrancy. One hundred and two people had also been taken to the lock-up as being drunk and incapable, but "released when sober."

Health care, too, seemed comparatively simple. Cases of both scarlet fever and diptheria had been reported, with seven deaths resulting, but cases of both typhoid fever and tuberculosis were negligible. The cornerstone of the Berlin hospital had been laid in 1894 and a women's auxiliary headed by the wives of the town's prominent citizens—Mrs. George Rumpel, Mrs. George Lang, Mrs. Catherine Breithaupt, Mrs. A. F. Bauman, Mrs. H. E. Lackner, and Mrs. E. P. Clement—had been active since 1895. By 1911 plans were underway for the creation of an isolation ward, but there is no evidence of any serious health or sanitary problems. For all intents and purposes, Berlin was a solid, sombre town of healthy and frugal factory workers and apparently the only vices were private ones. Public health and public morality seemed secure.

The Berlin Orphanage, Reverend C. R. Miller and Wards (Public Archives of Canada, PA 120926)

In its political life, too, Berlin lacked the flamboyant leaders of many larger urban communities. In its early years Berlin's councillors and its mayors had been the town's leading businessmen, merchants, and professionals and they shared a common view of their duty. They were "practical men," seeing themselves as agents of improvement and convinced that material progress was necessary and that it was measurable in terms of sustained growth. This could be best assisted by encouraging industrial development through a benevolent policy of favourable tax assessments or outright tax exemptions in return for the creation of employment for

Berlin's workers. Little thought was given to the effects of industrialization on the town's inadequate water supply or its precarious sewer system, let alone to the social impact of industrialization on Berlin's residents.[62]

Beginning in 1900, however, these issues would come to the fore. This potential conflict was heightened by a new provincial statute in 1902 which made the financial incentives to industries which had been an integral part of Berlin's philosophy subject to ratification by two-thirds of the eligible voters (the franchise in this case being restricted to those who owned property). While the statute was aimed at preventing the "bonusing" of companies by rival town councils, it had a distinct psychological impact on Berlin, where the businessmen and particularly the Board of Trade had always felt it necessary to obtain special assistance from the municipality in order to offset the "natural advantages" of other towns. It is not without a little irony that this same perception was shared by Berlin's labour leaders, the Trades and Labour Council, although not by all of Berlin's voters. After 1902 it became almost impossible to pass by-laws offering financial assistance to new industries,[63] and the owners of local companies whose tax exemptions were due to expire began to get nervous. The man who made them especially uneasy was one Allen Huber, destined in 1908 to become Berlin's most outrageous mayor.[64]

By 1900 Allen Huber had become a gentleman—that most ambiguous occupational category—after a career as a salesman for Berlin's industries. One could not have found a more enthusiastic booster of "Busy Berlin" than Huber, and his enthusiasm took him even to China and Japan to seek markets for Berlin's goods. When he returned to Berlin at the turn of the century, however, he found a town unlike that which he had remembered and promoted. He lost some of his enthusiasm, and in doing so, began a most peculiar political career.

Huber was quite successful in his career abroad, and he garnered enough commissions to enable him to retire to Berlin about 1900. Almost immediately he began to denounce some of those same businessmen whom he had previously served. He claimed that Berlin's businessmen were using the town's political system and were stirring up civic pride to serve their own interests, not those of the community in general. For Huber the proof of this assertion lay in the Williams, Greene, and Rome tax controversy of 1900-01 when the company's refusal to pay taxes was accepted by the town. To express his opposition Huber turned to Berlin civic politics, and in 1901 he ran for mayor against Dr. Bowlby. The report in the *Telegraph* of Huber's political appearance betrays both tolerance and amusement. Huber, the *Telegraph* declared, "was the fun of the evening."

> He was not brought out by the Board of Labor, Board of Trade, Grits or Tories. He said he had plenty of leisure to devote to the town. He was opposed to all bonuses and exemptions. He would raise wages of men on the street 25¢ a day. In all the bonuses voted no Council put in a stipulation that fair wages should be paid. That would not slip past him.[65]

Unfortunately for Huber, although the crowd laughed at him only fourteen voted for him in the 1901 election. He refused to accept defeat gracefully. On election night he went to the victor's headquarters and announced that he would have been a better mayor than Bowlby. He had lost because he had bought no drinks and had taken no beer barrels to the North Ward. The Bowlby supporters jeered him down, but Huber was undaunted. Throughout the new mayor's term, he continued to make his complaints.

The proposal that city council would grant money to the Board of Trade to promote a "yes" vote in the plebiscite to grant $25,000 for the proposed sugar beet factory outraged Huber. On a cold December evening, wearing his winter Tam'o'Shanter pulled down over his ears and over his white bushiness, he strode into council chambers and disrupted the meeting. He warned that he would take legal action unless the council stopped voting money for Board of Trade causes. The aldermen fidgeted, and Alderman J. M. Staebler admitted that the city solicitor had told him that the money was given to the Board of Trade illegally. Nevertheless, the cause was so important and so inherently just, he decided to sign the cheque in any case. Huber exploded with indignation at this explanation, at which point Alderman Aaron Bricker claimed that Huber had no right to address the council because he was a tenant, not a ratepayer. The constable was called, but in the meantime Huber fled into the night. But the council had not rid themselves of him.[66]

His Worship, Mayor Allen Huber

Huber offered himself once again for the mayoralty in 1902. On nomination night, which coincided with New Year's Eve, he let loose with a volley of charges against the town's leaders. He pointed out that the town's financial support of the Board of Trade had been declared illegal, that Dr. Bowlby should be charged with theft because he sold land for $3,000 to the Park Board, and that the town assessor had admitted his policy of unequal assessment. This time the *Telegraph* was not amused. It declared his address a waste of time and accused him of "slandering" Berlin's finest citizens. Berlin, the paper declaimed, "cannot afford to trifle with a man who seems to have no other occupation than to pose as a candidate at the elections." Huber's addresses at future meetings were not reported. Under his name was a short sentence: "This gentleman also spoke." Yet despite the poor coverage, Huber doubled his vote. But this was still only twenty-nine votes, and he lost the election by over seven hundred votes to John Eden.[67]

Huber ran yet again in 1903, receiving a grand total of thirty-nine votes and, of course, losing once more. The *Telegraph* editorially hoped that Huber would read the results as good riddance: "The comparison made by Mr. Huber in addressing the citizens of Berlin on Monday night, illustrative of his similarity of character and occupation to Moses, may be worthy of some recognition." Moses, the *Telegraph* observed, had prepared and worked for his achievement. "Instead of loitering about the streets of

Berlin smoking an old brier root," Huber should also spend forty years in the wilderness. But maybe forty years would not be enough for one with his deficiency in wisdom: only after sixty years should Huber consider coming back from the wilderness. Then, praise God, he would be too old to run for office.[68]

Perhaps Huber took the advice because one heard little of him until 1907. Then during a period of great controversy over the council's handling of financial affairs, he renewed his attack. On September 14, 1907, it was reported that:

> Between 600 and 700 citizens of Berlin gathered around the bandstand in the Market Square on Friday evening to hear Berlin's would be reformer, Allen Huber, discuss municipal matters. With the assistance of his copious notes he referred to what he was pleased to term "Berlin's Municipal Mess."[69]

And frankly it was a mess. The purchase of the street railway had proven more expensive than had been expected; the gas plant was inadequate for the city's needs; and civic finances were in turmoil. So were civic politics.

On nomination night fourteen names were put forward for the office of mayor but nearly all withdrew because it was believed that the popular former mayor, J. R. Eden, would run. At the last moment, however, Eden held back, leaving only two candidates in the field, W. V. Uttley, editor of the *News-Record* and a council member, and, of course, Huber. Even Uttley's rival editor declared that this amounted to an acclamation. At the nomination meeting Huber had performed in vintage style. He charged that the council had acted illegally in putting through a $83,000 debenture for the street railway purchase without citizen approval. Among examples of special treatment he cited was the grant of printing contracts to the *News-Record* by the council on which Uttley was a member. During his speech there was much shouting, commotion, and protest, and Huber barely escaped from the meeting physically intact. But during the campaign the town clerk and treasurer, Henry Aletter, was thrown into jail for misappropriating $1,800 of town funds. The jailing lent substance to Huber's charges and to his campaign. On January 6, 1908, there occurred "the Biggest Surprise in the History of Berlin." Allen Huber defeated one of the town's most prominent citizens by 896 votes to 890. That at least was the initial result; underneath the surprise headline was a "bulletin" with new results: Uttley 890 and Huber 886. Huber, it was reported, was rushing to City Hall.

Huber did not rescue his prize. On the next morning a shocked but relieved council declared Uttley mayor, refusing to accept Huber's plea to wait for a recount. The recount nevertheless began, and the judge in charge was shocked at what he found. The town clerk had been in jail, and no experienced figure replaced him. The result was chaos and over thirty serious irregularities.

In the meantime, however, George Rumpel had charged Huber with using grossly insulting language. At a public meeting during the election campaign Huber had declared that "old man Rumpel had stolen water from the town and should be in the penitentiary." Huber, when informed of the charge, replied: "Hit a dog and he squeals." In court he refused to deny his words and was given a suspended sentence. Council and Mayor Uttley saw this as justification for rejecting Huber's application for a new election and they did so. There was immediately a public uproar and provincial government intervention. The council resigned and a new nomination meeting was called.

George Rumpel, The Felt King of Canada

At the meeting Huber remarked that he really should be running for the sewer commission. Berlin, he observed, "needs good men on this commission to clear all the sewage out of town." Nevertheless, he ran for mayor with the motto, "God Save Our People." This time the field had widened: J. R. Eden was a candidate along with Uttley and the prominent businessman John Anthes. On February 19, 1908, Huber trounced his opponents, winning by over two hundred votes. This time he was a gracious winner. His campaign, he claimed, had cost him six cents for the first time and nothing the second. He denied the charges that he owned no property. In fact, he owned a vacant lot and a smoke house. In his conclusion, he rose to accustomed heights, comparing himself to Moses once again:

It took a long time for me to get there, but you know Moses was in the wilderness for forty years before he delivered the Israelites. I've done a lot of talking, but when you're in the bush you have to holler if you want to be heard. I'm going to stop talking now and get to work. It's too d—— cold.

With that he pulled his cap over his ears and walked off.

In those first days of his mayoralty, Huber gave interviews as freely as he had offered his opinions in the past. He let it be known that he considered the pipe one of "God's best gifts to man" and that he intended to smoke it in council. Nor would he wear the customary frock coat and white kid gloves to the opening council meeting. The result of these comments was a crowd of hundreds at the opening meeting. They came expecting an explosion; there was none. Huber did not smoke and he conducted council business with decorum and efficiency. He announced that he would work full-time on his mayoralty duties and would walk every street in town looking for cracked sidewalks or blocked sewers. Unfortunately, this was not so easy. On February 26 the *Telegraph* contained an unusual item: "Mayor Huber accuses police of treachery." Apparently a constable, unaware of his worship's purpose, tried to arrest him for loitering.

The Annual Summer Picnic of the Berlin Council

By spring the temperature of political feelings were moving in the same direction as the weather. Huber began smoking in council, declaring that he would rather give up his office than stop smoking. Moreover, on March 13 he stunned the Board of Trade when he announced to them that he was taxing all businesses at 100 per cent and that there would be no more bonusing. He added that he had a low opinion of the Board of Trade members and concluded: "Why should I pay your taxes and my own? Good Night Gentlemen."

The *Telegraph* was troubled; the *News-Record* demanded Huber's recall. The *Telegraph* did admit that the assessment scheme had been illegal, but businesses had come to Berlin because of it, and they had expected it would continue. Could the town end it now? The city council did not believe so and it refused to pass a motion introduced by the mayor which simply called for all laws to be enforced. The refusal signalled the battle. Huber declared war against the "foes" of the people.

The Annual Summer Picnic of the Berlin Council with Mayor Charles Hahn

He defied the Park Board and opened Victoria Park: in the people's park, no admission could ever be charged. Down came the fences which had enclosed the park. When Huber was summoned before the Park Board to explain himself, he expressed his belief that public property should not be limited solely to those who can pay. Mr. Breithaupt strenuously objected; Huber punched him squarely in the nose. Next came the Light Commission. Its members, Huber charged, decided matters that directly affected their own industrial interests. The introduction of the concept of conflict of interest provoked council retaliation; it rescinded a motion which had increased the mayor's salary. Huber promptly left the council chamber for the next two months, refusing to attend council meetings. When he finally returned, the council left. No one was paid because the mayor had final signing authority. The summer finally brought an armed peace.

In the fall, however, Huber made a final stand on the issue of the contract for Niagara power. He refused to sign a by-law implementing the agreement between Berlin and the provincial government, declaring that since this would cost ratepayers many tens of thousands more than had been promised, their opinion must be asked. "God save the people" was the answer that he gave angry councillors who demanded his signature. But God could not save Allen Huber in this case. The provincial government forced him to sign, and in December the extraordinary mayoralty of Allen Huber ended with only a few tussles, physical and verbal, to mar the final months.

The 1909 election which saw Mayor Allen Huber go down to defeat and Charles Hahn emerge as mayor over two other candidates, J. G. Gardiner and Louis McBrine, left Berlin's business leaders with renewed anxieties. McBrine and Gardiner were thought to have "split the vote" and it was suggested that the "labour vote" was largely responsible for Hahn's election.[70] The key issue in the election had in fact been concerned with the policy of special exemptions to manufacturers since seven of these tax exemptions were due to expire in 1909 and Gardiner had contended that McBrine was supported by the manufacturers who were hoping to have their assessments renewed at a "ridiculously low rate." From Gardiner's point of view, it was wrong to give "a low assessment to some wealthy manufacturers who could well afford to pay for higher assessment . . . to help pay the heavy burden of taxes which must necessarily fall upon the house owners."[71] In the election campaign Charles Hahn had occupied a middle ground between Gardiner and McBrine, promising only to provide efficient administration of municipal affairs.

Properly attired in a regulation Prince Albert suit for his inaugural, Mayor Charles Hahn must have seemed a pleasant respite from the vagaries of Allen Huber's mayorality. (Huber contented himself in his defeat, requesting an old armchair from the mayor's office as a symbol of his tenure.) Hahn's inaugural statement made it clear that council would work closely with the Board of Trade by promoting the industrial welfare of the town and by giving every "legal encouragement to manufacturing industries in the town." McBrine for his part returned to the Board of Trade where in 1910 he was elected as first vice-president. Despite Hahn's assurances, relations between council and the manufacturers remained strained. Several of Berlin's "old established industries" threatened to leave Berlin and only succumbed to the blandishments of the Board of Trade on the promise that the Board would meet with council to "devise some equitable system of dealing with manufacturers . . . regarding a fixed assessment of . . . ten years . . . [which would] settle this much vexed question of assessment for manufacturing industries."

Although Charles Hahn was re-elected without opposition in 1910, this was to be his last term as mayor. An increasing rivalry between council and the Board of Trade developed and an upswing in economic activity

throughout Canada and the United States led the Board of Trade to reassert its traditional leadership role in Berlin's municipal politics. Under the vigorous leadership of its president, James A. Scellen, the Board of Trade entered the battle for the mayoralty in 1911.

Mayor Hahn's Inauguration, 1906

J. C. Breithaupt, the prominent industrialist and a former mayor at a time when the industrialists had held the first magistrate's chair almost by right, announced his intention to defeat Charles Hahn. Breithaupt's rightful return to political power had seemed inevitable when in the last days of the campaign he was disqualified on the technicality that he had not resigned his seat as a member of the school board. Panic struck the hearts of Berlin's industrialists. At the last hour they turned to the Board of Trade for help and convinced the popular managing director of the Economical Mutual Fire Insurance Company (and by no coincidence also the treasurer and an executive director of the Berlin Board of Trade), W. H. Schmalz, to take on the task of unseating Charles Hahn. For his part, Hahn charged Schmalz with being "a tool of the manufacturers," much to the indignation of the Berlin *Telegraph* which saw this as a "dangerous and mischievous" tactic, endeavouring to set class against class, the working man against the manufacturer and businessman. Instead, suggested the *Telegraph* in an editorial so typical of the spirit of the day, "a vote for Schmalz is a vote for harmony and progress . . . for a man who will bring first rate business ability to the first magistrate's office."[72] In a sense, of course, Charles Hahn was right. Schmalz was clearly put up by the Board of Trade; the town's industrialists canvassed the wards on his behalf. The result was an overwhelming victory for Schmalz, who received particularly strong support in the East and Centre Wards while Hahn continued to do well in the working-class North and West Wards. Such divisions were not clearcut for, as the *Telegraph* observed, it was the vote of the women who turned out "in an unprecedented manner" that helped the successful candidate. Schmalz, who was personally very popular, had in fact won support in all of the wards.[73] The politics of Berlin would once again be the politics of business.

In Berlin the politics of business had come to mean active municipal support for policies that would serve as a foundation for the growth of industry in the future—in a word, for "progress." This had resulted in municipal ownership of the waterworks system in 1898, at a cost of $102,000; the Berlin Gas Company in 1903 ($90,000); the Berlin and Waterloo Street Railway purchased when its franchise expired in 1907 for $95,752; and in 1904 Berlin became the first municipality in Canada to establish a sewer commission.

In the campaign for municipal ownership, Berlin's industrialists served as canvassers, bagmen, and publicists. In the purchase of the waterworks, for instance, considerable opposition had arisen and some ratepayers stood aghast at the proposal to invest more than $100,000 in a utility and then run the risk of operating it. In its efforts to get its franchise renewed and in a direct appeal to the voters, the company had promised to actually lower its rates. Mayor George Rumpel, however, announced simply that if the town did not buy the waterworks, he would do so himself. ". . . [A]s the tide continued to run against the by-law [to purchase the system], Jacob Kaufman, John A. Lang and Hartman Krug made it known that if the by-law should be carried they were willing to take the purchase off the town's hands, make all the concessions offered by the company, pay the instalments of principal and interest and hand over one-half of the profits to the municipality."[74] However unusual this action may have appeared to those outside of Berlin, it was remarkably successful and the waterworks by-law was passed with a large majority. It would not be the last time that Berlin's business leaders would be forced to urge a recalcitrant council to action. When their campaigns ended in victory, however, the industrialists took their places on the light or water or sewer commissions which controlled the new "public" utilities. Seventy-five per cent of the collective membership was in fact made up of industrialists, at the same time as their active role on the town's council had begun to decrease.

The explanation for Berlin's leadership in public ownership can be traced to the businessman's belief that his town lacked natural advantages. Berlin's advantages had to be made.[75] There was also a fear that new technologies would favour the large city or plant. Only through united action could Berlin meet these challenges.[76] The result was special committees of the Board of Trade to consider Berlin's lighting and power problems as well as a solution to the pressing problem of Berlin's sewage—a product of industrial wastes, notably from the tanneries. The resulting sewage treatment system which was in place by 1908 became, ironically, a matter of great pride to Berlin's boosters and the amount invested in public utilities seen as a sign of the progressive nature of Berlin's community. By 1912 they could announce that "Berlin is an ardent friend of the public ownership principle. This may be due to the same cause which led seventy per cent of her citizens to become possessed of homes. German thrift sees in public ownership greater economics and improved services."[77] While all of this may have appeared to be true, a detailed examination of Berlin's tentative steps toward public ownership,

Improvements along King Street

and more particularly toward the provision of an adequate sewage disposal system to deal with industrial wastes, illustrates that council and Berlin's businessmen were extremely reluctant to proceed with improvements unless coerced by the courts. As Dr. J. Amyot, who investigated Berlin's sewage problems for the provincial Department of Health, candidly observed in 1908:

> The only reasons that the town had not up to this time been sued for heavy damages, was that those chiefly affected were Mennonites who are extremely adverse to forcible means. This was played on by the authorities of Berlin to the unbearable limit. It was a case of continuous promising and jollying. . . . The Mennonites finally rose to the occasion and entered suit. The town was beaten at every point.[78]

It is also true that the city ownership of public utilities was not so pioneering as civic boosters claimed. Nearby Guelph had run its gas and electric plants since 1893 and it too claimed to be the great innovator in municipal ownership. Moreover, as John Weaver has said with reference to Toronto's move to public ownership of street railways, the ingredients behind the movement were "a blend of naïve optimism and bald commercial ambition." The optimism was sometimes fully justified even if it was naïve in inspiration. The commercial ambition was less naïve and usually expressed less directly. The motives of Berlin's manufacturers in seeking hydro-electricity were similar to and as straightforward as those of the manufacturers in other surrounding middle-sized communities. Street railway expansion also assisted commercial interests. The merchants saw the railway bring passengers to their stores. The factory owners knew that proximity to the railway made recruitment of workers easier. The landowners knew that the expansion of the city depended in part on growth of the railway.

Nonetheless, in its overall record Berlin's advocacy of public ownership and its ultimate pride in the success and modernity of its sewage disposal system, clean water, inexpensive electricity, and public transit was seen to have served the needs of the community, not merely those of the economic elite. In many larger urban areas the principle of "privatism," or individual gain, seemed paramount and public ownership served as the means merely to obtain this end. As a result, a better quality of life was merely a fortunate dividend. In Berlin a greater sense of community seemed to persist, although, as the example of Mayor Allen Huber illustrates, the tensions were often close to the surface.

The social life of the community had contributed not a little to the harmony that carried Berlin through the difficult times of industrialization. In particular, Berlin's German clubs provided a milieu which drew the community together, for the great *Sängerfests* or song festivals were open to all and created an atmosphere of harmony. In the latter half of the nineteenth century these festivals had flourished in Berlin: between 1876 and 1906 nine were staged in the town, often with as many as sixteen choirs with more than eight hundred singers, attended by ten to twelve thousand people.[79] The song festivals were also an occasion for the release of tension and they provided camaraderie as well as a feeling of community well-being which transcended class or social divisions. For many, the song festivals and German industriousness were at the heart of life in Berlin. This is not to suggest that other forms of recreation were lacking. Sports, especially rugby, had long been organized, and since the coming of the railway in the 1850s Berlin's residents had had a surprisingly wide range of musical and dramatic productions to choose from. The railway had linked Berlin to touring companies from New York and Toronto. Along with other urban centres such as Ottawa, Kingston, London, and Stratford, Berlin was part of the "small circuit" bringing both New York drama and Shakespearean plays to town. At first these plays were performed in the Court House or the Town Hall, but after the opening of Abel Walper's Opera House in 1896 a proper theatre was available. Indeed, in 1896 the "greatest wonder of the age"—the cinematograph or silent movies—first opened in Berlin and by 1907 two new movie houses, the Theatorium and Allen's Star Theatre, entertained the townspeople. The programmes at the Star and the Theatorium were similar so that it was possible "to attend the first show at one theatre and then dash across the street to see the second show at the other."[80] Great events of the time were caught on film and shown in Berlin. The arrival of the movie theatres marked the beginning of the demise of Berlin's cultural uniqueness and hastened the weakening of that sense of community life which had brought Berlin relatively un-scathed through the complex processes of urbanization and industrialization.

BERLIN BECOMES KITCHENER

4

On June 9, 1912, Berlin celebrated the official proclamation of its city-hood. On that Sunday morning after church, Mayor W. H. Schmalz read the proclamation after which his words were drowned out by "the noise of bells, whistling, [the] cheering of crowds [and] cannon crackers . . . ." A band roused the crowd, ending with Berlin's dual anthems *Die Wacht am Rhein* and *God Save the King*.[1]

In February 1914 several of Berlin's leading citizens gathered at the *View of Berlin in 1912* Concordia Club for another celebration. Past and future mayors and parliamentarians raised their glasses in a toast to Wilhelm II of Germany's fifty-fifth birthday. Several of the speakers rose to declare their bond with the Kaiser, "the guiding star on the firmament of world history." This was the last birthday party for the Kaiser in "Canada's German Capital." As the war clouds darkened in Europe in the summer of 1914, a shadow was cast upon Berlin and its traditions.[2]

107

The Annual Summer Picnic of the Berlin Council in 1912. Mayor W. H. Schmalz is at the centre of the front row.

The *Berliner Journal* anxiously warned its readers on August 12, 1914: "The die is cast, the two greatest European empires face each other with weapons raised." Germans could love the fatherland but they must remember that they had accepted the invitation to live under the Union Jack. They must therefore not confront Canadians of different background. "Be silent, and face these hard times with dignity," the paper counselled. Duty and honour demanded that allegiance flow to the Germans' new *Heimat*. But the stream of allegiance could not flow so easily.[3]

As in the rest of Canada, the formal expressions of loyalty came quickly in those first days of August. Yet, like Canadians generally, Berliners did not expect much change. The German clubs continued to meet, ministers held German services in which Canadian loyalty was declared, and Kaiser Wilhelm benignly faced the newer statue of Queen Victoria beside the lake in Victoria Park. But the contentment of the Kaiser's gaze could not calm the animosity of Berlin's more militant patriots. In the early morning of August 22, local militia members tore the Kaiser's bust from its pedestal and tossed it into Victoria Park lake. A

Opposite page—Kaiser Wilhelm I Statue in Victoria Park

nearby family heard a splash, and on Sunday morning, the next day, the police recovered the bust still intact. The *Berliner Journal* reported that the bust would "probably" be restored soon to its original spot.[4] It was not; instead the Kaiser took wartime refuge on the Concordia Club's mantel. The vandalism was deplored by Mayor W. D. Euler, who pointed out that nearly all Germans were loyal to Canada and that the destruction of the Kaiser's monument would simply produce unnecessary and unwanted tensions.

The Kaiser is rescued after his dunking

The tensions nevertheless grew, especially after German instruction in the public schools was halted. This action seemed so unreasonable and so short-sighted that many of Berlin's most respected citizens publicly protested. L. J. Breithaupt led a public meeting of hundreds against this provincially inspired action. The audacity of the protest strikes a modern mind accustomed to the concept of total war as naïve. One must recall, however, that the Berliners in their lifetimes had known only peace. The duality of loyalty was never tested. It seemed so normal, and we must recall that the exclusivity of loyalty which the Great War came to demand is itself the creation and legacy of that first total war. This perception may not explain other problems of nationality, but it alone affords an explanation of that easy August assumption of Berlin Germans that the war would be somewhere else, some place beyond the familiar boundaries of their daily life.

By the end of 1914 this assumption was being tested. The speaking of German became less common, and Germans noted that their British-Canadian neighbours excoriated not merely Germany but also "German-ness." One who most excited British-Canadian suspicions was the Reverend C. R. Tappert of St. Matthew's Lutheran Church. Tappert, a German American who had come to Berlin in 1913, resented the British-Canadian propaganda, regarding it as a racist affront to the German people. In January 1915 he declared that Germans who had been naturalized owed Canada their loyalty but "an oath is simply an oath . . . the heart is not torn from the new Canadian's breast."[5] A few months later he wrote to the *News-Record*: "I am not ashamed to confess that I still love the land of my fathers—Germany. Yes, I love her! Indeed, I would not dare to look into an honest man's face, if I did not." Tappert's enthusiasm offended, but to confront it would only draw attention to an already nervous Berlin. Berlin's newspapers instead featured the contributions of the city to the Patriotic Fund which, in October 1914, were second in the nation per capita (Waterloo was first).[6] The authorization for the raising of the 118th Battalion in the fall of 1915 also captured much attention, but not so much as the recruiting campaign which followed.

The first Berliner to die in action was an Eby, the great-great-grandson of Berlin's pacifist founder. This event bore tragic irony, but it was in no sense symbolic. Few Berliners of German extraction enlisted in those early days. The local volunteers identified by the *Daily Telegraph* in January 1915 were mainly of British descent, and this fact prompted civic leaders to call for a more enthusiastic response to the recruiting appeal. The city council even provided a fund to promote recruitment in Berlin. The efforts, however, brought little success; and by January 1916, the 118th Battalion was still far below full strength, this despite the use of strong-arm recruiting tactics.[7] This "constant military featuring and coercion to enlist" annoyed Dan Detweiler at first, but by January 1916 he seems to have become convinced it was necessary. He recorded in his diary: "Young men [were] leaving for U.S. pretty largely to avoid enlistment." Detweiler's worries were reflected in a city council resolution of January 17, 1916, which called on relatives and friends to assist in every way "loved ones who are anxious to play the MAN in this great World struggle." The 118th Battalion, however, refused to rely upon the relatives' efforts, and they intensified their search for the young men who wore no khaki. They harried them on street corners, offered rewards for their apprehension, and threatened those who abetted the "slackers." Even the staunchly pro-war Galt *Reporter* was shocked at the press-gang tactics, asking querulously,

"Are these the Methods of the Kaiser's Berlin or Berlin, Ontario?"[8] The Berlin Trades and Labour Council similarly demanded that city council take steps to halt the battalion's "insults, molestations and interference" with Berlin's citizens. All was to no avail, for Berlin's meagre police force was no match for the 118th. Its best officer, Constable Blevins, rested with a broken jaw, the result of his attempt to arrest one of the most flamboyant soldiers, and a future mayor, Joseph Meinzinger.

Troops leaving the Berlin Station in 1914

As restraints vanished, demagogues flourished. Sergeant-Major Blood—an extraordinary but apparently genuine name—gave a "straight talk" to Berliners: "Once again, Be British. Do your duty or be despised. . . . Be British or be d——d." Even more fiery was Lieutenant Stanley Nelson, who claimed that he had witnessed Belgian babies thrust upon German bayonets. He warned Berliners that "the eyes of Canada" were upon them.

You have creatures in your midst who say success to the Kaiser, and to hell with the King; and all I can say is, round up this element into the detention camps, for they are unworthy of British citizenship and should be placed where they belong. Already the showing that the physically fit young men of North Waterloo have made is so rotten that I have heard an outside businessman say to a traveller from a Berlin wholesale house, "I'll not buy another damned article manufactured in that German town. Do you think I'm going to give my money to support a pack of Germans? If I did I'd be as bad as they."[9]

The anecdote was probably apocryphal, but it was often repeated and widely believed. On February 8, 1916, a Board of Trade meeting considered changing the name of Berlin, apparently in the belief that, as one participant quaintly observed, if a skunk lost its stripe, no one could think it would smell. It was claimed that business was being affected by the imprint "Made In Berlin." The war had brought many contracts; indeed it had created a boom. All could be lost if Berlin's patriotism was deemed to be lacking. This concern for the city's economic security was, therefore, the predominant sentiment behind the move to change the name. On February 21 city council passed a resolution imploring the provincial legislature to change the city's name. Perhaps the answer was amalgamation with Waterloo—what name could be more patriotic? Whatever the means, the result must be the removal of the stain of the Prussian capital.[10]

In the campaign to change the name, professionals and manufacturers led what they had begun. They thought that the provincial government would readily agree to their request; however, for technical reasons and because of concern for the effect of the name change on civic peace, the legislature's private bills committee refused to consider the proposed change. The offended petitioners returned to Berlin where an "Indignation Meeting" was held at the Star Theatre. The provincial government responded to Berlin's indignation with the passage of a private bill permitting the city to hold a plebiscite on the name-change question. Council did not hesitate and called a vote for May 19.

The legislature had first held back because they feared civil strife; the plebiscite assured such strife. One suspects that the name-change campaign stirred those passions which the decorum, civility, and restraint of small-city life had stilled in 1915 and 1916. In truth we really know little of what Berliners thought in those years. "Busy Berlin" was not a reflective town. One might suggest, however, that the reaction to the scattered incidents such as the Kaiser-dunking betrays a deeply rooted desire to avoid conflict, to regard the incidents as distortions of familiar patterns. Even in the private diary of Dan Detweiler one finds a reluctance to consider the dangers of the British-German war for Canada's most obvious German centre. And yet the incidents remained a part of the memory.[11] When the name-change plebiscite suddenly focussed the debate, the discrete incidents formed part of a pattern, thus gaining a new significance. This happened for both opponents and supporters of the name change. What had been ignored was now noticed and, more important, admitted.

*The first motorized de-
livery truck in front of
the Star Theatre, 1914*

The Kaiser's bust had been ignored since the war's early days; now its presence in the largely unused Concordia Club became an outrage. On February 15, 1916, shortly after the first proposal for the name change, some soldiers from the 118th Battalion broke into the Concordia Club, removed the bust, and paraded it down King Street. This proof of treachery aroused other soldiers and civilians who ransacked the club, seizing German memorabilia from the storage rooms, and destroying much of the clubhouse. The police did nothing; they could not. The next day the city's leaders tried to pick up the pieces. For their part, the Concordia Club members almost apologetically declared that the attack was unwarranted. The hall contained, they claimed, a portrait of George V draped in red, white, and blue bunting, not in German colours as the soldiers alleged. The German icons were in the storeroom and thus were not visible. The club asked for an impartial investigation. The investigation, however, echoed the report of the 118th's commanding officer, Lieutenant-Colonel W. M. O. Lochead. A Camp Borden court of inquiry led to no charges but rather to an explanation of the raid. The inquiry charged that

> conditions were allowed to prevail in Berlin that loyal British citizens found impossible to tolerate. . . . The Concordia Club, supposed to be a singing organization, was in reality a strong German club with a large membership of young men and everything we found in connection with the club went to show that it was an organization to foster and maintain a strong German spirit and love for the fatherland.

The whole responsibility was placed upon those authorities who allowed "conditions that were sure to bring trouble."[12]

There was to be no exoneration of the Concordia Club nor of Berlin's Germanness.

The Concordia Club raid freed the blacker spirits and suspicions of the community. Lochead claimed that he tried to restrain his men in the rampage which followed; others blamed outsiders for the new violence in civic life. There is not much evidence for either claim. All evidence points to a community rivened from within, with a gulf that the claims of economic gain and social harmony simply could not bridge. Thus when the distinguished businessman W. H. Breithaupt wrote a long letter to the *News-Record* presenting the traditional explanation of Germanism in Berlin, he was sternly and directly rebuked. Breithaupt claimed that "We are of German descent, and are not ashamed of it . . . we are not Germans nor are we German-Canadians or any variety of Germans or part Germans . . . . We are Canadians, and yield not an iota, to anyone, in devotion to our country and to the ideals of the British Empire." But W. G. Cleghorn, the chairman of the recruiting committee, believed that they must yield. Cleghorn angrily denounced Breithaupt's statement, "We are Germans and proud of it."

> Whom does he mean by "we"? Does he speak for the community, a certain element in Berlin, or only for himself? There are thousands of descendants of Germans in this city today who are NOT proud of the fact they are German. They approve neither of the purpose for which this terrible war was forced on the world, nor the ruthless manner in which it has been carried on. How any one can look back at the countless terrible outrages—women ravished, chil-

dren killed, non-combatants drowned at sea without warning, and still say "we are Germans and proud of it" is beyond our comprehension. We sincerely hope that Mr. Breithaupt is the only one who will flaunt such an assertion before the citizens of a British City at such a crisis. It is bad taste to say the least.

Cleghorn concluded with a charge that Breithaupt had not helped recruiting (despite a call in his letter for Berlin to do its "full duty") and that he was an American and not a British subject.[13]

Waterloo County Court House. W. H. Breithaupt is seated in the second seat from the front. He is wearing a fur cap.

Three days after Cleghorn's charges appeared, the 118th vented its fury on another "American," the Reverend Tappert. Tappert's 1915 comments had made his continuing presence an act of Germanic defiance in the soldiers' eyes. He had indicated that he would return to the United States on March 1, 1916. He did not, and on March 4 sixty soldiers led by Sergeant-Major Blood broke into his parsonage, demanding to know why he had stayed. Within minutes, Tappert was being dragged behind horses through the streets, his face bloodied, his body twisting as he fell into unconsciousness while the pavement scraped off his flesh. Three days later he was gone. Blood and another soldier were charged, but were given only suspended sentences. Blood, Lochead reported, had "particularly disappointed" him. "He is an awfully good fellow but suffers his enthusiasm for the British cause to drown his good judgment and sense of proper self-control."[14]

Not many had good judgment in Berlin in the next few months. The 118th Battalion became virtually a press gang, an arbiter of the public safety. The streets were theirs, as other young men vanished. Those who remained and spoke up were punished. When one clerk got "fresh" with women who urged recruitment, the *News-Record* warned "That this young

'Gentleman' will pay dearly for his indiscretion is certain for the soldiers have him on their list and woe betide Mr. 'Freshy' when they get their hands on him. Let this be a warning to Berlin's young men." The "list" grew longer as the year passed.

The name-change debate grew more acrimonious as the vote neared. The supporters of the change formed a British League to advance their cause; the opponents grouped themselves into an unnamed yet well-supported body. The latter group had within it some of the same people who had signed the original petition supporting the change, including such prominent manufacturers as August and George Lang and Jacob Kaufman. Some acted their parts in the patriotic drama that played in Berlin's streets and public places while they privately gave their support to the opposition. Just before voting day the *News-Record* published an advertisement arguing the opponents' case. The name change, the advertisement claimed, would really change nothing. It would, however, indicate approval of the intimidation that had ruled Berlin's streets since January. British democracy, if it meant anything, must not succumb to such intimidation.[15]

On May 19, 3,057 Berliners voted, but many others were denied that right when, for the first time in Berlin's history, the unnaturalized were challenged at the polls. Other "enemy aliens" were also turned away as opposition scrutineers failed to show up, fearing, it was claimed, that they would be physically beaten. But many women did vote, as did soldiers, and they apparently carried the day for the proponents. The name change carried by only eighty-one votes, but the promoters took to the streets led by the 118th soldiers. Skyrockets soared (a few did not, sailing straight into the celebrants), and Alderman Hallman cabled King George V, informing His Majesty that Berlin had "cast off forever the name of the Prussian capital." The opponents stayed home, but some did not escape the crowd's attention. A group went to the home of George and August Lang who, it was known, had paid for the opponents' advertisement and election-day cars. August, Berlin's wealthiest citizen (in 1916 his personal and property assessment was the city's highest), strode briskly from his door into the jeering crowd. Waving a large walking stick, Lang ordered the crowd to disperse. When they did not, he swung his stick wildly, striking a soldier and some civilians. Soon disarmed, he was carried back to the house, and the victorious crowd dispersed.[16]

Lang nevertheless derived some consolation when voting figures were published. His workers, if not his friends, had agreed with his stand. Most of those with calloused hands had marked their ballots "no." The working class and the "German" North Ward voted decisively against the name change. Not surprisingly, the opponents protested the vote, claiming that intimidation determined the result. But the protest achieved nothing. It merely irritated the change's supporters who became more convinced that traitors dwelt among them.

Wartime rubber workers   On the Monday following the vote the 118th Battalion left the city to train in London. Saturday, May 20, had been a public holiday as the 118th in a final public review marched through the streets that had been theirs. Even those who had deprecated the 118th's actions joined the rousing send-off. All could celebrate the battalion's departure even if motives were different. A sense of humour so long submerged reappeared. A newspaper joked:

> "Oh Nellie, don't speak to the four fellows coming. They are all members of the slackers' battalion."
> "Yes Ruth I know! They came back from Detroit as soon as the battalion left town."[17]

Poor wit, but a good indication that the battalion's departure removed some fears.

The remainder of the year passed without repetition of the earlier violence. The choice of a new name for Berlin was the immediate task, but this proved more difficult than anyone had believed. The original recommendations such as Dunard, Renoma, or Huronto were quickly—and understandably—rejected. A frustrated council drew up its own list of six names: Adanac, Benton, Brock, Corona, Keowana, and Kitchener. The last name was added after Lord Kitchener drowned and, not surprisingly, it was the popular choice—or at least the choice of the 1,055 who bothered to cast their ballots. Name-change opponents, now the Citizen's League, seized upon the low turnout to make one last attempt to halt the change. Their brief claimed that the majority for change was "insignificant": surely in so important a matter a mere majority was not enough. Within a short time, the Citizens' League had gathered 2,068 signatures on a petition opposing the change. But it was too late. On September 1, 1916, Berlin became Kitchener.[18]

Berlin City Council, 1915. Mayor Hett is seated at the centre of the first row.

This nominal patriotism failed to quell suspicions. Outsiders pointed to the strength of the Citizens' League, and in Kitchener itself, Mayor J. E. Hett's call for generosity and unity had little force. The *News-Record* became a forum where supporters and opponents jostled. H. M. Bowman, who had written the articulate opposition broadside "The Other Side, An Appeal for British Fair Play," and hydro promoter Dan Detweiler, exchanged angry letters in the *News-Record*. On October 3, ex-mayor W. H. Schmalz appeared in police court to answer charges that he tolerated pro-German appeals. Schmalz was a community leader in several fields such as music, the militia, and business. The general manager of the Economical Fire Insurance Company, he had, in 1915, joined W. J. Motz in the management of the *Berliner Journal*; and when the name change occurred, the *Journal* simply added after its name "verlegt und gedruckt in Canada" (published and printed in Canada). This refusal to change Berliner to Kitchener was, in late 1916, an act of defiance too bold to ignore. Suddenly Schmalz's past actions were perceived as part of a pattern of unpatriotic behaviour. It did not matter that Economical had pledged over $10,000 to the Patriotic Fund, the second-largest business donation. Dan Detweiler swore an affidavit that he had seen a notice in the Economical Insurance window in the early war days which called upon German reservists to serve their country. Schmalz's son, a graduate of the Royal Military College, saw his military prospects end. Schmalz was publicly embarrassed. Although nothing came of Schmalz's prosecution, it added to the atmosphere of suspicion and of personal anguish that suffused Kitchener's political air.[19]

An afternoon in Victoria Park (Ontario Archives)

The Citizens' League and the British League, fired to heights of enthusiasm by the contests of 1916, were both determined to control the city council elections which took place on New Year's Day, 1917. The button manufacturer, David Gross, who alone among aldermen had opposed the name change in early 1916, was the choice for the mayoralty of the Citizens' League. His opponent was W. E. Gallagher. Behind them, each League ran a slate of candidates. The British League moved quickly to strike "aliens" off the voters' list, and they were relatively successful in denying votes to some of Kitchener's oldest residents. This seemed an omen to Citizens' League members that their task would not be easy. Worse, there were rumours that the 118th would return to vote on New Year's Day. They might, of course, affect other votes through intimidation or even violence. Thus, Mayor Hett, who was a Citizens' League supporter, asked for the assistance of the military in maintaining order in Berlin on election day.

Surprisingly, election day was quiet until the sun set. Then citizens and soldiers took to the streets. The *News-Record* office posted the first results, and at once the winners were known. The triumph of the Citizens' League slate produced loud cheers for the League and for the *News-Record* which had supported it. But for Ben Uttley, the *News-Record*'s publisher, delight soon turned to fear. He hurried to the police station where he told the police chief and Major Baron Osborne that a gang was going "to wreck" the *News-Record* office. Soon the rumour became fact when an injured alderman-elect, Nick Asmussen, arrived at the police station reporting that the *News-Record* window had already been smashed. Mayor-elect Gross joined the crowd seeking sanctuary in the police station. Gross had learned that a party of 118th-Battalion soldiers had gathered outside his house. Osborne, who "knew from reports that a very bitter feeling existed" against Gross, wisely advised the new mayor to find safety in a friend's home for the night. Nevertheless, Osborne's report of what followed betrays little sympathy for the plight of the Citizens' League:

Major Baron Osborne on the right with General Douglas Haig (centre)

I immediately proceeded, with two military policemen [to the *News-Record*]. . . . There was a large crowd at this moment—several hundred people—outside the office. A few soldiers were mingled with the crowd, who seemed to be quiet and acting just as ordinary citizens, interested in the results of the poll. I went into the office, which was crowded with people more or less excited, all civilians. I there learned that Alderman-elect H. M. Bowman had been injured. This I found afterwards to be true, but it was only slight. I believe he struck one of the soldiers.[20]

The beleaguered celebrants in the *News-Record* office left on the orders of and under the protection of Osborne. With the victors gone, the losers marched down King Street singing *We'll Never Let the Old Flag Fall*. Fearing more trouble, Mayor Hett ordered Osborne to call in the 122nd Battalion from Galt to quell the high spirits of the losers. They arrived at 11:00 P.M., and confronted, with fixed bayonets, a "shouting, jeering, hooting" crowd on King Street. Other soldiers moved to guard Gross's home and his button factory and the *News-Record* building which now was in a shambles. By 1:00 A.M. the streets were clear of all but soldiers. During the next days the soldiers of the 118th who, Osborne "positively" declared, had no "part in the disturbance," returned to their London base and the new mayor emerged from his refuge to beg for a return to civility and peace in his troubled city. But in 1917 peace in Kitchener would be as tempting but as elusive as it was in Europe itself.[21]

The 118th Battalion at the Station

There were in fact some early attempts to heed Gross's call. The Board of Trade which had first promoted the name change elected as its president W. D. Euler, a prominent opponent of the change. The new president promised that the Board would avoid all political actions. The press, too, minimized conflict and hailed all signs of patriotic activity with feature headlines.[22] Business prospered as war orders continued to come to Kitchener's many industries. Even the *Berliner Journal* finally relented and became the *Ontario Journal*. The *Journal*, together with the *News-Record* and the *Telegraph*, followed the success of the Canadian Corps in the spring of 1917 with excitement and approval. When Prime Minister Borden returned from Europe in May and announced that conscription would be necessary to secure further Canadian and allied troops, his call received immediate and surprising support from the three Kitchener papers. The only loud voice raised against compulsion came from the Kitchener branch of the Social Democratic party. The party's next meeting was broken up by soldiers who warned the socialists never to comment on conscription again. The socialists were temporarily silenced, but more serious opposition soon appeared from the Independent Labour party, a local branch of which was formed in late May on the initiative of Berlin's previous mayor, J. E. Hett. In early June, Hett, a former Conservative, announced that he would stand in the next federal election as ILP candidate for Waterloo North. Hett's courage seems to have roused others who opposed conscription, although few followed him into the ILP ranks. The sitting Conservative member, W. G. Weichel, was most troubled by what he saw in his riding, and on July 5 his fears grew when the Board of Trade cast off the "non-political" raiment it had worn since January. At the end of a long meeting, when only thirteen members remained, the Board voted nine to four to support conscription. Immediately President W. D. Euler resigned, reminding conscription's proponents that he had promised no politics.[23]

Euler was a prominent Liberal, a former president of the Laurier Club, a fine speaker, prickly and perhaps even cantankerous in his outlook, yet a deft manipulator of men and their politics. From all he commanded attention if not affection, and his stand on a matter of principle naturally led others to think of him as a leader of anti-conscriptionist forces. By mid-July Euler was seriously considering becoming an independent anti-conscription candidate in North Waterloo.[24] Both Weichel and the Liberal candidate, Dr. J. F. Honsberger, had endorsed conscription; they would, therefore, split the conscriptionist vote, allowing an anti-conscriptionist to win. With this in mind, Euler responded to a delegation which met with him on August 13 asking him to be a candidate. This delegation included most of the *Conservative* executive but only two members of the Liberal executive (of which Euler himself was a member). More important, the entire Citizens' League executive came there beseeching Euler to run. He consented: he would be an "independent Liberal" anti-conscriptionist. His decision ruptured the intricate and carefully threaded fabric of party politics in Kitchener.

Confusion intensified when Borden formed his Union Government in October. The Liberals who clung to Honsberger were baffled. Euler demanded of them that he be recognized because, he correctly claimed, his stand on conscription, the "only issue," was the stand of Laurier. But the Liberal executive refused to abandon Honsberger and moved with him to the Unionist and conscriptionist side. On November 15, however, Honsberger finally was removed when a Unionist convention overwhelmingly supported the sitting member, W. G. Weichel. The next night a noisy meeting in the Roma Theatre confirmed Euler as the Laurier Liberal candidate. There were few of his former Liberal executive members there that evening, but their places were filled with many Conservatives who had left their first faith. Euler's address was characteristically bold. The war which Borden had declared Canada's own, Euler termed a distant conflict, unworthy of the spending of fresh Canadian blood. He alleged that the war had served mainly the rich and had led to "a nightmare of disregard for the public rights without parallel in Canada." How could this be a war for democracy? Borden was cutting down the supports for democracy at home.[25]

Left to right: W. D. Euler, W. G. Cleghorn, Herman Boehmer, and Harvey Sims, Lawn Bowling Champions, 1913

Euler's speeches got little coverage: the *Telegraph* and the *News-Record* both supported Weichel. We know little of what Euler said or to whom he spoke. What we do know suggests that the campaign in North Waterloo was, in a general sense, unlike all others in Ontario. The Laurier Liberal candidate neither shirked public meetings nor took refuge in ambiguity as nearly all other Ontario Liberal candidates did. Euler spoke every day at extraordinary length (two-and-a-half hours in one case) and with unusual vehemence. His frank rejection of the conscriptionist and Unionist sentiment that overwhelmed the constituencies around Waterloo startled his opponents, leading them toward greater virulence in their attacks. Thus the Liberal campaign manager in 1911, H. J. Sims, declared: "I do not say that all adherents to Mr. Euler are disloyal, but I do say that all disloyal citizens will vote for him, because his is the weaker war policy." Dr. Honsberger, the former Liberal candidate now invariably on Weichel's platform, claimed that Euler was "cold blooded, callous, and indifferent of the suffering of our boys at the front, and is afraid to express his true sentiments for fear of the righteous indignation of all loyal citizens in the riding."

The most unfair attacks on Euler came not from his political opponents but from some of the Protestant churches in Kitchener. The leading Anglican, Presbyterian, and Methodist ministers placed themselves at the forefront of the Weichel campaign. None was so emotional and none so inaccurate as The Reverend Charles Sykes of Trinity Methodist Church, ironically Euler's own church. Sykes claimed that while on American soil Euler had "declared that Canada would not suffer so badly under the Kaiser's rule." Euler, Sykes asserted, was an annexationist and so was Laurier. This was too much and Euler angrily responded. Sykes admitted that his comments were based upon mere rumour; now, thanks to Sykes, Euler would have a beneficial opportunity to repudiate the rumours.[26] This, of course, was scarcely an apology and there would be none in 1917. Euler left his adopted Methodism, returning to his (and The Reverend Tappert's) former church, St. Matthew's Lutheran. Even in prayer Euler was defiant.

The Lutheran and Roman Catholic churches did not share Sykes's enthusiasm for the Unionist cause. Their pastors shunned the public platforms of the campaign. Knowing that these two religions accounted for almost three-fifths of Kitchener's religious adherents no doubt consoled Euler. He had other reasons for confidence. To counter the English-language press opposition to him Euler produced his own broadside, *The Voice of the People*. His financial support reportedly was sufficient to distribute this pamphlet to all constituents during the campaign. Moreover, his canvassers delivering his literature did not hesitate to confront Unionists, even when it was the prime minister himself.

Sir Robert Borden came to Kitchener for a major campaign address on Saturday, November 24. Borden knew Weichel's chances were not good, but he does not seem to have appreciated the tense atmosphere in the city. On the evening of Borden's speech, about three hundred Euler supporters rallied beneath banners endorsing Euler as "the Common Peoples' Candidate" and Laurier as the saviour of democracy. They entered the auditorium where Borden was to speak, choosing strategic gallery positions. Not even the patriotic anthems escaped the gallery's boos. Mayor Gross, a former Conservative, but no Unionist, pleaded with the hecklers to desist. They refused. In a din of "tin whistles, hoots, and cheers for Laurier and Euler," Borden rose, tried to speak, and then angrily sat down. Weichel berated the crowd for their bad manners and accused Kitchener of supporting the war only when it involved economic gain. Other cities' newspapers carefully noted this view. In his memoirs, Borden recalled that, for the rest of Canada, "the Kitchener incident was much more effective than any speech I could have delivered." In Kitchener, however, its effect was only unfortunate.[27]

Euler quickly deplored the incident and pointed out that the pro-Euler forces did not have the endorsement of his campaign committee. The Unionist forces wanted more: a formal apology to Borden from the Kitchener city council. This they could not get, for seven of Kitchener's twelve aldermen refused to approve the proposed apology. The dissenting aldermen charged that the Unionists were using the incident for partisan purposes, but this simply angered the newspapers, in Kitchener and beyond, which cited the council's refusal as evidence of Kitchener's disloyalty. Berlin had changed its name but not its heart. The Kingston *Standard* thus declared: "The action of the Kitchener Council but confirms our earlier ideas that Kitchener is filled with Hun sympathizers and is in spirit, if no longer in name, a German city." The city councils of the nearby cities of Guelph and Brantford asked the government to remove the stain on Lord Kitchener's name by refusing "Berlin" the right to use it. The "loyalists," especially those who owned Kitchener's factories, were offered sanctuary in Guelph.

Kitchener from the air, 1919

The outside reaction shocked the Kitchener Board of Trade. At a special meeting Board of Trade president A. S. Capwell warned that Kitchener faced "the most critical time" in its history. "There is," he continued, "scarcely one manufacturer or businessman here who has not received letters and protests for the insults to Sir Robert Borden." The Board of Trade and the Kitchener Manufacturers' Association demanded that the seven "disloyal" aldermen resign. To force an apology, the Board of Trade and the manufacturers stated there would be an "Indignation

Day" on December 3. All factories would close for the day, and rallies would be held to demand action. Most factories did close, and on the evening of the third over a thousand swarmed outside a council meeting which passed unanimously a resolution containing an apology to Borden.

The protesters had brought telegrams indicating the cancellation of orders to the council hall, and these telegrams continued to be displayed at the city hall until election day. The economic impact of a "disloyal" Kitchener now became almost the sole theme of the Unionist campaign. Economic prosperity was unabashedly equated with Unionism in the press: "A vote for Weichel = a vote for prosperity. A vote for Euler = a vote for stagnation." The Board of Trade claimed that already Kitchener had lost $300,000 in orders since the Borden incident; how much more an Euler victory would mean was too frightening to imagine. Just before election day numerous manufacturers, including Breithaupt Leather, Lang Leather, and Kaufman Rubber, published an advertisement indicating their support for the Union government. The manufacturers asked citizens to read the cancelled orders, and "If after reading these letters with their story of cancelled orders running into hundreds of thousands of dollars, you desire to subject the industries of Kitchener to the risk of having this sort of thing multiplied and continued, then vote for W. D. Euler."[28] But on election day, December 17, most took the risk.

Euler trounced his Unionist opponent as the Unionists in North Waterloo suffered their most disastrous defeat in Ontario. Kitchener and North Waterloo still stood alone resisting the Unionist wave that swept so easily over their neighbours. Within a few minutes of the poll closing, the large crowds in Kitchener's downtown learned of Euler's triumph. The inevitable victory parade began with Euler in the lead car with sympathetic aldermen and Private Max Euler of the United States Army in the car behind. Following were the younger Liberals bearing a coffin with, according to different reports, this slogan: "This coffin is for Billy Weichel," "Here lies Bill," or "Here lies the Canadian Army." Unionists, already upset by the defeat, became enraged. In his committee rooms Weichel reportedly grabbed a Union Jack, leapt upon a table, and decried this latest insult. A private who claimed to have been spat upon called upon all British Canadians to leave town to permit the soliders to wipe out the remaining Germans with hand grenades. That suggestion was surely too much; a short time later the defeated Unionists simply went home, with Weichel muttering, "You can't beat the Kaiser in North Waterloo."[29]

The Kaiser cast no Euler vote in North Waterloo, but 5,405 Canadians did. Only 2,942 marked their ballot for Weichel. The turnout offered the Unionists no consolation, for 86 per cent voted. Euler carried the traditionally Liberal rural townships by extraordinary margins, winning the village of St. Clements by 189 to 9. But it was in Kitchener, where Weichel had won almost 60 per cent of the vote in 1911, that traditional patterns most dramatically changed. In 1917 only 40 per cent voted for Weichel, while 56 per cent marked their ballots for Euler. Weichel did win four Berlin polls, but his defeat came in those working-class polls that had given him the victory in the Reciprocity election of 1911.[30] The polls that Weichel won had Kitchener's highest per capita assessment and highest concentration of "British Canadians." Those that Euler won contained Kitchener's poorest and the "Germans." For Kitchener, as for Canada, this was a critical election where fundamental changes in old loyalties occurred. After 1917 the Liberals held North Waterloo for four decades.

The final scene of the wartime drama took place on December 2, 1919. On that evening the city council was considering a finance committee report which recommended that another plebiscite be held on the city's name. A crowd of five hundred, mostly made up of Great War Veterans' Association members, swarmed into and about the council chambers. The crowd's opinion was known. Council respected it, voting down the recommendation. Aldermen Bowman and Bitzer, however, had not voted and had remained in the hall outside the chamber. Such silence was deemed to be defiance by the crowd. Both aldermen were grabbed, dragged to the council table where the Union Jack was placed before them. Kiss it, they were ordered. They refused. Bowman was saved by the generally ineffectual police, but Bitzer was taken off to the Great War Veterans' Association Hall. There he did kiss the flag, but this display of "loyalty" did not save him from several subsequent dunkings in the lake at Victoria Park. The crowd then attacked the *News-Record* office, smashing the door and windows, and vandalizing the equipment. Alderman-M.P.P. Nick Asmussen was the next target. He met the crowd with a revolver, vowing to protect his family. The leaders told him "they did not want his better half, but him." Thus reassured he too went to the Veterans' Hall and under compulsion saluted the flag and swore his loyalty. Euler's turn was next.

The mob found the M.P. at his club. He made no attempt to hide or escape and "willingly" accompanied the mob to the Veterans Hall. Once there, he refused to kiss the Union Jack and shouted to the crowd that "under proper circumstances he would certainly kiss the flag, to do so under these circumstances would be to dishonor it." The demand nevertheless persisted, as did Euler's refusal. He was grabbed, struck, pushed down on the ground, and pummelled, but this time the mob had met its match. The Union Jack unkissed, Euler "departed from the hall under the protection of a few of those present." The next morning Euler was "on the street," telling all that his bruises did not hurt, and they would not last. His comments had more than their literal meaning.[31]

The war years had assured that Kitchener could never again be Berlin. In 1918 the German newspaper ceased publication, the victim not only of a federal order-in-council but also of the new life that Kitchener knew it had to lead. The belief that Kitchener could live apart, could have a double

Opposite page—
Visit of the Governor-General, the Duke of Connaught, May 1914

Opposite page—
Visit of the Governor-General, the Duke of Devonshire, June 1918. David Gross is on the right of the vice-regal party.

Duke of Devonshir[e]
Governor General of Cana[da]
and Duchess of Devonshi[re]
and daughters
Kitchener June 13. 1[9..]
Victoria Park

loyalty, could purchase respectability through productivity, had abruptly ended. The city was now a part of that national community whose contours the Great War had done so much to shape. In later days, few would talk about the Coffin, Sergeant Blood, the beatings, or the Kaiser's bust now melted down into souvenir napkin-holders; records of the community consigned those things to oblivion. Berlin thus died; its signs and icons vanished. Those who sought its monuments could not find them, and yet one knows that in those most private moments of public life, such as when they voted, all these things were still remembered.

The Economy in Wartime

Historians commonly look for the causes of political divisions in social and economic factors. On the surface, it seems that Kitchener's wartime divisions can be easily explained on the basis of ethnic differences. Certainly prewar rhetoric in the newspapers and the council chambers gave no hint that class differences were a source of antagonism in the community. And yet the voting pattern in the 1917 election does reveal a strong sense of class feeling. Moreover, during the election campaign Euler appealed directly to the disadvantaged and denounced the "big shots."

Workers at Merchant's Rubber

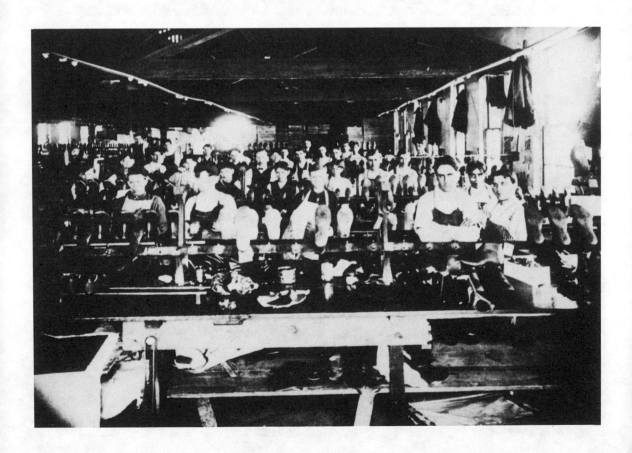

In fact, the war years showed that the comity that existed in the community was not so profound as Kitchener's prewar boosters imagined. There was resentment that occasionally burst through the veneer of racial co-operation. The domination of professional classes in Kitchener by those of British extraction was well established. The choice of Dr. John Scott as the first mayor is symbolic: those who transacted Berlin-Kitchener's relationships with the extra-urban environment through the courts, the schools, and the hospitals were more often British than German. The professional classes, with their historical intermediary function, were more like the Ontario community than other residents.

A recent study of occupational categories in Kitchener in 1916 has found that in the highest employment category (foremen, professionals, merchants, managers, manufacturers, contractors, travellers, city officials, gentlemen) those of British background make up 44 per cent of the category, considerably higher than the British background of the general population (28.9 per cent in the 1921 census). Moreover, the British pre-eminence in "intermediary" professions such as law, medicine, reli-

Caspar Braun Construction. Braun is standing on the top at the right of the future Dominion Rubber.

gion, and education was even more pronounced (54.9 per cent). "Managers" were a remarkable 59.2 per cent British, and government and city officials were 50 per cent British. Among semi-professionals (accountants, teachers, nurses, and related fields), 50.5 per cent were British in background. An interesting and related facet of this is the British prominence in Berlin's civic political life. Although Canada's German capital could point to a large number of Germans among North Waterloo's M.P.s and M.P.P.s, Germans were in fact underrepresented in municipal politics. If one examines the membership of the city council (including the office of mayor) between 1900 and 1917, one finds that the percentage of German councillors only slightly exceeded those of "British" background (55 to 45 per cent).[32]

The prominence of British Canadians in Kitchener's professional and political life might naturally lead one to conclude that British Canadians were similarly dominant in economic life. The congruity of economic and political power in prewar Canadian urban life has been demonstrated so often that we might assume there is a general rule. In Kitchener, however, wealth derived mainly from manufacturing, and Germans dominated the manufacturing field. Indeed, their pre-eminence in manufacturing was long and strongly established. The wealthiest manufacturing families— the Langs, the Breithaupts, and the Kaufmans—were all of German origin. Germans in Berlin were at the apex of the economic pyramid; they were also overrepresented at its base. Like some other ethnic groups, such as the Jews and the Huguenots, the Germans in Kitchener both thrived and suffered because of exclusion from the Anglo-Saxon society engulfing them. The sons and grandsons of the early German manufacturers in Kitchener did not seek the refuge of education and profession but rather remained in the factory and in the traditional family activity. They did so long after the progeny of the early Canadian manufacturers had sought out the sanctuaries of Oxford and Bay Street. But the sons and grandsons of old Berlin's German labourers also tended to follow their parents' patterns. While the German owners generally prospered as a result of their decision, the workers perhaps did not.[33]

The ethnic antagonism in wartime Kitchener at times took on the flavour of class division. The first opposition to conscription came from the socialists, and the rhetoric was bequeathed to the Euler campaign in which the prosperous businessman spoke of conscription of wealth and defence against oppression. The *News-Record* under Motz's editorship similarly identified the "injustices" that befell Kitchener's Germans with class discrimination. On the other hand, some newer groups, notably the Polish Canadians, resented the German predominance. This was especially true when Kitchener's economy paid the price for its citizens' Germanism.

Prewar Kitchener had felt few of the effects of the depression which had so affected other areas. Between 1912 and 1914, its population rose from 16,917 to 19,056 and its assessment from $8,891,583 to

Opposite page—
The Auto Age arrives.
Visit of the Prince of
Wales, 1919.

$11,187,861. The war years, 1914-18, saw population rise insignificantly (19,056 to 19,767) and assessment stabilized as well ($11,187,861 to $12,403,646, unindexed for inflation).[34] In the manufacturing sector, Canada's wartime prosperity was unevenly distributed within Kitchener. The rubber factories thrived. By 1916 the Dominion Rubber plant, completed in 1914, already employed 604 workers, while Merchants Rubber had 526 workers and Kaufman Rubber 466. Some smaller firms also benefitted from the war.[35] Berlin Robe and Clothing Company, which had specialized in imitation buffalo robes before 1914, quickly adapted to the military demand for overcoats. The manager of the firm, Mr. Walter Barrie, recalls that output, which was doubled, became entirely overcoats. When the war ended, there were too many overcoats, the market crumbled, and the company suffered the effects of pursuing short-term gain. During World War Two, the firm held to the rule that no more than 50 per cent of production should be devoted to war-related goods.[36]

The problem of reconversion occurred throughout Canada, but Kitchener's political problems were unique. As we have seen, contemporaries believed that the political difficulties were having a direct economic effect; hence the name change and the industrialists' opposition to W. D. Euler in the December 1917 general election. There can be no doubt that the letters from buyers threatening to cancel or cancelling orders from "Canada's Prussian Capital" were genuine. A recent study which compares Kitchener's economic performance in 1916-19 with that of surrounding communities concludes that Kitchener did not share in the wartime prosperity as fully as Guelph or Galt.[37] A firm conclusion is impossible because statistics are not fully reliable and because any comparison would have to take account of the demand for the types of goods the various cities produced. Nevertheless, it is likely that Kitchener's political problems during the war years did affect investment and production. That is certainly what most thought at the time, and there is no evidence that we should doubt their testimony.

KITCHENER BETWEEN TWO WARS

5

Progress Lost: Economic Developments in Kitchener

The First World War affected Berlin-Kitchener differently than other Canadian cities; the city's response to the war's aftermath also did not reflect national tendencies. The strife between labour and capital was not found in Kitchener's factories or on its streets as it was in so many Canadian communities in the spring of 1919. While Kitchener's workers shared many of the grievances of workers elsewhere, the wartime turmoil seemed to moderate their expression of these grievances.

During the spring of 1919, as Winnipeg's workers grasped the sinews of that city, Kitchener's Trades and Labour Council politely discussed with city council and the Board of Trade methods of maintaining comity in the city. The best example of this spirit was the founding in that year of the Kitchener Young Men's Club, the city's first service club. The club's purpose was to "stimulate and maintain a keen interest in all matters of civic welfare." This meant, in the context of the time, that the club sought to reunify the community and to speed the passing of civic leadership to a younger generation with fainter memories of wartime antagonism. Labour was represented, but the major activists were younger businessmen and professionals. These were the kind of men who would dominate the civic and economic life of the city between the wars.[1] In most cases the names were familiar. One might easily have found them in the second-generation characters of Mann's *Buddenbrooks*: their concern was accumulation and stability, and they moved more closely with the rhythms of their times than did their fathers. The sons of George Lang, Reinhold and Louis, are good examples. Reinhold remained in the tanning business, becoming its president, while Louis became president of the Waterloo-based Mutual Life Insurance Company, the area's most important financial institution,

and an adornment to boards of directors across the country. They were club men, more social, and more attuned to the business life of the nation than their fathers had been. They were not mechanics but managers.

L. O. Breithaupt, son of L. J. Breithaupt, managed and was president of the family's leather business and, like his father, entered politics. Elected as an alderman in 1919, he symbolizes the new generation which recognized the necessity of healing internal conflicts and establishing closer links with the prosperous southwestern Ontario society around Kitchener. In 1915 L. J. Breithaupt had led the protest against the end of German-language education in Berlin; in 1940 and 1941, L. O. Breithaupt welcomed government moves to suppress German activities in Kitchener. L. O. Breithaupt became Lieutenant-Governor of Ontario in 1952; his father could never have done so. L.O.'s attitudes and accomplishments are a measurement of the change between generations in the family and in the city.

If Breithaupt is an illustration of Kitchener's adaptation, A. R. Kaufman, son of Jacob Kaufman, is an example of the way Kitchener still stood outside. Kaufman possessed the entrepreneurial skills and spirit of the first generation and the paternalistic commitment to community so characteristic of an earlier age. Probably the city's wealthiest businessman after the 1920s, Kaufman expanded the rubber company he had founded with his father's assistance at the age of twenty-two in 1907. His interests also included extensive landholdings in the area, and, at a later date, the Superior Box Company and the Kaufman Furniture Company in Collingwood. In 1922, he became chairman of the Kitchener Planning Board, and he was an early promoter of town planning. In the early 1930s he founded a birth-control clinic, which soon became a centre of controversy and litigation. In his relationship with his employees he remained paternalistic, vigorously opposed to unionization; and his rubber factory was the only unorganized factory in the field in Canada. In short, he fits no category easily; neither reactionary nor progressive, he testifies to the different origins and affiliations of Kitchener's entrepreneurial elite. In the 1920s and later, the remarkable tenacity of the family firm in Kitchener contrasts with the disappearance of such businesses throughout Ontario. In Kitchener some old patterns lingered longer.[2]

This persistence of the past was as true for labour as for management. The Industrial Relations Commission's visit to Kitchener in May 1919 elicited the frankest assessments of industrial relations in the city's history to that point. Labour and business representatives agreed that there was no unemployment in Kitchener and that "unrest" was muted. O. Hughes of the Trades and Labour Council could not even recall any strike, only about "2 or 3 incidents." Both labour and owners recognized that there was potential for unrest in the changes occurring in the structure of industry. E. O. Weber, testifying for the furniture manufacturers, pointed to the breakdown of the apprenticeship system in that industry. The organization

Opposite page—
Krug home

of the factory had become different, and the result was specialization "in more elaborate lines." In response to Weber's testimony, Harry Weinstein, the secretary of the woodworkers' union, charged that apprenticeship failed because wages were too low ($2.50 per day) when unskilled rubber workers could earn considerably more. He also charged that employers had a "blacklist" of those workers who "held out for [their] rights." This was denied by George Lang, speaking for the Manufacturers' Association. Lang said that manufacturers did maintain a "labour bureau" with a full-time secretary, but the bureau's purpose was solely to assure that "right men" would find a "right place." Labour sent by the bureau was not "guaranteed" to the employer and no blacklist was therefore employed. The secretary also co-ordinated the collective buying of manufacturers. The symbiotic relationship of Kitchener industry had obviously not died with the wartime divisions.[3]

William Knell, second from right; Weyburn Doerr (later Dare), farthest right

Other characteristics had not changed either. Manufacturing remained the predominant economic activity of the city, employing 57 per cent of the labour force in 1921, and that labour force had an unusually high percentage of women in it. The shirt factories, the button industry, and other light industries found women a source of cheap labour. In the 1919 Industrial Relations Commission hearing, one button company owner said he paid men $3.00 to $8.00 per day, and women a fixed rate of $1.50 per day. Overall, Kitchener's postwar wages seem to have been lower than those in other manufacturing centres.[4] In any case, rapid postwar inflation made many Kitchener families dependent upon incomes from both husband and wife. There is no evidence that this altered family structures, although it is possible that women by providing cheap labour were the foundation of the remarkable growth of Kitchener industry in the first three decades of this century. More speculatively, it may be that the German tradition of the family, which Berlin-Kitchener boosters still regularly lauded, was particularly suited to industrialization, for it does appear that the traditional family and the modern factory fitted together very well elsewhere.[5] What is certain is the fundamental importance of women in the economic life of Kitchener.

In 1911 in Berlin, manufacturing employed 2,668 men and 1,148 *Workers in the 1920s* women. (At 30 per cent this percentage of women was considerably higher than the Canadian average; in nearby Guelph, for example, the comparable figures were 2,064 and 450.) In 1921, one finds the percentage of female workers in manufacturing somewhat lower (1,427 out of 5,292, or 27 per cent), and in 1931 lower still (1,613 of 6,883, or 24 per cent). In the 1930s those industries that employed women most often—manufacturers of shirts, buttons, and shoes—felt most keenly the depression's sting.[6]

In the twenties, however, depression seemed far away as the boosterist philosophy returned after the wartime gloom. Even in the immediate postwar doldrums, Kitchener managed to secure major new industries. In June 1919, T. H. Rieder, the former Kitchener entrepreneur, announced the establishment of a large tire factory which might employ six hundred people. (This eventually became the Goodrich Canadian subsidiary.) Another automobile-related company established in 1919 was Four Wheel Drive Company, a subsidiary of an American company. The announcement of its arrival occasioned special celebration because it was the first postwar company location. At a grand but dry dinner at the Walper Hotel, civic politicians proved they had not forgotten the booster's litany of prewar days, but there were some differences. Alderman W. T. Sass, a businessman himself, expressed regret that "the directors could not stay here to

live in the city. The real sentiment of the people could not be learned unless one lived here. . . ."[7]

There was never reluctance, however, only regret. The encouragement of "outsiders" continued throughout the 1920s with impressive results for the community. Taxable assessments grew continuously from $18,053,521 in 1920 to $25,686,732 in 1930. Population also advanced significantly from over 23,027 in 1920 to 30,274 in 1930. In the period from 1920 to 1928 over one thousand new houses were added to existing stock. The construction business prospered not only because of residential housing, but also because of the need for service institutions to meet the demands of this larger and more prosperous population. The civic government supported several large projects which considerably increased city debt: the expansion of the Kitchener-Waterloo Collegiate and Vocational Institute, an expanded sewage system, and a new city hall. The debenture debt per capita more than doubled from $.80 to $1.85 between 1920 and 1924, but such was confidence in the future that protest was insignificant.[8] In fact, the new expenditures such as the city hall were usually solidly supported by ratepayers in referenda.

The Santa Claus Parade, 1921

*Opposite page—
The W. H. Bowlby residence, converted into offices for the Canadian Goodrich Company*

*Opposite page—
Precision machinery in the workplace*

The twenties brought a richer material life to all classes in Kitchener. For the middle class, new conveniences provided leisure and pleasure. Automobiles were ubiquitous. Roads spread out to carry Kitchener holiday-makers to the countryside, often for picnics on lambent summer afternoons. The workers, too, benefitted from the general prosperity. After acute shortages in the early 1920s, housing became available at reasonable prices. The number of hours worked per week decreased to approximately forty-two by 1928, but higher hourly wages more than compensated for this shortened work week. This prosperity began to seem normal, as each year its symbols—new factories, grander homes, paved roads, and manicured lawns—multiplied in all city wards. A 1928 publication boasted: "Kitchener is a busy city, a beautiful city, an ever-expanding city; looking forward in a most hopeful, a most confident state of mind; assured by the qualities of its citizenship that the remarkable progress marking its career to date will be exalted in coming years."[9] The prophecy, of course, was false, but so tenacious was its appeal that Kitchener could not reject it even when the evidence disputing it appeared everywhere.

A picnic in the country with the 1928 Oldsmobile, 1929: Roxy Roche and Helen Archambault

When the great crash of 1929 came, Kitchener, judging by its politicians' remarks and its newspaper's attitude, assumed that the good times would stay. L. J. Breithaupt, the city's economic patriarch, assured his fellow Kitchenerites that "the town is going ahead fast and will continue to go ahead despite the little ups and downs." In December 1929, the *Record* polled the city industrial leaders and reported that they believed that "business is inherently sound and there is no substantial reason to

Opposite page— The auto comes to King Street

believe that the winter period ahead will be more perplexing or difficult than in any former year."[10] The perplexities, however, were only beginning as the worst continued to worsen.[11]

Buddell's Garage

Construction stopped first. Furniture soon followed, as Canadians suddenly stopped purchasing new chairs and couches. Production in the furniture industry in Kitchener fell dramatically from a value of over $11 million in 1928 to just over $1 million in 1932. By December 1930, there were 582 jobless Canadian males in Kitchener; a month later the number had doubled to 1,034.[12] For those who kept their jobs, wages usually fell. For male workers in Kitchener the average wage in 1930-31 was $961, below the median for Canadian cities above 15,000 in population. As Terry Copp and Blake Weller have pointed out, this wage was below the Canadian Welfare Council's "essentials" family budget of $1,040 per year.[13] But many fell far below this as the relief rolls of the city lengthened. By the summer of 1930 the city's allocation for relief, $10,000, was exhausted. In 1931, six hundred were on relief and the costs were over $85,000.[14] The Family Relief Board, which had been organized in the 1920s but whose existence in those booming times was rarely noticed or admitted, suddenly became the most publicized civic body. Its competent and sympathetic administrative secretary, Mabel Feick, captured as much newspaper space as city aldermen as relief expenditures swelled.[15]

By 1933, 4,500 men, women, and children lived on relief in Kitchener. Their monthly income was $26 per month, roughly a quarter of what the Welfare Council deemed a decent income. Incredibly, the provincial government declared this was too much.

In 1933, the Henry government warned Kitchener that it must conform to provincial standards or lose its financial support for local projects. Kitchener reluctantly agreed, and the city reduced costs by moving families to less expensive housing. Nevertheless, Kitchener during the depression managed to pay relief 25 per cent above the normal provincial levels.[16] In the earlier years of the depression the willingness to share, the commitment of the community, and, probably, memories of the past combined to moderate protest. In 1932, for example, the Young Men's Club organized the distribution of over twelve hundred bags of groceries to the needy. A year earlier, the Kitchener Community Relief Campaign had raised $40,000 which was contributed to community relief costs. Merchants gave credit; barter became once again a normal method of business. The diversity of Kitchener's churches undoubtedly contributed to private acts of assistance. Although churches such as the Lutheran, the Evangelical, and the Swedenborgian were not in the tradition of the Social Gospel, they were especially concerned to protect their own people. There was a familiarity in the pews that fostered generosity, and yet for all this there was anger, bitterness, and discontent.

For Canada and for Kitchener, 1933 was the depression's hardest year. Unemployment continued, but gradually the situation improved. By 1936 the city could speak of "rapid growth":

Table 1

The Impact of the Depression

	1933	1934	1935
No. of employees	6,916	7,612	8,034
Salaries and wages	$ 6,206,187	$ 7,028,649	$ 7,505,880
Gross value of production	$25,549,350	$32,457,335	$34,929,052

By 1936, the worst of the depression had passed, and for the majority of Kitchener families the standard of living of the 1920s had returned.[17] However, it was then that labour troubles began.

There had been no significant labour disturbance in the early 1930s. The number of union members in 1933, 301, was over 250 less than in

1923.[18] In January 1934, nevertheless, a major strike occurred as hundreds of woodworkers walked out. This strike, organized by the Militant Furniture and Woodworkers' Industrial Union, was Kitchener's first industrial strike. The victory went to the workers who secured higher wages, better working conditions, and recognition of the union. Encouraged by this, shoe and leather workers were organized by the communist-led Workers' Unity League. Their strike was less successful, and in 1935 the labour turmoil subsided.[19]

In 1936 industrial unionism came to Kitchener to remain. In 1935 and 1936, the American Congress of Industrial Organizations had an early success in the rubber industry in Akron, Ohio. Kitchener, of course, was the "Akron of Canada," with several plants which were subsidiaries of Akron enterprises. Now American labour followed American capital across the border.

In both cases Canadians extended the invitations. Alfred Mustin, a worker at Merchants Rubber, secretly organized support at Merchants. When he thought support was sufficient, he and some sympathizers drove to Akron to ask for support.[20] They got it in the person of C. D. Lesley, a United Rubber Workers organizer who, by Christmas 1936, had organized a local at Merchants. In successive months beginning in January 1937, locals were chartered at B. F. Goodrich, Dominion Rubber, and Kaufman Rubber. On March 24, 1937, workers at B. F. Goodrich "sat down," and the test of strength began.

Dominion Rubber

Goodrich immediately agreed to negotiate with the union, and both union and management agreed to principles to govern the strike which included no picketing. The company's readiness to negotiate is probably explained by the experience—sometimes violent—of Goodrich in Akron, for the Kitchener local at Goodrich was not strong. Its membership included roughly half of the Goodrich employees, and the "sit-down" strike probably had been employed because union leaders feared they lacked the strength to close down the plant if union members simply walked out. The union leaders' aim was recognition, but, publicly, wages were declared to be the primary goal. Obviously fearing a long strike, the union settled quickly and the strike ended on April 3. The workers got raises of 5-1/4 per cent, but the union did not obtain recognition through a written agreement. The civility of the dispute contrasted sharply with events in Oshawa where automobile workers clashed bitterly with management and government at the same time. The Kitchener strike left no scars, only hopes.

Workers in other rubber factories hoped that they too could receive the benefits their Goodrich counterparts had won. The management of Dominion Tire and Merchants, hoping that the moderate demands of the workers at Goodrich would continue, generally agreed to similar terms in the summer of 1937. Both these companies were American-owned and no doubt felt the constraints which their parent companies, concerned about labour relations in the United States, exerted. A. R. Kaufman, president of Kaufman Rubber, had no such concern. When over six hundred men and women at Kaufman Rubber walked out on September 23, 1937, they soon learned that Kaufman was different. The union's demands at Kaufman were higher than those at Goodrich, and the union seemed to believe that this privately owned firm was an easier target. It was wrong; Kaufman proved an exceedingly tough bargainer. Indeed, he refused to bargain seriously during most of the strike. When the union proposed that it be consulted in questions of lay-offs and seniority, Kaufman responded with a demand that he be given a voice in the composition of the union executive! Tensions grew, and by the strike's third week the police were constantly present at Kaufman's plant. Only provincial government intervention finally brought the strike to an end in early November, by which time Kaufman had made clear the seriousness of his threat to close the plant for the winter. The union gained nothing; it merely recovered the status quo before the strike.

In 1938 the U.R.W.A. lost members in Kitchener and failed even to protect the gains of 1937. Only when companies took advantage of this quiescence to reduce wages did unionist forces swell. In February 1939, workers walked out at Dominion and Merchants, this time with an explicit demand for a signed agreement between company and union. Again the union had misjudged its strength. Non-union workers organized parades against the strike demanding a secret ballot on the question of whether the union genuinely represented the workers. After initial agreement with this request, the union refused, losing considerable face. Criticism came from numerous public figures, but the union persisted, encouraged by organizers from Akron where recent strikes had been successful. The year 1939 was a relatively prosperous one, and the companies feared loss of their profits. Thus they settled, granting the union the signed working agreement with sole bargaining rights. Alfred Mustin, the president of the Merchants local, did not boast when he claimed, "We are going back to work stronger than when we went out."[21]

The U.R.W.A. strength ebbed once more in a month-long strike at B. F. Goodrich in the late spring of 1939. The strike began in the rubber footwear division and expanded to the tire division within a few days. This time, the union lacked resources for a long strike and the company was more adamant in its position. The strike affected the city more than others because violence came with it. The city government was especially concerned because the King and Queen were visiting Kitchener on June 6, and it pressed hard for settlement. Goodrich nevertheless held out, and when settlement was reached on June 9, the union did not have the signed agreement. The U.R.W.A. had taken a step back.

There it remained until war began in September 1939. Nevertheless, in those last years before the war, international and industrial unionism had grounded itself firmly in the economic structure of the city. It would never again be rooted out. And yet its growth was truncated. Locally owned firms proved especially resistant to its development, and the community, as reflected in its public officials and its newspaper, was more suspicious of unionism than other industrial centres in Ontario. But suspicion was less prevalent than optimism in that last summer before the war. The gloom which the depression had cast over the city had lifted, and both workers and owners were prepared to grasp the economic opportunities that war would bring.

Planning the Modern City

Kitchener's boosters in the 1920s suggested that the city was a uniquely successful blend of humanity with nature, where sylvan retreats stood beside hives of industry and where all elements found their proper place. But that was simply not so. Kitchener was, as its greatest booster Dan Detweiler admitted, a city that "like Topsy just grew." To shape growth and to eliminate old mistakes, Kitchener's civic leaders took up the concept of planning with great alacrity.

The city's problems were easily enumerated. As with so many other Canadian cities, the railway caused a large part of the problem. The mainline railway tracks split the city, and well into the twentieth century the Margaret Avenue overhead bridge was the sole direct link with the city's North Ward. Moreover, the positioning of the tracks had created a street pattern that was irregular, with certain streets running parallel to King Street and others parallelling the tracks. Too many streets were not continuous, and they were difficult to extend. This was especially so in the case of streets in the direction of Waterloo. Mount Hope Cemetery blocked the extension of several streets that might have connected the two cities. As a result, travel between the two communities was largely restricted to a congested King Street. There was also congestion created by the crowding together of factories and residential areas. And there were always too many people and too few houses.

The famous Five Points Grocery at the corner of Frederick and Lancaster Streets

The first attempts to create a city plan took place before the war. A group of civic leaders met in November 1912 to discuss the possibility of such a plan.[22] At the meeting, which Dan Detweiler chaired, there were many complaints. Some participants grumbled about the lack of a city centre, others pointed to the inadequate sewers and street railways as impediments to rational growth, and others condemned the building of houses in laneways. The meeting condemned obvious abuses, and Detweiler sought, as he had with hydro, to draw in other nearby municipalities. With Waterloo this need was obvious, since the twentieth-century expansion of both towns had drawn their social and economic lives more closely together. Although not yet the "twin cities," they were certainly very close cousins connected by a street railway, a joint hospital near the city boundaries, and, of course, their main street. Nevertheless, the response to Detweiler's appeal was negligible, and Berlin had to proceed on its own.[23]

The Board of Trade, with the encouragement of the mayor and council, formed a Civic Association which hired a noted planner, Charles Leavitt, to produce a city plan. Waterloo also participated at this early stage. Visiting the city intermittently from his New York base, Leavitt managed to produce a tentative plan by November 1913. His plan envisaged connected parkways, quaint vistas, three-hundred-foot boulevards, and civic structures approaching the monumental. It also provided for "zoning"—that is, the separation of industrial, residential, and commercial areas. This was a heady brew and much too strong for the city's frugal burghers. Interest continued, but the resolve abated. The immensity of the plan seemed too much for a city which still extended only a mile from the main intersection of King and Queen and where most of the population still lived within a half-mile radius of that intersection. Then in August 1914 war came, sending so many civic dreams into limbo for its duration. When they returned after armistice day, their form was no longer the same.[24]

The war and the attendant slowing of population growth eased the demand for "planning" until the war's end. There was so much else to worry about. These early attempts at planning had very little effect. Nevertheless, they did accustom Berlin and Waterloo to think of themselves as part of the same functional area. The possibility of union of the two communities was considered with a degree of seriousness for the first time. The "efficiency" of such a union was emphasized by the very nature of the civic planner's approach. Indeed, the Ontario Planning and Development Act of 1917 defined a city's urban zone as extending up to five miles. Thus Waterloo was clearly within Kitchener's urban zone, and its interests had to be considered in Kitchener's future plans.[25] After the war Waterloo worked more closely with Kitchener in joint planning efforts, although Waterloo's work was usually a response to Kitchener's initiatives.

Kitchener was the first municipality in Ontario to establish a City Planning Commission in response to the 1917 act. Its first chairman was W. H. Breithaupt, who persuaded the young entrepreneur A. R. Kaufman to join the board. In 1922 Kaufman became chairman, a post he held for almost four decades. In that same year the commission hired the distinguished planner Thomas Adams to draw up the city's first plan, a plan that would also apply to Waterloo. Adams and Kaufman both rejected notions of civic grandeur and emphasized what Adams termed "orderly development" which would, through planning and proper zoning, "produce beauty without seeking beauty as an end in itself." Adams himself went to the United States, but he did remain as a consultant. Horace Seymour, who drew up the plan, nevertheless reflected Adams and Kaufman's views. In 1925 the city council approved the Seymour plan. Waterloo, which had been most co-operative to this point, did not follow Kitchener's lead in adopting the plan. Informally, however, the plan naturally influenced Waterloo.

In announcing the new plan the *Journal of the Town Planning Institute of Canada* lauded "the fact that at last a Canadian city of the size and importance of Kitchener has passed into law a comprehensive town plan." The *Journal* admitted that there were some cases where "private interests"

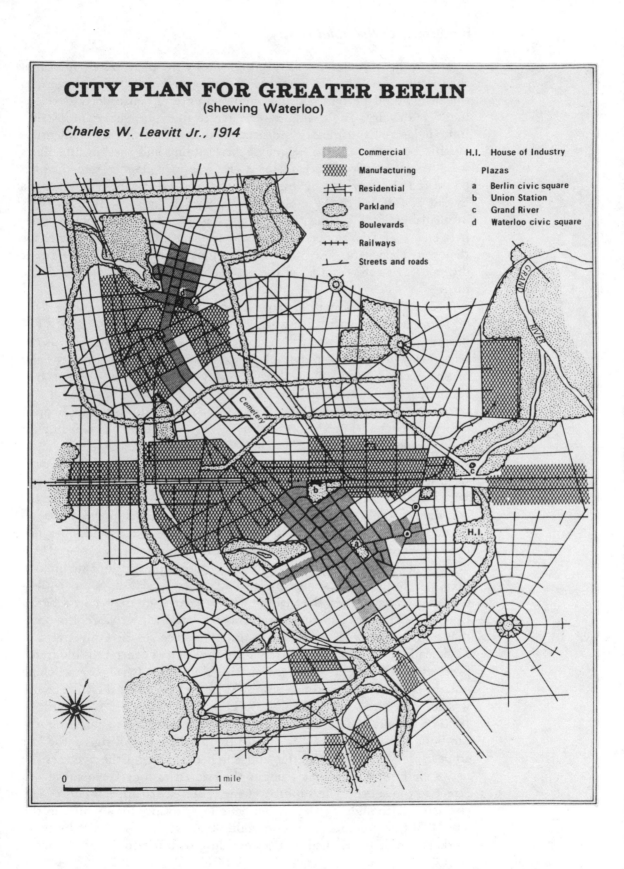

CITY PLAN FOR GREATER BERLIN
(shewing Waterloo)

Charles W. Leavitt Jr., 1914

Commercial
Manufacturing
Residential
Parkland
Boulevards
Railways
Streets and roads

H.I.   House of Industry

Plazas
a   Berlin civic square
b   Union Station
c   Grand River
d   Waterloo civic square

Cemetery

GRAND RIVER

H.I.

0   1 mile

received some concessions, but, on the whole, the plan was a triumph of the planners' art. The "comprehensive zoning by-laws" that characterized the plan would protect housing values and create "an orderly development" of the city. The zoning by-law created five zones: heavy industrial, light industrial, business, residential, and detached private residential. Within each district, the height of the building and the building lines were regulated. Twelve years later A. R. Kaufman claimed that the plan had saved the city money and that "the protection which Kitchener's by-law has offered to real estate, especially in the residential districts, is incalculable."[26] What the plan brought was security. Homeowners benefitted most, and developers were not as active in the planning movement as they were elsewhere. The plan's modest aims were its greatest appeal. It did not redress the disorder of the past; it prevented such patterns in the future.[27]

The Adams-Seymour Plan of 1924 illustrates generally some patterns of Kitchener's growth during the next fifteen years (see p. 153). The barriers to expansion, especially the sewer farm and cemeteries, can also be seen. Many of the projected developments, however, had to await the end of the Second World War. The depression slowed but did not halt residential and commercial development. The proposed residential districts in the South Ward (Queen Street South) and in the Westmount area, which had been planned before the First World War, were partially but not fully developed by 1940. The city's face had nonetheless changed. In October 1940, Walter Cunningham, a former city editor of the *Record*, returned for a visit after a twenty-three-year absence. He saw "a new city with but a few of the old landmarks left to remind him of the days when the community took issues bitterly and the papers went into headlines on points of high controversy." To be sure, many of the old landmarks had gone. The old city hall disappeared in the early twenties to be replaced by a neo-classical structure of grey stone, with Queenston and Indiana mouldings. The building, designed by local architect W. H. E. Schmalz, and the site were far from the elaborate civic centre envisaged by Charles Leavitt. There was also the large rubber factory where Ward Bowlby's modest mansion with its charming grounds once stood. Only traces of nineteenth-century Berlin now remained in the city's centre; the old frame post office was a relic displayed on the ubiquitous local postcards one bought in the new department stores. What impressed local citizens more was the new seven-storey Dunker Building on King Street West built in 1930 on the site of an old planing mill and drive-shed. The building was symbolic of a shift of the city toward the northwest, closing up the last empty spaces between Waterloo and Kitchener. During the twenties the new suburb of Westmount brought the two cities together below King Street to the south. The suburb's name reflected its upper-middle-class character. Although the depression halted its advance for a while, in the later 1930s new homes spread out along boulevards often built by relief workers. These homes had to meet building requirements that restricted

*Opposite page—
Adams-Seymour Plan,
1924*

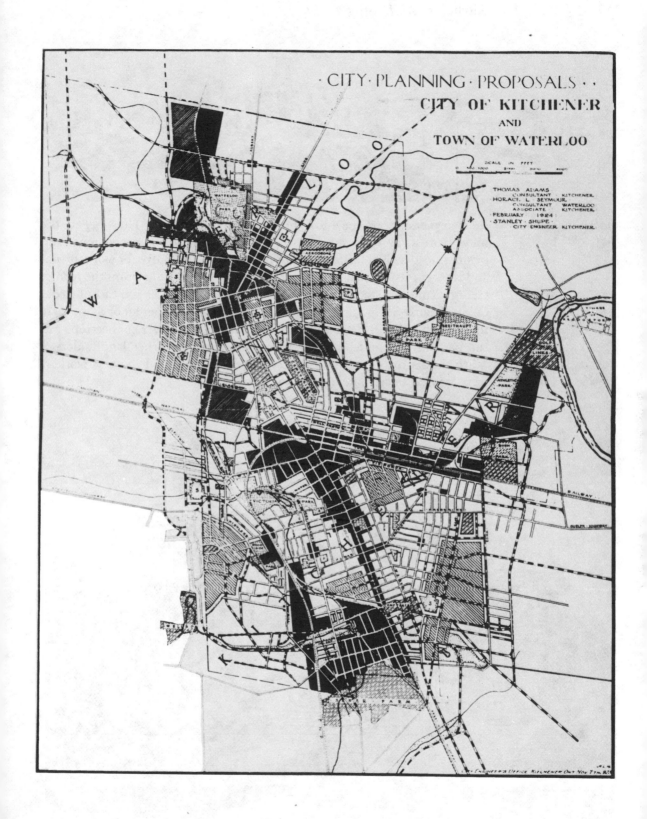

CITY·PLANNING·PROPOSALS··
CITY OF KITCHENER
AND
TOWN OF WATERLOO

SCALE IN FEET

THOMAS ADAMS
CONSULTANT KITCHENER
HORACE L. SEYMOUR
CONSULTANT WATERLOO
ASSOCIATE KITCHENER
FEBRUARY 1924
STANLEY SHUPE
CITY ENGINEER KITCHENER

Kitchener's new City Hall, 1925

Home designed by City Hall architect W. H. Schmalz

their ownership to the most prosperous in the city. Thus began the movement away from the centre of the city where the professional and business leaders had earlier dwelt. There were new suburbs for workers too, and the depression made their cost relatively low as well. From the former George Rumpel estate, Forest Hill (south of King Street and east of Cedar on the Adams-Seymour map), the city sold land for $1 per lot or $7 per acre in December 1939. Each house had to pay $60 for sewer connection, but the bargain was undeniable and much resented by other landholders.[28] With the depression's end, industry was ready to expand and new workers were needed once more and so were their houses.

Society and Politics between the Wars

Middle-class residence of the 1920s

The wartime political and social turmoil described in the previous chapter left its imprint on the decades which followed. The celebrations to end the war were muted in Kitchener, and not simply because wartime prohibition had stopped the flow of spirits. Tension lingered because the city remained smaller or, perhaps, more enclosed than its numbers suggest it should have been. In the newspapers, for example, the editors continued to assume an intimacy of social life; hence this item in the *News-Record* in May 1919: "A request has been made of the *Record* by a highly respected citizen, the bride of a local soldier, recently returned from overseas, to give an emphatic denial to certain rumours on the street, false and malicious, regarding herself, which have been current." Because so much of the rumour, the tension, and the life of the city remained "on the street" and not in the newspapers, the re-integration of the community often seems like a play where most of the time the actors perform while the lights are out.

The record of the interwar years nevertheless suggests that the re-integration was successful. There were industrial problems, economic hardships, and political brouhahas, but the turmoil that so marked Kitchener during the war did not recur. Contemporaries gave much of the credit for the restoration of calm to civic affairs to the Young Men's Club which had been organized with the objective of assuring continuity and calm in city politics. The club resembled in its social and service functions the Rotary and Kiwanis Clubs that proliferated on the main streets of North America during the twenties, but unlike them it had an explicit political purpose. The club, which limited membership to one hundred males, chose a slate of candidates for the municipal elections. In the memory of one club member, this selection was done secretly; he recalls meeting for the selection in a remote hall in Bridgeport. In any event, electors seemed to know who the nominees were, and in the 1920s these candidates did consistently well at the polls. In 1920 the *News-Record* hailed the election to aldermanic posts of the young businessmen L. O. Breithaupt, Charles Greb, and F. H. Ahrens as a victory for the "Young Men."[29] The next year, a "young man," Charles Greb, captured the mayoralty from five-time Kitchener mayor J. R. Eden. Eden's approach to the electors reflected his view that the newcomers to civic politics such as Greb represented too narrow a segment of the community. On nomination night, the *News-Record* reported, Eden claimed that "during his term he had played no favourites. He had treated all classes alike. He stated that he spoke and wrote German and English and was fair to all." The electors, however, found the younger candidate Greb fairer as he carried the election 1,398 to 1,161.[30] The Greb administration emphasized harmony, a budgetary surplus, and civic expansion which included plans for a new city hall. These plans were approved, along with Mayor Greb himself, in the 1921 civic elections in which Greb trounced Eden and another political veteran A. Bricker.[31]

Table 2

Comparative Civic Finances

City	Assessment per capita	General debenture debt per capita	Mill rate	Population
Hamilton	1,112	61	33.50	114,766
London	911	105	38.82	59,281
Brantford	890	53	39.00	30,000
Kitchener	828	34	30.00	22,717
Stratford	660	37	35.70	18,871
Guelph	755	33	36.00	18,027
Galt	820	57	38.00	13,300

During the campaign the "Young Men" emphasized civic responsibility which in their view was epitomized in the reduction in the general mill rate from 20.40 mills in 1919 to 18.74 mills in 1921.

Kitchener's civic position was compared favourably with surrounding communities during the campaign. The comparative figures do speak well for Kitchener's civic administration.[32]

In the 1920s, however, the debenture did rise as the cost of the new city hall exceeded expectations. Between 1920 and 1925 debenture debt more than doubled. The frugal businessmen who had spoken so eloquently of the importance of thrift and a low mill rate had forgotten the promises so solemnly made in the aftermath of war. Even the heady prosperity of the early 1920s did not erase the memory of the promise made in harder days.

By 1925 many of the men who had entered politics through the Young Men's Club withdrew, perhaps because they thought civic unity was restored, perhaps because they found civic management more difficult and certainly less lucrative than managing their own businesses in the increasingly prosperous twenties. As many of them withdrew somewhat from Kitchener politics, others of similar background took their place, but a few familiar names from the past returned and some new politicians, quite unlike the "Young Men," moved forward. One of these was C. Mortimer Bezeau, an eloquent but rather eccentric politician whose flowing white locks and long, black coats were intentionally reminiscent of Sir Wilfrid Laurier. He had studied commercial law in Chicago, and after his return had worked in the organ and furniture business. After 1914 he wrote articles for business publications under several *noms de plume*; and, like most writers, he was thought rather peculiar. His first political foray for alderman was disastrous: he finished twenty-second with 512 votes in 1923. Bezeau finally appeared on city council in 1925, a year in which Nick Asmussen, the political veteran who had been dunked so unceremoniously in Victoria Lake only a few years before, was re-elected mayor. In 1928 Bezeau ran for mayor against W. P. Clement, a young lawyer from a distinguished Kitchener family. His was the campaign of the outsider, the foe of established interest and traditional ways. "In private life," Bezeau opined,

> Mr. Clement is a splendid young man; as a citizen we might well be proud of him. If he were mayor of this city I believe he would carry with him all the grace and charm that belongs to the position—a grace and charm which is characteristic of the family from which he sprang. If those qualities were the only qualifications required to fill the position, I would retire in his favour.

The contest, however, was not between personalities. It was "to decide whether the mayor of this city is to be the representative of a clique from the Young Men's Club, or whether he is to be the representative of the taxpayers at large."[33] Clement responded to this and other charges with an advertisement that implicitly dismissed his opponent as a crank. Clement, his appeal claimed, had "No Grudge; No Grievance; and No Axe to Grind." When challenged, he defended the Young Men's Club, praising "the work which it performed in healing the breach which separated the people of this city during war days." On election day the prosperous Centre and West Wards voted heavily for Clement, and he carried the election by 238 votes.[34]

These wards carried Clement through the 1929 election, but in 1930, with the depression's effects already being felt in Kitchener, Bezeau won.

It is interesting to note how the Bezeau-Clement contests reflect political divisions which had antedated the war and which were intensified by wartime experience. These divisions appeared not only in civic elections but also in federal and provincial elections. Throughout the interwar period W. D. Euler remained the federal Member of Parliament for North Waterloo, and his large majorities followed the new pattern he established in 1917 for the Liberal party in that riding. Kitchener's North Ward, the working-class and "ethnic" section, was the core of his support. This was also true for Nick Asmussen.

Although Bezeau, Euler, and Asmussen were very different in personality, they shared their Liberal politics and an understanding that their political success in the city required that they never move too far from those who bore the grudges from 1917 or from those who lived materially less well than others. On this foundation a powerful political machine was built, as was a reputation for eccentricity which has surrounded many of Kitchener's most notable politicians.

Like Allen Huber, Bezeau's ideas lacked the flair of his appearance. Kitchener voters soon learned that behind the gaudy plumage and stirring rhetoric, there lay little that was new. To be fair to Bezeau, there was not much that any mayor could do; there were no miraculous nostrums the wisest economists could find in those early depression years. As delegations of unemployed besieged the council, he could offer little. At the same time, property owners, themselves suffering from the depression, demanded lower taxes. Both demands could not be met, and as a result neither was. Bezeau nonetheless brought some colour to those drab days. Many years later his obituarist remembered Bezeau in 1931:

> Hostile spectators jammed the city hall to jeer aldermen as they came to council meetings. Mayor Bezeau's way with council soon turned them to admirers. He could inject bitter humor to silence an opponent, solid philosophy to guide a vote, flamboyant fireworks to cow the timid.[35]

After two years the timid were no longer cowed nor the opponents silenced. In the election of 1932, he lost every polling district but one, and that he won by a single vote.

The victor of 1932 was Henry Sturm, an aldermanic veteran and a respected businessman. Having tried flamboyance, Kitchener returned to familiar patterns, electing a businessmen's council: over two-thirds of the 1933 council members were from the business community. But this group did not accomplish much more in ending the depression. There was a tightening of relief rules, but this brought strikes by the relief workers in

May 1933. There were charges of intimidation and radical infiltration. It was alleged that relief workers who wanted to work were beaten. The city met the strike with adamant opposition, and the strike leaders were arrested. This ended the strike, but surely not the bitterness.

By the end of the decade, in 1939, Kitchener's voters were ready to take a chance again in the person of Joe Meinzinger, the mayor who served Kitchener longest and probably most strangely. His story, however, belongs in the next chapter.

If Kitchener's politics were often flamboyant during the interwar years, its social life largely mirrored that of surrounding cities. The twenties in Kitchener, as in North America generally, were a decade where traditional belief and modern actions mingled uneasily. In December 1920, for example, city council halted dancing in the market building. Alderman Ratz argued that dancing in public buildings lowered the morality of the city. Alderman Bowman agreed, adding that the dancers' germs would make the building unsanitary for the market produce. Alderman John Lang dismissed their concerns and called Ratz's "morality stuff . . . all bunk." The morals of a minority, he claimed, should not spoil the fun of the majority.[36] Lang's arguments took a deeper hold as the decade progressed, and "public morals" became more difficult to enforce. The raid on the hotels on New Year's Eve became a ritual. The police entrance was invariably "heralded by the ringing of bells and buzzers," and in most cases the offenders escaped with only a sudden end to their revelry.[37] With automobiles, movies, more money, and more leisure hours, all the forces of public morality could not keep the freer spirits reined in. By the 1930s their attempts at enforcement were much feebler.

This was a time when the young were more numerous. When the new Kitchener-Waterloo Collegiate and Vocational School opened in 1924 it had 550 students. Eight years later there were 1,418 students. Not only were there more young people but they stayed in school longer, especially the women. In the 1930s, however, the growth stopped and by 1938 there were only 1,309 students. That Kitchener's young people shared the fears and, perhaps, anger of other Canadians during the depression is suggested by a 1933 editorial in the school newspaper, *The Grumbler*.

> We, of the present generation, will soon have placed on our shoulders a tremendous responsibility—that of reconstructing the economic and political basis of the world. . . . It is only too apparent to any intelligent person that our present system of economics faces extinction.[38]

The fears of the young were shared by many of the old. A. R. Kaufman, worried that society could not support so many children, established a birth control advisory clinic, the Parents Information Bureau, in the early 1930s which may have influenced the drop in the birth rate during the depression years.[39] But Kaufman's enthusiasms or worries do not reflect those of most of his class at the time. In the twenties and

thirties, club life thrived. For the more prosperous, the Westmount Golf
Club became a focus of social life. Others played at the Rockway Municipal
Golf Course, also built in the 1930s. Most Kitchenerites, of course, were
spectators, and for them the success of the Kitchener Panthers football
team which won the Canadian intermediate championship in 1927 was
occasion for community celebration. Kitchener was also an especially
fertile source for hockey players, producing during these years the great
goaltender George Hainsworth and Boston's immortal "Kraut Line" of
Bobby Bauer, Milt Schmidt, and Woody Dumart.

*The Kraut Line: Bobby
Bauer, Milt Schmidt,
and Woody Dumart*

Games became more organized, less the whim of the moment than
the reflection of a more structured, less familiar society. Social and service
clubs which provided structured opportunities for meeting people
proliferated during the interwar period. The Young Men's Club was
followed by the Rotary, the Kiwanis, the Gyro, and the Lions, all branches
of international clubs. Similarly, women entered into local branches of
national organizations, such as the Rotary and the National Council of
Women, ending such uniquely local events as the Bachelors' Ball, a high
point of the social season in old Berlin. Other forms of social activities

reflected what people did elsewhere, and in the 1920s and 1930s what people did very regularly was go to the movies. The city had as many as six theatres, and in postwar newspapers the reports on the new movies often exceeded coverage of municipal affairs. One senses in reading these advertisements and reviews (invariably favourable) how the movies affected sensibility. The local theatre all but vanished; Kitchener became a part of a broader international experience. In 1925, in Kitchener as in New York, one could see Rudolph Valentino in *Cobra*, in which the great lover proved helpless in the power of "certain alluring women." So popular were the movies that special streetcars had to be put on at the time the theatres closed, and the theatre owners had to call the car barns ten minutes before their programme concluded.[40]

And yet the main focus of social life probably remained what it had always been in Berlin-Kitchener: the churches. Kitchener stood outside the religious patterns of the nation, and perhaps for that reason the churches' hold upon the community was more tenacious. That the German Lutheran and Baptist churches served a special function in maintaining the German cultural heritage was obvious during the war. After the war they continued in this function. Dr. Herman A. Sperling, the pastor of St. Peter's Lutheran Church, whom pro-war groups had excoriated and sought to have interned in 1916-17, became once more a leading figure in the

Chicopee Tennis Club, 1944: left to right—P. R. Hilborn, Wm. H. Sims, H. Ballantyne, R. H. Dickson, H. J. Sims, D. G. P. Forbes, J. A. Martin, D. J. MacDonald, J. K. Sims, W. G. MacDonald, J. O. Beynon

community, preaching regularly in German to his parishioners. The
ill-fated C. R. Tappert's church, St. Matthew's Lutheran, even broadcast
its German services over the new radio station. This was not an act of
defiance but an assertion of cultural and religious faith. Other churches,
such as the Swedenborgian and the Evangelical, were insignificant in
numbers nationally; but in Kitchener they were important congregations
whose membership included such leading families as the Schneiders
(Swedenborgian) and the Breithaupts (Evangelical). The Catholic community continued to grow and its institutions assimilated Catholic newcomers with ease. The diversity of religious belief produced strength and,
perhaps, tolerance.

Historians have frequently argued that religious toleration was the
outgrowth of religious diversity in the seventeenth century. In the case of
Kitchener, cultural diversity was in marked comparison to other Ontario
cities where Canadians of British background predominated. Before the
First World War Kitchener had been overwhelmingly German (70 per
cent). After the war the "German" population dropped continuously (to
55.6 per cent in 1921 and 53 per cent in 1931). Part of this decline is
explained by the transformation of Brauns into Browns and Schmidts in
Smiths during the war. More important, however, are other factors.

There had been relatively little German immigration between 1911
and 1914 and, of course, after 1914 there had been none for some time.
During the war, workers came to Kitchener's factories from outside the
city, and these workers reflected the Anglo-Saxon background of most of
the surrounding area. There were, moreover, other reasons why Kitchener
was becoming more closely linked with the world beyond Waterloo

County. The automobile's influence is obvious, but more important is the impact of the new media—the movies, the radio, the mass magazines. Just as Canada was becoming more North American in its outlook, so too was Kitchener losing those styles and tastes that were European. Canada became less British, Kitchener more Canadian, but in both cases the death of the past was protracted. And there were a few who would not let the past die.

The German press in Kitchener died in 1918 when the *Journal* was forced to close by an order-in-council which banned publications in the German language.[41] The *Journal*'s publisher, W. J. Motz, nevertheless retained much influence as he and W. D. Euler bought the *News-Record* in October 1919. In July 1922 Motz and Euler purchased the *Daily Telegraph* and thus controlled the community's sole daily newspaper, now called *The Daily Record*. The *Record* remained sensitive to the "German" question. It recognized that the unique German-Canadian community of Berlin could not continue to exist, but it resented the slurs upon its memory. The continuing suspicion of, and attacks upon, Germans in the Canadian press did not escape it; nor did the orders-in-council of 1919 which forbade the immigration of Germans as unsuitable and Mennonites because of "their peculiar customs, habits, modes of living and methods of holding property."[42]

These restrictions ended in 1923 when Canada once again was more disposed to tolerate "peculiar customs" and when Canadian industry required immigrants to underpin its expansion. After 1923 a large number of Germans did come to Waterloo County, many of them *Volksdeutsch* from southern and eastern Europe. There were several hundred families of Saxons from Romania, and hundreds of Swabians from Yugoslavia. The largest group was Russian Mennonite; about 2,700 arrived in Waterloo County, but many soon moved on to western Canada where land was so much cheaper. Because these people came in groups they tended to emphasize traditional ties, especially those of religion. The immigrants from Germany itself were, perhaps, more open to community involvement. In 1925 a group of recent German immigrants, along with some older Concordia Club members, formed the *Deutschen Verein* in Kitchener. This club kept alive old traditions through its sponsorship of a German school, a German cinema and theatre, and various athletic and cultural "fests."[43]

This limited renewal of Germanism reflected the influx of new immigrants, the remarkable strength of the prewar Germanness, and the impact of historical revisionism upon the perception of the First World War. The *Daily Record* paid close attention to the revisionist historical scholarship which questioned whether Germany was in fact "guilty" as the Versailles Treaty deemed it to be. The peacemaking laurels bestowed upon German Chancellor and Foreign Minister Gustav Stresemann were also carefully noted. The point made was subtle yet powerful: good and evil did not run along national boundaries or ethnic lines but bisected every human heart. No people could be indicted as wholly evil and no cause in wartime could be wholly good. Unfortunately, at a time when Kitchener's Germans were benefitting from the recognition of this fundamental human truth, many in the fatherland were forgetting it once more.

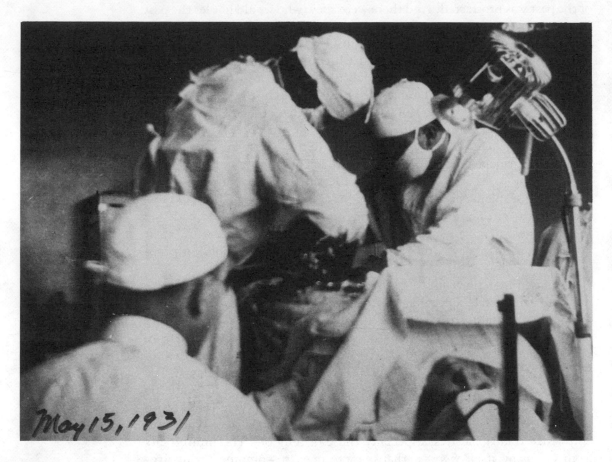

May 15, 1931

Modern medicine in Kitchener, 1931: Drs. Louis Lang, Victor Traynor, Charles McCarville

When Adolf Hitler took power in Germany, Kitchener was still Canada's "German capital." The satisfaction which had marked Kitchener's view of Germany's responsibility and progress in the later 1920s had given way to bafflement as the Weimar Republic disintegrated in the depression of the 1930s. Most feared the victory of communism in Germany. Editor W. J. Motz of the *Record* thus welcomed Hitler as one who would halt Germany's tumble toward collectivism at the same time as he questioned some aspects of Hitler's own reform programme. The newspaper's president, W. D. Euler, told a gathering of publishers that they had a responsibility to present the European news in a "relaxed" and "unalarming" fashion. The excitement of the First World War was too fresh in Kitchener's memory; the embers must not be rekindled. Those who blew the flames of hate would regret their actions. F. W. Claussen, the president of the Kitchener-Waterloo Rotary Club and of Waterloo College, in a March 1933 speech referred to a Jewish protest against Hitler in New York City and warned: "I am going to say that the people at the New York meeting will be ashamed of themselves in two weeks. I can say that from what I know of the German." The Jewish "problem," Claussen argued in another address, could be better appreciated if Canadians recognized that many Jews in Germany were newcomers and Marxists.[44] A more sensitive reaction to Jewish persecution in Germany came from W. J. Motz who, in a report from Germany, deplored the lack of justice in the treatment of Jews but suggested it was "no different than the Canadian reaction to those of German heritage during the First World War."[45]

It was, of course, much different. Gradually Motz and most German Canadians realized this. From the start there was nervousness and a fear that the tensions of the Third Reich might explode in Kitchener. The advice of the *Record*, of civic leaders, and, indeed, of Kitchener's Jewish leaders was unanimous: extreme statements must be avoided and a cautious distance must be reflected in Kitchener's observation of the Third Reich. An attempt by an unemployed German, Otto Becker, to organize a Swastika Club in Kitchener in 1933 failed. Even those who had themselves praised Hitler denounced Becker's attempt to import Germany's problems to Canada. Becker nevertheless called a meeting at the Wintergarden on King Street for August 14, 1933. He strode into the meeting wearing a brown shirt with swastikas on his sleeves. Immediately the booing began; the heckling continued through his speech, until finally the police broke up the meeting, citing the need to preserve public order. The same night, the city council passed a resolution deploring "any organization that among their [sic] aims and objectives brings oppression and discrimination upon any creed. . . ." Becker, who was not naturalized, was deported ten days later, an action he blamed on Jewish conspirators.[46]

Becker's failure did not discourage others. In early 1934 five Waterloo County Germans organized the *Deutsche Bund Canada*, a militant, pro-Nazi group. The *Bund* was supported by the German government, which quite correctly regarded it as a propaganda instrument for its causes.[47] The reaction of Kitchener's Germans to the *Bund* was not enthusiastic and the group's headquarters soon moved to Montreal along with its leader, Karl Gerhard. The *Bund* nevertheless maintained a coterie in Kitchener which caused the traditional German clubs considerable trouble in 1935.

In that year, the local *Bund* president, Ernest Woelfle, announced that the Ontario German reunion would be held in Kitchener. Its purpose was solely cultural, and it would affirm that Canadians and Germans should not be antagonistic. The Concordia Club was understandably sensitive; it had already emphasized that its purposes were purely "social." It decided to boycott the event and did so. Others, however, did not. On the afternoon of Sunday, September 2, the high point of the reunion occurred in the Kitchener auditorium. The ceremony was colourful as groups marched in carrying their banners and flags, and their leaders took their places on the platform where the Union Jack and the swastika intertwined. Yet German blood was little stirred. On Monday morning most returned to their "social clubs" avoiding carefully the political undertones of Sunday's meeting.[48]

The fears and sensitivities of Kitchener in those last few years before the war were obvious to all.[49] By 1936 the *Record* had ceased to extend "sympathetic understanding" to Hitler, and tended to emphasize the distinction between Hitler and the German people. Indeed, the *Record*'s view of Hitler possessed more objectivity and perceptiveness than most Canadian newspapers and, for that matter, politicians. Editor Motz, a Liberal, was genuinely offended by the racism, the authoritarianism, and the violence of the Third Reich. Rather oddly, W. D. Euler, the newspaper's president and the North Waterloo Member of Parliament, was less critical. He attended the German reunions, spoke too eloquently about the "shackles" of Versailles, and recalled with too much enthusiasm his visit to Germany in 1936 and the accomplishments he saw there. These words and actions were not forgotten when war finally came and they were a factor in Euler's removal from the Cabinet and appointment to the Senate. Euler's loyalty was beyond reproach, but his memory of the First World War and his desire to justify his actions in those years affected his judgment of Germany and of his German-Canadian constituents. He was too frightened that the past would return. Fortunately, it did not.[50]

In February 1914, some of Berlin's leading citizens gathered to toast the Kaiser. Hitler received no such honours in 1939 in Kitchener. Indeed, support for Hitler was small, his opposition overwhelming. Lita-Rose Betcherman's claim that "Kitchener remained very sensitive throughout

The Royal Visit, 1939

the thirties on the subject of Hitler" can be easily misunderstood. Sensitivity there was, but sympathy came only from a fringe group, made up largely of recent immigrants, most of whom had left by 1939. The *Deutsche Bund* simply disappeared in August 1939, and some who had flirted with its ideals renounced them quickly once war began. The *Record* reported that "one man who 'Heiled Hitler' in a Kitchener public building less than a week ago, absolutely denied that he ever had wanted to return to the Fatherland and certainly had no desire to go back now." The Concordia Club and other German social clubs immediately closed down lest their purposes be misunderstood and community leaders moved quickly and aggressively to assure outsiders that Kitchener was "loyal" and that suggestions it was not would be confronted and resented. L. O. Breithaupt, Board of Trade president, thus demanded that the Chief Censor protect Kitchener against "foul rumours": "Those who lived through the last war in this community will always remember the unfairness that marked under the guise of patriotism sought to impugn the loyalty of the city."[51]

Kitchener's patriotism was not impugned. In this war, its recruiting offices were crowded, its antagonism muted, its sympathies clear. Kitchener had moved far from the Germanness of Berlin, and the reaction to the Second World War revealed how much more Kitchener had become like the communities around it. The new roads, radios, and economic activities had broken down the uniqueness of Kitchener in southern Ontario. Lacking a continuing stream of immigrants, Kitchener lost its European flavour and became more fully part of the North American way of life. The mood of 1914-18 was lost. Kitchener was a different city, Canada another country, and the Second World War a different war.

KITCHENER AFTER 1940   6

The First World War had divided the community of Berlin and isolated it from its neighbours; the second renewed the City of Kitchener and drew it closer to the national economy and the national mood. As late as July 1939, over nine hundred unemployed Kitchener men were applying for ninety-seven jobs allocated to Kitchener by the Grand River Conservation Authority.[1] A year later there was no unemployment, and Kitchener's industries began to look far beyond the city's boundaries for workers. Kitchener shared fully the benefits of the renewal of Canadian manufacturing in the first years of war. An economic and psychological transformation took place which established the economic base of the community for over a generation.

Economic Growth after 1940

The parts which came together to form that base were present in prewar Kitchener. Kitchener was truly the "Akron of Canada," and a modern war moved along on rubber tires. Its food-processing industry was also prepared to supply the Canadian meat the empire consumed in wartime (but not so eagerly in peacetime). Kitchener's balance of industries was particularly suited to respond to the needs of war. Before war began, the city ranked fifth in manufacturing output in Ontario with only Toronto, Hamilton, Windsor, and Oshawa ahead. Throughout the war, it would maintain that position as it began to spread its economic influence more widely in the Waterloo County region and beyond.

There were, naturally, fears that Kitchener's Germanic reputation might affect the readiness to place orders, as it apparently had in the First World War. These doubts soon disappeared as Kitchener's young men swarmed into recruiting offices, and a sudden efflorescence of patriotic gestures and organizations showed that Kitchener would not be "Berlin" in this war. When a delegation of Kitchener businessmen returned from

Ottawa in early December 1939, they reported that the city could expect a boom from the war orders that would begin in January. The orders came, and so did the boom. Within a year the number on relief had dropped from slightly over thirteen hundred to only four hundred, and those were mainly the halt and the lame. The value of building permits rose by over $500,000.[2] During 1940 city assessment increased by $1,016,213 and the level of civic indebtedness was the lowest since 1922. By the end of 1941 the relief rolls were so scant that the relief administrator, the industrious Mabel Feick, no longer had a job.

In 1941 the contracts came for foodstuffs, electrical goods, trucks, and tires. In February Kaufman Rubber received a $17,920 order and Four Wheel Drive one for $29,760. In March Kaufman received another order for $10,075, and B. F. Goodrich and Dominion Electrohome garnered lucrative contracts of $90,594 and $88,213 respectively.[3] There was not, however, unrestrained joy among Kitchener manufacturers. The year 1941 was one of unprecedented labour unrest in the city as workers took advantage of the labour shortage to push their demand for collective bargaining rights under the federal government's P.C. 2685, which established the right of workers to fair working conditions, wages, and representation. The troubles began in April 1941 when two Waterloo businesses resisted attempts by the Canadian Congress of Labour to organize their factories. Resentment spread to the point that there were other walkouts and even a threat of a sympathetic general strike. Mayor Meinzinger, who had fussed about communists in the labour movement during the 1930s, reflected the general pro-worker mood coupled with worry about the legitimacy of strikes in wartime.

> The sooner the manufacturers come to their senses and admit the workingman is a cog in the wheel, the better for them. Strikes are not the best thing for both parties. They cause trouble and create ill-feeling, but sometimes they are necessary. You [the worker] have a right, however, to organize and the right to share in the profits in whatsoever industry you are working in.[4]

Despite Meinzinger's hopes, walkouts continued and on June 2, 1941, the federal Minister of Labour, Norman McLarty, ordered a conciliation board, established to settle the strike at Dumart's Meatpacking, to issue a special report on "the reasons behind the trouble in Kitchener."

"Trouble in Kitchener"—the words surely caused many residents who remembered the last war to tremble. Still the strikes and walkouts continued. The conciliation board report on the Dumart strike clearly favoured the workers. It claimed that the Dumart strike and, by implication, the labour troubles in Kitchener generally were not so much the product of wage dissatisfaction as of the reluctance of employers to bargain fairly with employees. The city council reacted to this by establishing its own conciliation committee which urged a settlement on the terms of the conciliation board report. Dumart's settled, and other companies saw that their contracts, markets, and, in labour-short Kitchener, their employees

could disappear. Hence, labour peace came by the end of 1941. That *Wartime industrial* memories of the troubles lingered was shown in the 1943 election when *troubles* North Waterloo elected John Cook of the C.C.F. as its member in the 1943 provincial election.

There was another important reason for the industrial peace that settled upon Kitchener until the war ended: the benefits of wartime prosperity did flow downward in a fashion that the depression generation could never have imagined.[5] An important survey of the Kitchener area carried out in late 1943 and early 1944 for the Canadian Chamber of Commerce offers a remarkably clear view of how the war changed the economic landscape of the area. The survey covered the cities of Kitchener and Waterloo as well as four nearby villages and the surrounding rural area. It was, by modern standards, remarkably extensive, covering all city businesses and 11.1 per cent of the city households. What it showed was, in the survey's own words, "an industrial revolution." The following table shows that the Chamber of Commerce was guilty of only minor exaggeration.[6]

Table 3

Economic Growth in Kitchener-Waterloo,
1939 and 1943 (thousands of dollars)

	1939	1943
Payroll	$15,149	$ 30,331
Manufacturing payroll	10,973	24,519
Aggregate sales	74,000	146,250
Manufacturing sales	53,700	115,500

This astonishing growth bestowed widespread benefits on all classes. The average wage rose substantially:

Table 4

Wages in Kitchener-Waterloo,
1939 and 1943

	1939	1943
All occupations	1,120	1,663
Manufacturing	1,076	1,708

The result of this prosperity was a meaningful redistribution of income.

Table 5

Household Incomes in Kitchener-Waterloo, 1939 and 1944

	Under $1,500 (%)	$1,500 to $2,600 (%)	$2,600+ (%)
1939	57	29	14
Early 1944	36	45	19

The city thus took on that middle-class aspect that has marked it since. The survey aptly concluded that "there can be no doubt that in material comforts the population of Kitchener-Waterloo lives, on an average, considerably better than it did in 1939—in spite of heavier taxation and even after purchasing War Bonds and War Savings Certificates to the tune of $17,500,000." Indeed they did, and the remarkable 91 per cent increase in bank deposits between 1939 and 1943 was further proof of this claim.

This burst of economic activity affected all areas of community life. The survey revealed a society constantly in motion. In 1939 the community employed 9,239 men and 4,288 women. During the next four years, 3,198 men and 131 women enlisted in the armed forces. Nevertheless, in 1943, the community employed 11,411 men and 6,824 women, a net addition to the work force of 8,037 employees. Where had the workers been found? Two thousand came from the community itself and had been "retained in, or drawn into employment because of war conditions." At least four hundred others had become commuters to the city's factories from their farms or villages. The rest were "sucked into" the city from towns and farms of southern Ontario. The countryside as well as the city had been transformed:

> The result of [the wartime growth of industry] is that, from approximately 2,500 farms in the four townships canvassed, more than 1,200 members of farm families have left in the past four years—or almost one from every second farm; and, in addition, there has been a loss of more than 700 hired men who had been employed on a permanent basis until war broke out—or not much less than a loss of one hired man from every third farm in the district.

And yet fewer farmers produced more products. The symbiosis between country and city was thus strengthened, and Kitchener's metropolitan influence deepened and broadened.

Kitchener's residents, like most in Canada, worried lest the war's end bring a return to the depressed conditions of the 1930s or a replay of the bust and boom cycle which followed the First World War. They worried needlessly. The recovery that came was economic, and also a matter of confidence. As the survey confirmed, in 1944 Kitchener-Waterloo's residents possessed this confidence in abundance. After the war they wanted—and expected—a richer material life. Above all, they wanted houses and automobiles, and this boded very well for Kitchener's industries. Moreover, wartime savings were sufficiently large to finance over 60 per cent of the anticipated purchases. Their fears allayed, Kitchener's factories adjusted with relative ease from meeting the demands of war to fulfilling the rewards of peace.

The survey's prophecy proved correct, as Kitchener responded easily to postwar consumer demands. Unemployment in the first quarter of 1946 was less than 4 per cent of the labour force, and overall employment was up considerably. But, as a recent study observed, expectations were high, and "the vast majority of [Kitchener-Waterloo] union members were psychologically ready for a confrontation which they hoped would guarantee them a fair share of post-war prosperity."[7] A rash of strikes hit the Kitchener rubber industry in 1946. These strikes undoubtedly established the "credibility" of the United Rubber Workers in Kitchener. Although Kaufman Rubber remained unorganized, the other companies recognized that the union was "a powerful organization which the rubber companies had to learn to live with."[8] This they did for two decades during which industrial peace reigned in the organized rubber industry.

The survey had indicated that the major consumer demand would be for housing. Contractors and the civic politicians scurried to meet the need. The Veterans' Land Act assisted many returned soldiers, but more generous lending provisions under the National Housing Act were probably more important. The reasons for the housing demand are clear in the city's demography. Between 1941 and 1951 the number of Kitchener residents between the ages of sixteen and forty rose from 15,591 to 18,408, but in 1951-61 the comparable figures were 21,706 to 32,399. Even more important was the zero to fifteen age bracket, which rose from 23.2 per cent of the population in 1941 to 31.1 per cent in 1961. The babies not only needed to be housed; they required schooling, feeding, and recreation. The economic life of the city benefitted from the construction of the Kitchener Memorial Auditorium, completed in 1951, a new Kitchener-Waterloo Hospital, and from the building of schools. In 1953 alone three new schools—Prueter, Smithson, and Queen Elizabeth—were opened.[9] In the later 1950s post-secondary educational expansions contributed to the continuing health of the building trades, even though Kitchener residents were surely disappointed that Waterloo now had two post-secondary institutions, and it had none.

Kitchener Memorial Auditorium, 1954

The University of Waterloo was brought into being by area businessmen who recognized the need for a more skilled work force and who shared the common late-1950s assumption that education was a powerful ingredient in economic growth.[10] This incentive also arose, in part, because businessmen realized that future prosperity was by no means

*King and Breithaupt
Streets in the early 1950s*

assured unless the future was anticipated. This lesson was clearly implied in the failure of several traditional industries to share the benefits of postwar prosperity. The button industry, for example, lost out to foreign competition, and by 1964 only one company, the American-owned Kitchener Button Company, survived. More striking in its decline was Kitchener's first major industry, the leather industry. The Lang tannery declined quickly after wartime sales ceased, and operations ended in 1954. The Breithaupt leather empire began to atrophy in the 1920s when the branch plants in Listowel, Woodstock, and Burke's Falls closed. In 1950 the Kitchener tannery closed not long before its centenary. In other cases, individual firms thrived while others who engaged in the same business stumbled or collapsed. This was particularly true in the case of the footwear industry, where Greb and Kaufman continued to grow with total employment in the industry remaining at the 2,000-3,000 level in the 1960s and 1970s. In other sectors the prosperity was uniform although considerable consolidation took place. The meat-packing industry came to be dominated by J. M. Schneider, which grew at a continuously rapid pace during the postwar years. By 1980 Schneider's employed 2,500 in the Kitchener area and its Courtland Avenue home sprawled over two large blocks. J. M. Schneider continued to be controlled by the Schneider family, but two other major packers of the war years, Dumart's and Kitchener Packers, became a part of the Calgary-based Burns Meats.

Other industries had an exciting but rougher ride through the postwar years. Although Cluett Peabody's Arrow shirts acquired a national reputation for excellence, foreign competition was a constant worry. The electrical industry, which had advanced so rapidly during the war years, had similar difficulties. Electrohome, controlled by the Pollock family, became Kitchener's most exciting company in the late 1960s and early 1970s. In 1974 it employed 3,400 and was the city's largest employer. Yet within three years its losses were large and its work force had been almost halved. Many blamed unfair foreign competition; others blamed management for a failure to respond to changed circumstances. All hoped that the technological advances of the 1980s would restore to Electrohome the vitality of the middle years of this old Kitchener business.

Kitchener County Buildings and part of Centre Ward, 1954

Opposite page— J. M. Schneider's Head Office and Plant on Courtland Street

Electrohome's fate in the late seventies was shared by those factories which were dependent upon the North American automobile industry. B. F. Goodrich and Uniroyal expanded in pace with the industry in the

*King and Breithaupt
Streets in 1979
(compare p. 175)*

1950s and 1960s, but in the 1970s problems appeared which were similar to those the industry faced throughout North America. In the case of both companies the physical plants were old, and investment by the American-controlled parent companies tended to flow to areas of Canada—and the United States—which were thought to be more salubrious. Nevertheless, the two companies employed over four thousand in the late 1970s, and Kitchener remained the Akron of Canada, although one heard that reminder of the declining capital of the American rubber industry much more rarely in later days. The other major employers who have depended on the automotive trades are Budd Canada, a maker of automobile frames, and Lear Siegler, an automotive spring and seating manufacturer. Budd was the Canadian subsidiary of an American manufacturer which established the Kitchener plant as a result of the 1965 Automotive Trade Agreement between Canada and the United States. Lear Siegler also expanded rapidly after the automotive agreement. At their peak in the mid-1970s, these two companies provided high wages to over four thousand workers. The automotive parts industry, however, is highly cyclical, and in the late 1970s both companies moved downwards with the cycle. Budd alone laid off well over one thousand workers in nine months when it lost its contract with Ford. It also gained a new parent as the American Budd was taken over by German interests. In the light of Kitchener's German-American history, the takeover was especially appropriate.[11]

These automotive-related industries were nearly entirely foreign-controlled. The effect of this on the community is a broader topic than could be considered in this book. Foreign ownership of industry is, of course, characteristic not only of Kitchener but of the surrounding communities in southwestern Ontario. A 1971 study of nearby Galt entitled *Galt, U.S.A.* asserted that over 80 per cent of industrial assets in the "Kitchener-Waterloo-Preston-Hespeler-Galt complex were controlled outside Canada." The figure is certainly too high for Kitchener where several major companies, notably J. M. Schneider, Electrohome, and Kaufman Rubber, were not only Canadian-controlled but locally controlled. Except when the foreign-controlled plants run into difficulty, Kitchener residents, like those of Galt, probably would respond as did the business reporter of the Galt newspaper: "Erosion of culture? Asserting our identity? His pay cheque: that's what the working man is concerned about." In that respect, the generations after 1940 had far less concern than their predecessors.[12]

The pay cheques, however, tended to come from different sources. In the postwar era more workers tended to fall into the service sector than into manufacturing. This was, of course, an international trend, not merely a

Kaufman Strike, 1960

local one. In the Waterloo region there were significant differences in the fashion in which this trend was followed. In 1970 a local government review showed Kitchener-Waterloo had about 35 per cent of its labour force characterized as craftsmen in comparison to a figure of 43 per cent for Galt and Preston. Kitchener-Waterloo also had less than 50 per cent working in manufacturing in comparison to 62.9 per cent for Galt. Significantly, Galt, with an average annual family income of $5,573, was behind Kitchener's $5,905 and Waterloo's $6,848. Although Kitchener-Waterloo were clearly one economic unit, Waterloo had become the home of more white-collar workers; Kitchener remained more the home of the workers. The review concluded that the Kitchener-Waterloo region was an economic unit which was not directly related to the Galt-Preston-Hespeler portion of Waterloo County nor, for that matter, to nearby Wellington County.[13] All parts of the area, nevertheless, "tried to reach out towards Highway 401, particularly for industrial and commercial expansion." The extension of that super-highway from Milton to Kitchener in 1960 brought the region more closely into the so-called Golden Horseshoe which surrounded Lake Ontario and which was dominated by Toronto. The Waterloo region, the review perceptively declared, "is one that in many ways could be said to be of, but not in, Toronto."[14] As the horseshoe glittered, so did Kitchener, but the city had to bear the tarnish as well.

Few saw that tarnish until the 1970s. In 1972, *Galt, U.S.A.* began by asking what happened to the "spirit of 1944." The question is especially appropriate to end this discussion. In the cases of Kitchener and Galt the spirit of 1944 arose from the success of the war effort and from the reconstruction of the economic life of the community. That sudden burst of industrial growth in the war years established the structure of Kitchener's future development. By the 1970s, parts of the structure were crumbling, and cosmetic repairs were simply not enough. And yet in terms of 1944, the citizens of Kitchener had little cause for complaint. That richer material life the depression generation wanted had been attained. The legacy bequeathed on a new generation in Kitchener in the 1970s was sufficiently large to give that generation the opportunity to make its way in the new activities it had to undertake.

Politics and Society since the War

Kitchener's politics during the Second World War were not dramatic; this fact, however, was not due to the lack of colourful events and characters. The war years saw the integration of the labour movement into civic affairs, and the beginnings of a more activist role for the civic government in the encouragement of industrial and commercial development. In evaluating what happened in civic elections, J. E. Rea's conviction that, in a free society, there is no such thing as a non-partisan election is worth recalling. "Voters," Rea observes, "make their electoral choices for a variety of reasons including whim, prejudice, self-interest, ideology, religion, ethnicity, and so on."[15] In Kitchener, one sees a variety of interests that have influenced civic politics and what may seem simply whim often reflects deeper social and economic tensions in the community. This was true for Allen Huber's mayoralty before the First World War and for the entry into politics of the Young Men's Club in the 1920s. It is also true in the case of Joe Meinzinger, the North Ward's favourite, Kitchener's longest serving mayor, and probably its most controversial politician.

"Vote for Joe the man you know" was Meinzinger's slogan in 1939. He was an orphan who, after finishing grade school, had worked in Kitchener factories. When first elected to city council in the early depression, Meinzinger presented himself as a voice of labour, a representative of the common man. His response to depression issues, however, reflected no consistent ideology. Jack Walter, a fellow alderman and a founder of the C.C.F., thought that Meinzinger's efforts for the working man were pure flim-flam, loud sounds that signified nothing.[16] Perhaps; but his appeal is undeniable, and many times Meinzinger's maverick attitudes reflect those of significant parts of the community.

In 1939 Meinzinger played the demagogue to excite fears and to stir sympathy. During the Dominion-Merchants strike Meinzinger, alone among Kitchener aldermen, supported non-union workers in their demand that American professional agitators be expelled. When Mayor George Gordon called a special meeting of the relief board in August 1939, Meinzinger charged that Gordon, an optometrist, acted at the behest of communists:

> If the Mayor continues to grant privileges to Communists that are denied to others I think that the time for a showdown is at hand. So far as I am concerned no Communist will ever again be permitted to air his views in the city council chamber.
>
> Years ago I broke with the Bezeau-Gordon outfit because of its views on communism and I think it is high time the Mayor declared himself one way or the other on this important issue.[17]

There was, of course, nothing to declare; the damage was nonetheless done. Next came the police force which Meinzinger accused of corruption and moral turpitude. Constable Douglas Stevenson, accused by Meinzinger of stealing a can of tomato juice, sued for libel. The suit was subsequently dropped. Meinzinger declared himself vindicated and turned upon the chief, William Hodgson, hinting vaguely at moral irregularities.

There were, admittedly, problems with the police: their efficiency was certainly unimpressive during the strike violence, but the attacks were unfair and the innuendo justly resented. The city council thus refused to grant the investigation Meinzinger had demanded. Denouncing this refusal as a "whitewash," Meinzinger announced his candidacy for the mayoralty. The *Record* declared him a "dark horse."[18]

Joe Meinzinger getting the results in 1945

Reading the *Record* today one has the impression the newspaper supported Meinzinger, although that does not appear to have been the case. The impression derives from Meinzinger's skillful manipulation of political emotions. On September 30, 1939, two months before the election, Meinzinger told a reporter that he had met an old friend and a fellow orphan at a bazaar in support of the orphanage. The *Record* reported the conversation:

> "The day you left the orphanage Joe, I never dreamed that some day you would be the general chairman of the bazaar to raise funds to assist it."
> "And neither did I. . . . It's a queer world."

Other Kitchener residents also began to believe the world was "queer" as the mayoralty election loomed. The "dark horse" was running well against two strong candidates, A. J. Cundick, long-time Board of Trade treasurer, and Alex Schaefer, a respected businessman. Both had run very well in previous aldermanic contests. Mayor Gordon made the first error when he made a comment that seemed to question Meinzinger's loyalty. The local Legion compounded the error by censuring those who attacked the police chief, William Hodgson. This was, of course, a censure of Meinzinger. On November 29, an advertisement-letter appeared in the *Record* signed by Rudy Schultz, "a veteran," which deplored the Legion's stand and pointed out that Meinzinger was himself a veteran and a "worker." Two days later another advertisement-letter appeared, this one signed by a well-known insurance man, Irvin Erb. Erb challenged Meinzinger to tell the "truth" about his war record. The next night he did, in another advertisement.

> As an impetuous young soldier I struck a police officer when he attempted to arrest me for a minor offence. I was unwise to have lost my temper and certainly unlucky in that the blow I struck broke the jaw of the police officer. I was tried in a Kitchener Police Court and sentenced.

After expressing regret for the incident and pointing out that he had paid the price in jail that society exacted, he continued:

> There can be no doubt about Irvin Erb's motive in asking me to publish these facts. He stooped to such a challenge for the purpose of injuring my standing in this community on the eve of an election. Twenty-five years ago, I acted impetuously and have regretted it ever since. Most people have been willing to let that incident be forgotten during the quarter century that has passed in which time I have proved to my fellow citizens that I, too, could have become a serviceable citizen, respected by his fellow man. IN THAT TIME, I WON THE FORGIVENESS AND FRIENDSHIP OF THE MAN I INJURED.

He concluded with the promise that he would be as forthright with all citizens as he had been with Mr. Erb.

The statement was not as forthright as it seemed, but it was exceedingly effective. On election day, the battle between "the businessman and the product of the factory," as Meinzinger put it, ended in a Meinzinger victory by sixty-eight votes. Meinzinger trailed all evening behind Cundick as the upper-middle-class areas gave the businessman extraordinary margins. The poll in the new restricted Westmount subdivision showed Cundick leading by an eight-to-one margin, but Meinzinger did not worry even when he lagged behind in the vote count. "Wait for Alberta Street," he told his supporters. That working-class poll reported last; Meinzinger won 103 votes to only 13 for Cundick. The mayoralty was his, and would remain so for five years.[19]

Meinzinger won on the votes of the less prosperous and the workers, sweeping the North Ward as other mavericks like Allen Huber and Mortimer Bezeau had before him. They were different men in different times, but the pattern is certainly suggestive. Meinzinger fits far better into this pattern than into national ones. At a time when wartime expenditure seemed to be supporting the Canadian left's argument that state intervention and expansion were the best means of preventing depression and the distress of the poor, Meinzinger, elected by those who felt the depression's sting most fully, prided himself on his cutbacks in expenditure and on his reduction of the tax rate. His antagonism toward international unions, interestingly, did not much hamper him in his appeal to workers in 1939. During the war, however, he did express sympathy for workers in some strikes, notably that at Dumart's Meatpacking. In 1941 he was even supported by the Labour Council in an election he won by a large majority over Dr. S. F. Leavine, a highly respected alderman and future mayor. But he was always unpredictable, and in this unpredictability lay much of his attraction. In 1945 he was elected to the provincial legislature, and at Queen's Park he defied the party whip regularly. His party affiliation was as vague as his political ideology. He was once again mayor of Kitchener when he died in 1962.[20]

In Joe Meinzinger's first mayoralty year, 1940, an era ended when W. D. Euler resigned as Member of Parliament to enter the Senate, but not before he held the seat in the 1940 general election with a 7,478 majority. In the August by-election which followed his resignation (a resignation compelled by Prime Minister King who had grown antagonistic towards Euler), L. O. Breithaupt held the seat for the Liberals. Breithaupt and King were on friendlier terms, but the distinguished Kitchener businessman did not seem to enjoy the political rough and tumble. He hesitated about running again in 1945, but agreed after King insisted. During the war years, Breithaupt worked to ensure "that the good name of [Kitchener] and North Waterloo would not be besmirched the way it was in the last war." To King, he expressed pride in his work: "The fact remains that not one district in Canada has surpassed our war record and the flag flies high here."[21] In any case, the Liberal flag flew high in North Waterloo in 1945 and 1949 as Louis Breithaupt ran up large margins. He became Lieutenant-Governor of Ontario in 1952, and another Kitchener businessman with a familiar name, Norman Schneider, retained the seat for the Liberals. When the local Liberal association approached Schneider, they emphasized the importance of having a businessman represent Kitch-

ener and, on that basis, Schneider accepted.[22] The same tone, so characteristic of the 1950s, affected civic politics. In 1953 a young businessman,
Donald Weber, was acclaimed as mayor after general agreement among
council members that he was the best choice to succeed fellow businessman
Bruce Weber. Donald Weber told the press that he felt a municipality
should be run like a business. The *Record* did not mind this attitude, but it
lamented that so few showed interest in civic and political affairs.

Mackenzie King returns to Woodside

> Perhaps the people in the Red satellite countries of Europe did not know any
> more about public affairs than the average Canadian. . . . A lively interest in
> the affairs of their community and their country might have saved them from
> being engulfed by the wave of Red slavery.[23]

The *Record*'s lament stirred few, for in 1953 only 32.04 per cent voted in
the municipal election, and in 1954 it dropped even more to 31.7 per cent,
as Don Weber was acclaimed mayor once more.

These were prosperous times for the city and politics reflected that
mood. In the mid-fifties, the city's growth remained among the top ten of

Canadian cities. Commenting on the city tax returns in 1956, the *Record* pointed out that the middle class predominated. Sixty per cent of the population filed returns indicating taxable incomes between $2,000 and $4,000 compared with only 6 per cent who had incomes over $6,000. Issues tended to be minor.[24] In 1956, for example, 250 persons attended the municipal nomination meeting at which the greatest civic problem seemed to be downtown parking. The municipal elections, nevertheless, resulted in an upset in which six new candidates who were identified as the "downtown block" were elected. To them, downtown parking was truly important as was the issue of night shopping.[25] In the 1950s and early 1960s these were the political issues that preoccupied council debate, and they did so because the downtown merchants were so prominent in council ranks. The presence of Joe Meinzinger on council assured that dullness would not predominate. His return to the mayor's office in 1958 meant that boredom would be exceedingly rare.

Kitchener Centennial Committee

Nationally as well as locally, 1958 was an exciting political year. The Liberal hold on Waterloo North was broken by the Diefenbaker tide which carried O. W. "Mike" Weichel to Parliament. The popular Weichel was the first Conservative elected since 1917, and he was also the first member since 1917 who was not a wealthy Kitchener businessman. Weichel's energetic work for his constituents kept Waterloo North Conservative in 1962 and 1963.[26] In 1965, however, the Liberals recaptured their traditional stronghold under Kieth Hymmen. They kept it in 1968, 1972, and

1974, when Joe Flynn succeeded Hymmen in the new Kitchener riding. Although John Reimer captured the riding in 1979, the Liberals won again with Dr. Peter Lang in 1980.

Norman Schneider congratulates winner, O. W. "Mike" Weichel

Provincially the Liberals maintained pre-eminence throughout most of the period. In 1963 Kitchener's M.P.P. and Ontario Liberal leader, John Wintermeyer, was defeated in a controversial election in which Wintermeyer's stand on insurance questions offended that important Kitchener-Waterloo interest. Jim Breithaupt recaptured the new Kitchener seat in 1967, winning a fifty-two-vote victory over New Democrat Morley Rosenberg. Breithaupt, a respected Opposition member at Queen's Park, has retained the seat with large margins in subsequent elections. He is now the longest-serving provincial member in the history of Kitchener-Waterloo North riding.[27]

The Liberal success is striking, especially at the provincial level where the Conservatives have held power continuously since the war. There appear to be several factors which have led to Liberal victories. First, and most important, there is the Liberal tradition established in 1917 when voters of German and working-class background in Kitchener shifted decisively toward the Liberals. Secondly, later immigrants of German and other backgrounds tended to prefer Liberalism in Kitchener, as they did elsewhere in urban and industrial Ontario. Thirdly, the Liberals had strong organizational and personal support. The Sims family, for example, offered three generations of financial and organization support beginning with Harvey Sims, Mackenzie King's campaign manager in the early 1900s, and reaching into the 1980s with Peter and Elizabeth Sims, who have held senior party offices. Fourthly, the New Democrats failed to take advantage of the large working-class and unionized population as they did in Brantford, Windsor, and Oshawa. After the C.C.F. victory in 1943, the C.C.F.-N.D.P. came close only in the 1967 provincial election, and that election may be seen as one where Kitchener's attraction to an outspoken political maverick was mainly responsible for the N.D.P.'s near triumph.

Liberal generations: Peter Sims is the baby; Harvey Sims is behind him; Kenneth Sims is at far right; Prime Minister King is beside Harvey

The maverick was Morley Rosenberg, highly articulate and politically shrewd, who later became the city's mayor and, to general surprise, a Conservative candidate in the 1980 provincial election after running five times provincially and federally for the New Democrats. Rosenberg was at the centre of Kitchener's greatest controversy of the 1960s and 1970s, the building of the Market Square development in downtown Kitchener. In the 1960s downtown businessmen had been an active force on council, not least because of the evidence that downtown Kitchener faced serious problems in the core area. Dilapidated buildings, cramped space for the automobile, and strong competition from suburban shopping centres bothered them. By concentrating too fully on their own concerns, however, they gave Rosenberg an easy target, and he seldom missed. Throughout the late 1960s and the 1970s "Morley" was a dissenter who won even more public favour. His popularity at the time speaks to the resentment

*King Street and the
downtown in 1954*

that many Kitchener residents must have felt about the direction of their
civic life during that period. He, too, was Allen Huber's heir.

Kitchener's resentments extended much beyond its own boundaries.
During the council meetings on the Market Square plan, Alderman Alan
Barron would invariably ask where a speaker lived. He reflected Kitchener's suspicion of "outside" interference as well as its belief that it
shouldered too many of the burdens of the surrounding municipalities.
Years earlier the city's planning director, W. E. Thomson, had urged that
the solution to Kitchener and Waterloo County's future economic and
governmental problems lay in regional planning. This notion fitted per-
fectly with that of the Ontario government. In February 1970 a Waterloo
Area Local Government Review, established by the Department of Municipal Affairs, after a local initiative, issued its report. Commissioner Stewart
Fyfe expressed his belief that "Many of the difficulties in carrying out such
functions as slum clearance, urban renewal, town planning, pollution
control and area development arise as much from the complexities and
fragmentation of local government as from any other source." Fyfe urged
reorganization but thought that "the strength of the interest in common
between urban and rural areas and between the two urban complexes does
not seem strong enough to warrant one government for the whole Area at
this time." He recommended a reorganized city-county system rather than
a single "regional government." When, however, the provincial government acted, it chose a two-tier regional structure where the regional
municipality took over responsibility for numerous functions, including

police and social services; but municipal and township governments remained, while members of those local councils formed a regional council on the basis of proportional representation. It was a compromise that satisfied few. It nevertheless recognized that modern government was more complicated than government in the past. Whether it could be more successful was a question unanswered in Kitchener as elsewhere.[28]

Politics affected all those who dwelt in Kitchener, but politics were not the major interest in the lives of most. In the most contentious political debate of the 1960s and 1970s, the Market Square controversy, only two-fifths of the population voted in the referendum on the question. A greater percentage went to church the following Sunday. The churches probably remained the main focus of social life of Kitchener for most of the postwar years. During this period Kitchener's religious pattern became closer to that of the area around it.

Kitchener's Market and City Hall

In 1941 the Roman Catholics became, for the first time, the largest religious group in the community with 21,249 adherents as opposed to 20,031 Lutherans. By 1971 the Roman Catholic community had increased to 79,313 and the Lutheran to only 38,085. By this time the United Church had taken over second place with 38,945 members. Beyond these large religious groupings there remained an abundance of smaller sects that played an important part in the community. Some of these were the fundamentalist groups, such as the Pentecostals, which grew so rapidly elsewhere in English Canada. Others were long-established churches whose roots extended far into the early days of Berlin, such as the Mennonites and their numerous branches, and the Swedenborgians. One of the most venerable local churches disappeared in 1968, when the Evangelical United Brethren Church, which had first come to Berlin from Pennsylvania in 1837, merged with the United Church of Canada.[29] But new churches appeared, such as the New Apostolic, whose headquarters were in Kitchener, and the New Testament Church of God which was established in 1973 to minister to the growing Caribbean community in Kitchener. Ethnic groups continued to turn to the churches to preserve their heritage. The churches in turn responded to the spiritual and cultural needs of the newcomers. The Lutheran and Roman Catholic churches thus responded quickly to the flood of postwar German immigrants, and later the Roman Catholic Church also made certain that it became a haven for Portuguese and Italian immigrants.[30]

In the case of the Roman Catholic Church and several other religious groups, education was an important focus of the church's effort. The Beth Jacob Synagogue taught the children of Jewish families Hebrew and Jewish history. The Mennonite Church established a private high school, Rockway Mennonite, which attracted many Mennonites from Kitchener and the surrounding community. In the 1970s Kitchener fundamentalists opened a private "Christian school." Roman Catholics, of course, continued to maintain their separate schools which were state-supported to the Grade 10 level. There were, in 1980, twenty-two elementary separate schools as well as two separate high schools, St. Mary's for girls and St. Jerome's for boys. They continued to flourish into the 1980s and indeed were expanding their physical facilities as the public school system remained static.

The public school system ceased to grow because it had expanded so rapidly in the postwar decades. Until the mid-fifties Kitchener-Waterloo Collegiate Institute remained the city's sole public high school, one which also trained most from the surrounding area as well. The baby boom ended this and led to the establishment of Eastwood Collegiate in 1956. By 1980 there were no less than eight public secondary schools in Kitchener and Waterloo and students wandered across civic boundary lines. This was a natural outcome of the regionalization of the school system which occurred in 1969. The Kitchener and Waterloo High School Board merged into the Waterloo County Board of Education, a body which administered a larger budget than the regional municipality. What did this all mean? Those closest to it were unsure. In the official publication honouring the 125th anniversary of Kitchener-Waterloo Collegiate Institute, the author claimed it was not easy to judge the events and the education which had occurred in the previous twenty-five years. "These years," he wrote, "have been crowded and often confusing. 'Like the front hall between classes?' Perhaps."[31]

Whatever they learned in school, Kitchener's young people stayed in school longer and those who did tended to have better jobs. The 1976 census revealed that well over half of Kitchener's youth (57.94 per cent) had more than a Grade 10 education. This was, significantly, much lower than the figure for Waterloo (71.73 per cent).[32] Waterloo had developed an increasingly middle-class hue, not least because it became the area's centre for post-secondary education. Waterloo College graduated its first six students in 1927. The depression stunted the college's growth, but this Lutheran institution survived until the influx of postwar students returned its early vitality. In 1958 the college separated from the University of Western Ontario, which had bestowed degrees upon the college's graduates, and became Waterloo Lutheran University. In 1973 the university, lured by the promise of full provincial funding, broke its ties with the Lutheran Church and took on another name, Wilfrid Laurier University. During its metamorphosis, Waterloo College had shed an educational skin which became the University of Waterloo. This university emerged in 1958 from a cocoon known as the Associate Faculties Division of Waterloo College, a division which since 1956 had offered engineering courses. By the mid-1960s, a university with numerous faculties had taken form. The university offered courses in nearly all areas, but it retained the scientific and technical flavour which its local businessmen founders wished it to have. A community college, appropriately named Conestoga College, trained Kitchener's young people in more technical fields. By 1980 the universities and Conestoga College were the community's largest employers, profoundly influencing the cultural and economic life of the community.

Learning in Kitchener did not occur solely within the classroom. Forms of popular entertainment changed Kitchener in a fashion which reflected the communications revolution which occurred throughout Canada. In the early postwar years Kitchener went to the movies and, much less often, to local dramas, especially those produced by the Kitchener-Waterloo Little Theatre. K-W Musical Productions and the K-W Community Concert Association also attracted many to their events and, more important, offered opportunities for local talents. The Kitchener-Waterloo Symphony Orchestra grew out of a meeting in October 1944 at the Waterloo Band Hall, and it has become an increasingly professional symphony, one which in the classical music field exerts an influence over the surrounding area and attracts attention throughout Canada.[33] In 1981 Kitchener's Arts Centre opened in Mackenzie King Square in Kitchener's downtown. The Centre indicated the community's commitment to its symphony and to its cultural traditions. The controversies which surrounded its construction were forgotten on opening night as one of the Centre's most vigorous opponents, Mayor Morley Rosenberg, proudly hosted a gala to celebrate the appearance of the new civic gem.

The controversy surrounding the Arts Centre is of some interest. Its opponents argued that the Centre's appeal would be narrow while its supporters pointed to numerous hockey rinks the city had built without civic murmur. Both sides had a point. Civic government since the war had

Opposite page—
K-W Dutchmen, Allen Cup Champions, 1952-53

Opposite page—
Welcoming the Dutchmen home

bestowed many blessings on athletes and those who watched them. In 1948 the Queen Street Arena burnt, perhaps to the delight of some of the hockey players and spectators who had complained about its rickety structure. Its replacement, the Kitchener Memorial Auditorium, could hold six thousand people, and on several occasions Kitchener's sports fans crammed the auditorium's corners to watch the highly successful Kitchener-Waterloo Dutchmen in the 1950s and early 1960s. The Dutchmen represented Canada in the Olympics in 1956 and 1960, unfortunately losing both times. Although one observer claims that the 1960 loss—to the United States, of all nations—was the death blow to senior hockey in Kitchener, it is possible that television, which brought the National Hockey League into Kitchener's living-rooms, was mainly responsible.[34] Whatever their inspiration, local or distant, Kitchener's young continued to participate in the city's five minor hockey leagues which produced several players who made "the big time." So did the golfers Moe Norman, Gerry Kesselring, and Gary Cowan who learned their skills on Kitchener's civic-owned Rockway Golf Course (built by depression workers on the old sewage plant site), or at the Westmount Golf and Country Club at which the city's business and professional elite golfed and socialized.[35]

Business, sports, and social life continued to intermingle in the city. In the shadow of the cultural giant of Toronto, Kitchener sought to maintain its separate merits and existence. Increasingly it showed that Toronto had not suffocated its indigenous growths but rather had nourished them. By the 1980s there was no doubt that the local efflorescence would endure.

Housing and Planning in Postwar Kitchener

Like nearly all Canadian cities, Kitchener emerged from the depression and the war much in need of new housing and fuller municipal services.[36] By late 1944 the Chamber of Commerce survey had indicated that housing would be the major consumer demand of the postwar period. Moreover, the survey showed that Kitchener's residents and those of surrounding areas had the savings to fulfill their hopes. Even those who lacked the savings, especially those from the middle and lower-middle classes, could now purchase their own home through the assistance of the National Housing Act which greatly expanded the number of Canadians who qualified for mortgages. In Kitchener, as in Canadian cities generally, the problem was to create supply—the bricks and mortar—to meet the sudden demand. The house was "not just a mere assemblage of brick, stone, steel, wood, and glass, built to protect its inhabitants against severe climactic conditions and to provide a shelter where they may procreate and nurture their young." The house was a home, "an impressive and intricate material apparatus," which made possible a psychologically desirable way of life. For postwar families, the house was what was wanted, and it expressed what families wanted to be.[37]

   This perspective is useful in understanding the growth of suburban Kitchener during the postwar era. Until 1965 Kitchener's planners constantly coped with population growth greater than they had anticipated. They also faced a consensus that single-family homes were an essential part of the "good life" to which postwar Canadians aspired. This consensus on homes was parallelled by a similar consensus on the right to education and on the need for adequate recreation facilities. As a result, whereas the cost for land and services amounted to very little of the total cost of a home in the mid-nineteenth century, these costs could amount to over half of the total by the mid-twentieth century. This meant that civic authorities had to take a more active part in the direction of civic growth. This caused difficulties. The past invariably influenced the present as old roads, rules, buildings, and attitudes affected the planners and developers' hopes. In Kitchener, as in other Canadian communities, "the most common form of planning . . . in the years after the middle of the century represented an uneasy compromise between regulation and *laissez faire*."[38]

   In the early postwar years the old downtown attracted little attention compared to the question of where and how Kitchener was to expand. Kitchener had to increase its physical limits, and this created a need to co-operate with surrounding communities. It also, quite naturally, brought conflict. Because of the character of Kitchener's physical boundaries, Waterloo Township to the north was particularly appetizing to the city's taste. To the south and the east, the Grand River created a natural barrier to expansion, and to the west a rolling topography made industrial expansion too expensive and limited housing to the more expensive variety. Recognition of common interests as well as possible future conflicts led Kitchener, Waterloo, and Waterloo Township to form the joint Kitchener-Waterloo and Suburban Planning Board in April 1947.

   This board only had authority to advise subsidiary planning boards (Waterloo did not have an official plan until 1948), but, in the judgment of Professor Ralph Krueger, it was "surprisingly successful."[39] In 1949 it adopted an official plan for roads which incorporated a "ring road" plan. This road's planned route was approximately the same as the one followed by the Conestoga Parkway which was opened two decades later. Although the parkway was long delayed, much dislocation was avoided because much of the right of way had been purchased earlier. In 1953 the board adopted an official parks plan, in co-operation with the Grand River Conservation Authority, and by the early 1960s the parks plan had been fully implemented. These successes, however, were less noticed than the frustrations which continued to mark Waterloo County planning in the 1950s and early 1960s. It was not so much that there was no planning; in retrospect, it is clear that the Waterloo region suffered from too much planning and too many plans. A local government review in 1970 identified at least eighty-six planning studies completed in the previous nine years. Some of these studies were carried out in ignorance of other relevant studies. As the review commented, "the multitude of authorities in the

Area may plan exhaustively, as they have done and are continuing to do, but unless the plans are translated into action and the community begins to take the shape conceived in the 'Plan,' the planning process is indeed sterile."[40]

The planners nevertheless deserve sympathy, for the problems they faced were remarkable. The population of Kitchener grew from 35,657 in 1941 to 44,867 in 1951, 59,562 in 1956, 74,485 in 1961, and 93,255 in 1966. Waterloo, for most of the period, grew at an even more rapid pace (9,025 in 1941 to 29,889 in 1966). By 1961 over 50 per cent of the housing stock in both cities had been built since 1945, a figure considerably above most Canadian cities as indicated in Table 7.

Table 6

Comparative Housing Characteristics of Canadian Cities, 1961

| City | No. of dwellings | Tenant occupancy (%) | Period of construction | | |
			Before 1920 (%)	1920-1945 (%)	Since 1945 (%)
Kitchener	20,600	29	25	24	51
Halifax	21,501	50	48	27	25
Sudbury	19,526	42	9	41	50
St. Catharines	23,287	25	25	26	49
Toronto	172,809	43	54	31	15
London	47,428	34	35	18	47
Windsor	33,061	36	34	47	19
Guelph	10,770	29	43	17	40
Waterloo	5,558	22	23	21	56
Ontario	1,640,750	29	34	22	44

Source: Kitchener Planning Department, *Town Housing* (Kitchener, n.d.), 113. Compiled from census materials.

Not only did Kitchener's citizens want many houses, but they also had particular tastes. A 1955 survey showed a definite preference for ranch-style and split-level homes over two-storey homes even though the latter required less land and were cheaper to build. There never seemed to be enough houses to meet the demand. The first postwar housing appeared in the southwest area near St. Mary's Hospital and then in the east in the area around the new Kitchener Memorial Auditorium. More expensive but fewer homes were built in the Westmount area, and this reinforced that area's reputation for exclusiveness. In some cases, for example the area south of St. Mary's, housing now appeared that had been planned for since the first decade of the century.[41] In 1953 the city assessment commissioner R. V. Alles urged that some proposed housing projects should be delayed since it was too expensive to service an area which was not already developed. His concern did not halt demands for housing and for new land, demands to which politicians necessarily responded.

In 1952 Kitchener annexed 3,541 acres, mainly from Waterloo Township, justifying the land as essential for Kitchener's population and industrial growth. But this was not enough. By 1956 Kitchener was asking for 12,000 more acres. Waterloo Township complained that Kitchener acted as if it did not exist, yet by 1958 Kitchener had taken 4,345 more acres of township land.[42] In these new areas services were much more expensive to install, and expansion brought special problems with garbage, water supply, and sewage. In the case of the first, Kitchener turned from incineration, which was costly, to land-fill as a method of disposal, offering for a price to accept Waterloo's, Bridgeport's, and Waterloo Township's garbage as well. In the end, Kitchener paid a price as its

The Rumpel residence in 1958

land-fill site in the 1970s developed a serious problem with methane emissions which prevented its intended use as a recreation area and which also affected some nearby housing developments. In the case of water and sewage, which the mayor declared Kitchener's major problems in 1957, there was a recognition that meeting future demands would be more expensive than in the past. Kitchener's water commissioners in the mid-1950s, Carl Knell and Egbert Seegmiller, warned that the wells which had supplied the city's needs for so long would be inadequate in the future. Kitchener would have to depend on others for this most fundamental need.[43]

Fairview Park Mall   The opening of Highway 401 in 1960, the development of a K-Mart store on the access road (Highway 8) from Kitchener south to Highway 401, and, most of all, the plans of Fairview Shopping Centres to open a large shopping mall along the access road, but closer to the city, once again emphasized to Kitchener's politicians and businessmen the need to work with surrounding communities. Simultaneously Kitchener began to fear the loss of economic predominance by its downtown merchants. Indeed, after a decade and a half, an atmosphere of growth and optimism which had derived from the city's swelling boundaries and the well-scrubbed new subdivisions gave way to worries about the deterioration of what had been the city's heart. The city's new planning director, W. E. Thomson, bluntly expressed this concern in 1962, warning that the downtown would suffer the fate of American metropolises whose urban ills were documented nightly on the television. Kitchener must not become a naked city, stripped of its civility and urban richness. The message was clear. There must be green belts, new parks, more planning, and a more diversified civic life.[44]

The Age of Rock on the King Street Mall, 1966

On November 20, 1962, the same day on which the Waterloo Trust Company announced that construction would start next year on a twelve-storey skyscraper in downtown Kitchener, the Chamber of Commerce held a "smoker" for 250 of the largest taxpayers in the city. City officials told the taxpayers that there would be major problems with growth in the future. The problems of air pollution, inadequate housing for an expanded civic bureaucracy, and urban transit were discussed. The downtown, it was stressed, was in very bad shape; perhaps it should be relocated. There was much to do and very little time. The future could be truly splendid with Kitchener the commercial and cultural centre of a community of half a million people—or it could be catastrophic. The opportunities must be grasped: "To do this we must plan together and grow together, making no little plans but big plans to stir men's blood."[45]

The first HiWay Market

In the next few years, some blood did stir and some was also spilt. In January 1963 a Kitchener Urban Renewal Committee was formed to give direction to the process of urban renewal. Kitchener was not alone in pursuing urban renewal, and the federal and provincial authorities were willing to assist financially. These funds became available once the city had presented an urban renewal scheme. By 1964 there was a flurry of activity resulting in numerous reports on various aspects of Kitchener's future. The most important of these were "Kitchener 2000," "Downtown Kitchener—Economic Analysis for Redevelopment Planning," and, in 1965, the Kitchener Urban Renewal Committee's "The Plan—Downtown Kitchener." The first of these led to the development of a fuller official plan based on Kitchener's needs by the end of the century. The other two concentrated on downtown urban renewal. At the same time the provincial government, having observed too many squabbles and too much confusion, established a Waterloo County Area Planning Board charged with the responsibility for preparing an official plan to embrace all Waterloo County communities. For Kitchener, then, the problems involving its periphery were to be handled by involvement in a broader planning exercise. The problems of its core, however, were still its own.[46]

The core difficulties were much more Kitchener's own when in 1968 the federal government, responding to criticisms of the bulldozing approach to urban renewal, froze funds for urban renewal. In June 1968 city council had adopted an urban renewal scheme that would bring major changes to the downtown. The shopping district with its decaying façades, vacant upper storeys, narrow sidewalks, and gasoline fumes would be rebuilt so that it could challenge the allure of the new shopping centres. To the east of the downtown, in the old Centre Ward, a civic centre would take form consisting of an art gallery, a concert hall, and a new city hall. To fulfill the plan's hopes $16,385,000 was needed. Half was expected from the federal government; in the event, less than one-sixteenth was given.

Kitchener's character was at the core of the problem. In 1965 the city showed the highest growth rate of any Canadian city, but of all the Ontario census metropolitan areas it had the lowest average wage in the manufacturing sector. It was the retailing centre for the area, but the new roads which civic boosters lauded could carry shoppers to Waterloo, Toronto, or, much more worrying, to complexes just beyond the city's edge. Only continued growth, it was thought, could assure a broader sharing of the city's prosperity.

But in the late 1960s some began to question the value of growth and some began to see urban renewal as the cause of, not the cure for, the problems of North American cities. Such were the differences of opinion when Oxlea Investments approached city council in the spring of 1971 with a plan for the re-development of the City Hall and Market Square area. The Kitchener Urban Renewal Committee saw the Oxlea plan as a godsend after the freezing of federal funds had scuppered action on earlier plans. It heartily supported the plan and the secrecy which Oxlea insisted upon before it presented the plan to council. Council agreed to the secrecy as did the local news media. The significance of the planned development, it was believed, justified the secrecy. When, however, the story broke in the University of Waterloo student newspaper, *The Chevron*, it became clear that many disagreed. Very soon the proposed development, which involved tearing down the old city hall and market, became a subject of great controversy. Morley Rosenberg, who had originally supported the secrecy of the negotiations, quickly took the lead in opposing the development. Despite Rosenberg's N.D.P. affiliation, he did not carry the labour movement with him. It saw jobs in the project and its leading spokesman, council member George Mitchell, was a strong supporter of the project. The debate became stormy with supporters denouncing the shaggy manes of the mostly-young opponents and pointing to the fact that many of them came from Waterloo. The opponents responded with charges of manipulation, deceit, and corruption. The Oxlea project, they angrily declared, was the work of a "Kitchener Kompact." The Ontario Municipal Board decided that the matter should be put to a vote, and the referendum was held on December 6, 1971. The supporters won 15,689 to 11,513, and the project gained Municipal Board approval.[47]

Morley Rosenberg pro-testing. Jim Breithaupt is seated behind him at the right.

Looking back, the debate seems very much an event of a time when the future of cities seemed most unclear. The opponents were too often stereotyped, as, for example, by Bill Thomson, who described them as a "small, immature and exotic minority section of our society."[48] So, too, were the proponents, who were not simply a "Kitchener Kompact." This concept of a civic elite acting together on all fundamental matters affecting the city's political and economic life is very misleading. On many political and economic issues organized labour, financial interests, manufacturers, and the media were divided. In the late 1960s their unity came from a growing fear that the city core was disintegrating and that the consequences would be most serious. Jack Young exaggerated, but his sincerity is unquestionable in his belief that "The core of the city must not be permitted to decay except at the risk of permitting degeneration of the economic and ultimately the moral fibre of the community itself."[49] The Market Square fight was symbolic, and the rhetoric reflected the turbulence of the early 1970s. Ten years later, as Morley Rosenberg occupied the mayor's chair in the new city hall which overlooked the Market Square development, the debate seemed very much of the past.

Opposite page— Oxlea Mall is at the centre (Eaton's)

The Market Square development did not take quite the form its promoters had originally planned. The remainder of the urban renewal

The new Waterloo
County Court House

scheme has also been only partially fulfilled. By 1979 some elements of the scheme had been incorporated into Kitchener's city centre, but the 1979 closing of downtown Kitchener's most familiar landmark, the Walper Hotel, and its subsequent dilapidation symbolized the inner core's continuing problems. Some of the gloom dissipated when the Centre in the Square, with the long-promised art gallery and a concert hall, finally opened in the civic square area in the heart of the old Centre Ward. The Centre graced the square, its sloping eaves blending elegantly into the park above it. Behind and beside it remained tattered reminders of the Centre Ward's old prosperity. And the city hall stayed in the office building on Frederick Street. Still, the Centre, the public library, and the two courthouses facilitated urban life and enhanced the urban landscape.

Beyond the downtown, by 1980 it was clear that Kitchener in the year 2000 would not be what W. E. Thomson had imagined it would be in his 1964 report. Regional planning had come with regional government in the early 1970s. Kitchener developed its own official plan which was approved by council on January 20, 1975, and which fitted into the new region's official plan. The Kitchener plan anticipated population growth of 3 per cent in the 1970s and 2 per cent in the 1980s, and it recognized that what happened in Kitchener would be much affected by regional and provincial actions. It re-committed the city to "the downtown core as the focal point of the Region" and to "the highest residential densities around the downtown." There was also recognition that other "centrums" would exist in the city, communities in their own right. Older communities would be more carefully tended as change took place. The plan embodied the concerns of the mid-1970s just as the Kitchener 2000 plan represented the ebullience of Kitchener and Canada in the mid-1960s.[50]

Growth had brought ebullience, but it had also obscured the longer cycles of civic and national life. The future would not be like the present, and the contingency of a city's fortunes was too often forgotten. In the 1980s, as the city's population stabilized and its once vital industries lost their strength, the gloom was perhaps greater than was warranted because hopes had billowed so much so recently. It was surely doubtful, however, that the landscape would ever again alter so much as it had in the years since the war.

The People of Kitchener

Centre in the Square

As the landscape changed greatly so did the people of Kitchener. The interwar years had made Kitchener more a part of the Canadian community. When Canada and Germany went to war in September 1939, Kitchener had not, for several years, proclaimed itself Canada's German capital. Hitler had embarrassed most German Canadians in the later 1930s, and when war came there was no discussion of double loyalty as there had been in August 1914. In the 1941 census, for the first time less than half of the population identified itself as German in contrast to over two-thirds which had identified itself as German in 1911. Moreover, in Canada if not in Germany, race had become a much less respectable manner in which to define individual and community characteristics. And yet memories of the pain the community suffered during the First World War remained, and the first months of war reflected the community's nervousness. On September 12, 1939, the city council applauded the Concordia and Schwaben Clubs for ending their activities; it further suggested that the clubs' doors remain closed for the length of the war. The *Record* agreed and reported enthusiastically on the large crowd which milled in front of the armouries where recruiting took place. On September 27 the *Record* commented that German and even Pennsylvania Dutch had been seldom heard on Kitchener's streets after the declaration of war.[51]

In a few years the uneasiness had disappeared as Kitchener contributed arms and men to the war in quantities which surpassed or equalled the most British communities in Canada. Some groups, notably the Mennonites, faced continuing difficulties, but conscientious objection had become more generally acceptable and many Mennonites simply joined the armed forces or accepted alternative service because their commitment to nonresistance had disappeared. When local conscientious objectors left Kitchener for alternative service in western Canada, the *Record* reported that "3,000 People See Conchies Board Train." This "huge crowd was the largest to gather at the station since the royal visit."[52] The contrast with the first war could not have been greater, and the mood explains why Kitchener did not witness any repetition of the ethnic tensions which had so marked its political and social life a generation earlier.

The absence of ethnic tension made postwar adjustment easier as well. As soon as the war ended the devastation of Europe aroused Canadian sympathy. Just before Christmas 1946 the Canadian Society for German Relief was organized in Kitchener.[53] Christmastime the next year the first German refugee families came to Kitchener. They were among the first fifty Germans who had fled or had been expelled from eastern Europe who came to Canada.[54] These *Flüchtlings* who could no longer live in the homes in Romania, Yugoslavia, Poland, or Russia which their ancestors had built generations before came to Waterloo County in large numbers. They could immigrate to Canada before Germans who lived in the *Reich* itself. The latter group could only enter Canada in 1950. Most of those who came had relatives among Germans who had come to Kitchener in the 1920s. The Schwaben Club readily accepted the hundreds of German-speaking refugees into its fold. A new club, the Transylvania Club, was founded in 1951 to offer social and cultural facilities for the 275-300 Romanian Saxon Germans who settled in the Waterloo region. Like the Schwaben Club, this club had a very practical purpose: it provided sickness and death insurance for its members, an important function in the years before medicare in Canada. The oldest German club, the Concordia, was more exclusively social. It re-opened in 1948 with 130 members. Such was the conviviality that filled its hall that the Concordia's membership had reached three thousand by 1977. By that time Kitchener was once more extolling its German past and present.

Postwar immigrants to Kitchener

In 1951 the founding meeting of the German-Canadian Alliance took place in Kitchener. Six years after Hitler's fall this alliance proclaimed its purpose to be "the furthering of the German tradition, speech, song, music, literature, and sport" and the promotion of better understanding between Germans and Canadians by acquainting both with each other's culture and tradition.[55] This alliance flourishes still and has done superlative work in maintaining and explaining the German tradition in Canada. There was one German tradition that those who met at the Schwaben Club on April Fool's Day in 1951 to form the German-Canadian Alliance could never imagine passing easily to Canada. In those parched days when Ontario's liquor laws assured that drinkers could not seem to enjoy it, an Oktoberfest seemed ludicrous to contemplate. In the late 1960s and early 1970s, as Canada shed its Victorian garb, Kitchener put on lederhosen and dirndls and enjoyed a rollicking Oktoberfest which brought as much joy to the treasurers of the German clubs as to the celebrants themselves. The German content often seemed less than the alcoholic content. This disturbed some but surely not those older Kitchener Germans when they reflected how such an exuberant German celebration would have been unthinkable in their youth.

Oktoberfest chairman Bill Renaud sampling products

When Oktoberfest became the major tourist attraction of the Waterloo region, few Kitchener Germans actually recalled Oktoberfest in Germany except when they visited as tourists. The German "economic wonder" of the 1950s and 1960s reduced the flow of Germans to Kitchener to scarcely more than a trickle. In the late 1960s and 1970s new groups came to Kitchener, often living in the same areas where Germans had dwelt on their arrival in the early postwar years. By 1980 Germans were not the major participants in the Kitchener-Waterloo Regional Folk Arts Council and Multicultural Centre. The largest ethnic communities in Kitchener were the Portuguese and the Greeks, mainly of Cypriot origin, two groups of whom there was scarcely a trace three decades before. They were, like most of the immigrants before them, refugees from lands where political turmoil abounded in the 1960s and 1970s. The Waterloo region has roughly three thousand Greek Cypriots today and nearly all arrived in 1974 and 1975. Their communities remained strong, but by 1980 Portuguese and Greek Canadians were found throughout the economic and social activities of the community.[56]

Other groups, such as the Poles, depended upon reproduction rather than immigration to increase their numbers. That assimilation occurred is most clear in the case of Sacred Heart Church, Kitchener's "Polish" church, founded in 1916. By 1979 most of the masses were in English and only 50 per cent of the six thousand parishioners were of Polish background; and of these only half understood Polish. And yet the church did remain a centre for the Polish community, and in its sanctuary the seasons of a Pole's life in Kitchener—birth, marriage, and death—continued to be marked.[57]

In the postwar period numerous other new groups appeared. The Indian, West Indian, and Chinese communities grew very rapidly in the 1970s, and in this respect Kitchener mirrored the changes in most surrounding urban centres. Until the late 1970s the growth was exceedingly rapid. A few statistics paint a sharp portrait of the pace of change in the community. Between 1971 and 1976, the city's population rose from 116,966 to 131,870 (12.65 per cent). In 1976, 21.5 per cent of Kitchener's citizens had a mother tongue other than English. In that same year, one of nineteen Kitchener residents had immigrated during the last five years. In the majority of the city's census tracts, over 50 per cent of the population had moved during that same five years. In some newer areas in the south and southwest, over two-thirds were newcomers to the area.[58] Kitchener was a city where men and women were very much in motion.

In the later 1970s the city caught its breath as population growth slowed. House and land prices stabilized. Some, such as developers, suffered; others, such as school administrators, welcomed the relief from swollen classrooms. The planners trimmed their projections as politicians promised that the new day would be better. Perhaps it would. Whatever the future held, Kitchener could be satisfied that, when growth had been so rapid, its pains had been relatively few.

CONCLUSION

A city is more than its people, and it is a part of much more than itself. Kitchener in the twentieth century has shared in the experiences of southern Ontario and Canada. It has become an integral part of the modern North American economic system, reflecting the patterns which have marked that system, whether depression, as in the 1930s, or boom, as in the postwar era. The future will inevitably reflect the past, and Kitchener's fate now depends on the adjustment the southern Ontario region, and Canada generally, makes to new technology and new economic forces.

Like cities elsewhere, Kitchener's fate is less of its own making than was the case with tiny Berlin a century ago. Its industries today produce tires and automobile frames that speed along California freeways and electronics that compete with East Asian counterparts for international markets. Kitchener has become intricately linked with the world economy, and local influences upon its direction are not so meaningful as they were when Bishop Ben Eby's little settlement grew into a village and then a town. As the town became a city, and as the small shops became factories, much that was distinct was lost. This loss occurred in surrounding communities such as Guelph, Brantford, and Hamilton; but in Kitchener's case the effect was probably greater.

Even in the 1830s what happened in the Grand River valley was directly related to events beyond North America. Kitchener was settled by German immigrants who were a part of the great migration of the nineteenth century. The large majority of early Berlin's settlers shared the Western European background of other settlers of the region, but Berlin was distinctive in this overwhelmingly British region because it was German. In the nineteenth century, many of the particular industries which developed in Berlin—especially leather, buttons, brewing, and furniture—did so because of the skills that the German immigrants possessed that British immigrants did not. These industries prospered because of these special skills, yet their prosperity drew them and the community more tightly into the social and economic world of North America. Those who feared the loss of their distinctiveness, notably some of the Mennonites, retreated from the city to remote and rural areas. Most of Berlin's residents, however, adapted to the changes easily until the First World War.

The First World War is the most significant event in the city's history. It forced the city to confront the problem of maintaining its cultural distinctiveness while attempting to participate fully in the Ontario economic and political system. More than the name of Berlin was changed in the First World War. Although Kitchener continued to reveal some different traits from its neighbours, as in the case of its political behaviour, the city after 1918 came to recognize that it must become more a part of the broader Canadian community. Today Kitchener is less obviously "multicultural" than some of its once "British" neighbours.

Kitchener's history shows the limitations of "multiculturalism" or of the "mosaic" as an explanation of Canadian development. It also shows the force of international influence upon local development. Kitchener's future is now tied closely to what happens far beyond its legal boundaries. In that respect, as in so many others, it is like the province and the nation where it finds itself. Ben Eby, the product of Europe's sixteenth-century religious wars, would not have been surprised.

NOTES

Chapter One

[1] Jacob Stroh, "Reminiscences of Berlin," in Waterloo Historical Society (WHS), *Annual Report* 66 (1978), 78.

[2] For a detailed account of the Indian lands and their subsequent development, see E. A. Cruickshank, "The Reserve of the Six Nations Indians on the Grand River and the Mennonite Purchase of Block No. 2," in WHS, *Annual Report* 19 (1927), 303-27. See also Charles M. Johnston, *The Valley of the Six Nations: A Collection of Documents on the Indian Lands of the Grand River* (Toronto, 1964); and Virgil Emerson Martin, *The Early History of Jakobstettel* (St. Jacobs, 1979).

[3] E. A. Cruickshank (ed.), *Correspondence of Lieutenant Governor John Graves Simcoe with Allied Documents Relating to his Administration of the Government of Upper Canada* (Toronto, 1923), vol. 2, 59; and E. A. Cruickshank (ed.), *Correspondence of the Honourable Peter Russell with Allied Documents Relating to the Government of Upper Canada* (Toronto, 1932), 48ff.

[4] Cruickshank, "Reserve of the Six Nations," 321.

[5] The best account of the response of the Mennonites to the American Revolution can be found in John L. Ruth, *'Twas Seeding Time* (Kitchener, 1976). For a more general treatment, see Frank H. Epp, *Mennonites in Canada 1786-1920: The History of a Separate People* (Toronto, 1974).

[6] E. A. Haldane, "The Historical Geography of Waterloo Township, 1800-1855" (M.A. thesis, McMaster University, 1963), 39.

[7] I. C. Bricker, "The History of Waterloo Township up to 1825," in WHS, *Annual Report* 19 (1934), 84, 85, 87. Bricker provides extensive detail about the arrival of the first settlers and the speculative intentions of many of the early Mennonites.

[8] Mabel Dunham's *The Trail of the Conestoga* (Toronto, 1924), 111-15, seems to have begun this tendency which has been faithfully followed by most other authors.

[9] Cruickshank, "Reserve of the Six Nations," 323-26, provides a fascinating account of the intrigue over the sale of these lands; Martin's *Jakobstettel*, 13-22, gives new details drawn from a variety of primary source documents.

[10] Dunham's account in *Trail of the Conestoga* has been adapted as a play and recently produced as a film. At no time, however, has any critical revision been suggested to the *fictional* version first set out by Miss Dunham in 1924.

[11] Cruickshank, "Reserve of the Six Nations," 330-32.

[12] Bricker, "Waterloo Township," 90.

[13] Each shareholder was to receive at least two farms as part of his purchase. Since there were 64 shares there would be 128 farms of 448 acres each and the balance of the property would be divided into 32 smaller farms of 83 acres each. Augustus Jones was commissioned to complete a survey on this basis. See the map on p. 7.

[14] J. D. Wood, "Historical Geography of Dumfries Township, Upper Canada: 1816-1852" (M.A. thesis, University of Toronto, 1958), 48.

[15] L. A. Johnson, *History of Guelph, 1827-1927* (Guelph, 1977), 3-27.

[16] Marilyn Tone Gray, *And Now We Are Many* (Toronto, 1971), 6.

[17] Haldane, "Waterloo Township," 46.

[18] "Berlin, 1835," cited in M. H. Snyder, *Hannes Schneider, Their Descendants and Times* (Kitchener, 1937), 301. (Hereinafter cited as *Schneider*.)

[19] There is a remarkable folklore about the choice of the name Berlin. While most traditions correctly identify the date as 1833, the place of honour has been variously designated as a carpenter shop, a tavern, or Gaukel's hotel. Both Bishop Benjamin Eby and Joseph Schneider have been credited with bestowing the name of Berlin upon the village (W. V. Uttley, *A History of Kitchener* [Waterloo, 1975], 37).

[20] According to M. Walker, *German Home Towns, 1648-1871* (London, 1971), "[After 1830] There were more apprentices and journeymen awaiting mastership than were being absorbed, and they became mobile wage earners who were socially depressed and excluded from the community" (334).

[21] Gerald M. Craig, *Upper Canada, The Formative Years* (Toronto, 1963), 124.

[22] There are a variety of sources dealing with immigration to Canada in the nineteenth century. Of these, Norman Macdonald's *Canada: Immigration and Colonization: 1841-1903* (Toronto, 1966), is particularly helpful. Gottlieb Leibbrandt's *Little Paradise, The Saga of the German Canadians of Waterloo County, Ontario 1800-1975* (Kitchener, 1980) provides a detailed account of German immigrants to Canada (49-50). See also Gladys Heinz, "German Immigration into Upper Canada from 1783 to the Present Day" (M.A. thesis, Queen's University, 1938), 104.

[23] Macdonald, *Immigration and Colonization*, 148.

[24] The entire text of Philipp Lautenschlager's letter was recently made available in a translation by Albert I. Hunsberger, assisted by Anne Wiebe, and published in WHS, *Annual Report* 66 (1978), 41-45.

[25] Clayton Wells, "A Historical Sketch of the Town of Waterloo, Ontario," in WHS, *Annual Report* 16 (1928), 27.

[26] A. E. Byerly, "Henry William Peterson," in WHS, *Annual Report*, 19 (1931), 250-61.

[27] See also M. Sokvitne, "Reflections of Our Religious Heritage," in Wendy Collishaw and Barry Preston (eds.), *Recollections of 125 Years* (Kitchener, 1979).

[28] For a general overview of this era, see C. F. J. Whebell, "Robert Baldwin and Decentralization, 1841-9," in F. H. Armstrong, H. A. Stevenson, and J. D. Wilson (eds.), *Aspects of Nineteenth-Century Ontario* (Toronto, 1974), 48-64.

[29] *Canada Museum*, July 27, 1837; and *Schneider*, 176H.

[30] See Haldane, "Waterloo Township," 57, 58, 65, 135, for population figures. By 1851 practically every lot in the township has been taken up and many farms were at least 50 per cent cleared by 1855 (116).

[31] The following account relies largely on an interview with the Honourable James Young published in 1906, "Old Time Reminiscences," in *The Chronicle-Telegraph Semi-Centennial Number* (Waterloo, 1906), 11.

[32] J. W. Connor, "Historical Sketch, Berlin Yesterday" (1906), reprinted in *Schneider*, 224.

[33] The following account of Berlin's urban landscape relies heavily on the reminiscences of Jacob Stroh which were reprinted in WHS, *Annual Report* 66 (1978), 71-122. Stroh's account is supplemented by the assessment records for 1853 which may be found in the Kitchener Public Library.

Chapter Two

[1] James Young, *Reminiscences of the Early History of Galt and the Settlement of Dumfries*, 230, cited in J. D. Wood, "Historical Geography of Dumfries Township, Upper Canada, 1816-1852" (M.A. thesis, University of Toronto, 1958), 106.

[2] D. W. Kirk, "Southern Ontario: The Areal Pattern of Urban Settlements in 1850" (Ph.D. dissertation, Northwestern University, 1949), 10. In 1852 Preston had 1,180 inhabitants while Berlin had 782.

[3] H. K. Kalbfleisch, *The History of the Pioneer German Language Press of Ontario, 1835-1918* (Toronto, 1968), 30-31.

[4] *Chronicle* (Berlin), July 9, 1856.

[5] Ibid., August 20, 1856.

[6] Ibid., August 13, 1856.

[7] L. A. Johnson, *History of Guelph, 1827-1927* (Guelph, 1977), 147-77.

[8] *Chronicle* (Berlin), June 18, 1856.

[9] The details of the railway schemes have been fully explored by Mary H. Farmer, "The Preston and Berlin Railway Company," in WHS, *Annual Report* 48 (1961), 16-22.

[10] J. M. S. Careless, "Some Aspects of Urbanization in Nineteenth-Century Ontario," in F. H. Armstrong et al. (eds.), *Nineteenth Century Ontario* (Toronto, 1974), 70.

[11] W. V. Uttley, *A History of Kitchener* (Waterloo, 1975), 101-102.

[12] Ibid., 102-103.

[13] Ibid., 66.

[14] *Advertiser* (Guelph), October 26, 1848.

[15] *Canada Gazetteer* (1867), 38.

[16] E. Ronnenberg has provided an extremely useful biographical series in the *Kitchener-Waterloo Record*, one of which is "Emil Vogelsang . . . the Button Capital" (June 29, 1975). See also I. Zimmerman, "Birth of the Button Industry in Canada," in WHS, *Annual Report* 45 (1958), 17-25.

[17] Uttley, *Kitchener*, 158.

[18] *Daily News* (Berlin), February 20, 1878. See also W. H. Breithaupt, *Sketch of the Life of Catharine Breithaupt, Her Family and Times* (Berlin, 1911), for additional details about the career of Louis Breithaupt.

[19] Cited in Uttley, *Kitchener*, 193. Uttley, however, failed to notice that the resolution before council called for support for *new* manufactories. Council *Minutes*, April 5, 1875.

[20] *Daily News* (Berlin), September 1, 1879.

[21] Ibid., September 28, 1878.

[22] *Chronicle* (Berlin), July 8, 1857.

[23] Cited in *Schneider*, 150B.

[24] Careless, "Urbanization," 70.

[25] Gottlieb Leibbrandt, *Little Paradise* (Kitchener, 1980), 29.

[26] Alan Artibise, *Winnipeg: An Illustrated History* (Toronto, 1977), 38-44; and Max Foran, *Calgary: An Illustrated History* (Toronto, 1978), 82-89.

[27] The description of the festivities taken from the accounts in the *Berliner Journal* (May 1871).

[28] The text has been reprinted in WHS, *Annual Report* 54 (1966), 78-80.

[29] E. Ronnenberg, "Hugo Kranz Helped Establish Economical Mutual Insurance Co.," *Kitchener-Waterloo Record*, July 5, 1975.

[30] *Telegraph* (Berlin), January 21, 1859.

[31] *Schneider*, 230.

[32] Cited in *Daily News* (Berlin), September 19, 1879.

[33] Council *Minutes*, October 5, 1874.

[34] All subsequent quotations are from the account in the *Daily News* (Berlin), September 17, 1879.

[35] Council *Minutes*, October 5, 1874.

[36] For a detailed account of the impact of the school system, see Patricia Pearl McKegney, "Germanism, Industrialism, and Propaganda in Berlin, Ontario During World War I" (M.Phil. thesis, University of Waterloo, 1979), 45-52; and Patricia Pearl McKegney, "The German Schools of Waterloo County, 1851-1913," in WHS, *Annual Report* 58 (1970), 54-67.

[37] McKegney, "German Schools," 58.

[38] McKegney, "Germanism," 52.

[39] *Daily News* (Berlin), November 13, 1879.

[40] Ibid., September 3, 1879.

[41] The names appear to have been changed in 1854 at the time of Berlin's incorporation as a village, but Schneider's Road continued to be used for the area of Queen Street South at least into the 1870s.

[42] Scobie's survey of 1853 is the earliest general survey of Berlin, but it was not until the coming of the Grand Trunk and the survey commissioned by George Grange that a proper survey of the village could be said to exist.

[43] T. Marklevitz, "Public Space in Downtown Kitchener" (B.Arch. thesis, School of Architecture, University of Waterloo, 1978).

[44] E. D. Weber, "Waterloo Township, German Company Tract Lot Number 16," in WHS, *Annual Report* 58 (1970), 12.

[45] *Telegraph* (Berlin), November 25, 1853.

[46] Ibid., December 9, 1853.

[47] Ibid., August 12, 1859.

[48] Ibid., November 23, 1853.

[49] *Schneider*, 229.

[50] Uttley, *Kitchener*, 193.

[51] *Daily News* (Berlin), April 27, 1878.

[52] There is virtually no evidence of serious labour unrest during this transitional period. In March 1879 a strike did take place at Breithaupt's tannery by workers demanding a ten-hour day, but it appears to have been amicably resolved (*Schneider*, 310).

[53] *Telegraph* (Berlin), November 21, 1856.

[54] Ibid., March 6, 1857.

[55] *Chronicle* (Berlin), December 2, 1857.

[56] *Daily News* (Berlin), December 26, 1879.

[57] The editor of the *Daily News* was fined $100 plus costs.

[58] Town of Berlin, By-law 200, September 1, 1873.

[59] *Daily News* (Berlin), March 12, 1878.

[60] Artibise, *Winnipeg*, 86.

[61] Leibbrandt, *Little Paradise*, 127-43 and 165-87, describes the dominant German social activities in great detail.

Chapter Three

[1] A. Bridle, "Trip Over a Gas Producer Plant," *Engineering Journal* (1906), cited in *Berlin Today* (1906).

[2] Quoted in Paul Tiessen (ed.), *Berlin, Canada* (St. Jacobs, 1979), Introduction. This book is a reproduction of the 1912 publication *Berlin, 1912: Celebration of Cityhood*.

[3] Tiessen, *Berlin*.

[4] Ernie Ronnenberg, "George Rumpel Made Kitchener the Centre of the Felt Industry," *Kitchener-Waterloo Record*, October 17, 1975. The name "Furniture Centre of Canada" is in *Berlin, 1912*. Ronnenberg provides the description of Rumpel as the "Felt King" of Canada.

[5] City of Kitchener, Assessment Records, 1879, 1895, 1905, 1915.

[6] *Mail* (Toronto), Special Supplement, n.d., 1886. The *Mail* also observed: "What Berlin is especially noted for at the present time, however, is its factories."

[7] *Globe* (Toronto), August 3, 1889.

[8] Board of Trade *Minute Book* (1886), 180. We are indebted to the kindness of Mr. Archie Gillies for permission to examine the Board's historical records.

[9] D. A. MacMillan, *The Chartered Banks in Kitchener* (n.p., 1927), cited in W. V. Uttley, *A History of Kitchener* (Waterloo, 1975), 323-24.

[10] *Telegraph* (Berlin), December 31, 1901.

[11] The following served as both mayor and president of the Board of Trade: L. J. Breithaupt (1888, 1889), H. L. Janzen (1890), J. C. Breithaupt (1896, 1897), J. M. Staebler (1891), C. H. Mills (1912). Other prominent members of the Board of Trade who also served as mayor were: Hugo Kranz, W. H. Schmalz, Carl Kranz, Daniel Hibner, George Rumpel, and J. R. Eden. Thus, the interrelationship remained extremely close throughout most of this period.

[12] The *Sängerfests* were of course also sponsored by the musical societies and aided by grants from the municipality of Berlin, but the congruence of the interests was clearly spelled out in the 1905 exhibition which brought together the two "great interests" of Berlin.

[13] Reports on industrial conditions in Berlin may be found in the *Ontario Labour Gazette*, in the *Telegraph* (Berlin), and in the *News-Record* (Berlin).

[14] For example, when the Williams, Greene and Rome Company moved to Berlin from Toronto, with a labour force of 365 females and 60 males, it soon found it had "outgrown the labour furnishing capacity of Berlin." Cited in the *Globe* (Toronto), August 3, 1889.

[15] Ibid.

[16] See K. M. McLaughlin, "Race, Religion and Politics: The Election of 1896 in Canada" (Ph.D. dissertation, University of Toronto, 1974).

[17] *Globe* (Toronto), June 15 and 16, 1896; and *News-Record* (Berlin), June 18, 1896.

[18] *Telegraph* (Berlin), 1901, passim; and Daniel Detweiler diary, Kitchener Public Library.

[19] Detweiler Papers, especially the diary.

[20] Ibid., Snider to Detweiler, February 14, 1902.

[21] *News-Record* (Berlin), June 10, 1902.

[22] This series of publications is available at the Kitchener Public Library and is generally referred to as the series on "Busy Berlin."

[23] *Berlin Today* (1906).

[24] Ibid.

[25] This much-quoted figure was derived by comparing the number of names on Berlin's voters' list with the number of individual property owners. In 1905 this calculation produced a figure of 65.6 per cent. Subsequently the notion of home ownership became firmly incorporated as part of the mystique of Berlin and is found in almost all "boosterish" publications.

[26] In 1916, for instance, Dominion employed 604, Merchants 526, and Kaufman 466. Cited in Patriotic Fund record, John Lang Papers, Public Archives of Canada.

[27] Tiessen, *Berlin*; interview, Mr. A. R. Kaufman, 1974; T. G. Reive, "The Industrial Background of Waterloo County to 1914" (B.A. thesis, Wilfrid Laurier University, 1970); and *Berlin Today* (1906).

[28] Based on the R. G. Dun reports and municipal assessment records.

[29] *Telegraph* (Berlin), January 13, 1911.

[30] Ibid., January 4, 1911.

[31] Gottlieb Leibbrandt, *Little Paradise* (Kitchener, 1980), 180.

[32] Cited in Uttley, *Kitchener*, 120.

[33] Cited in Alan Artibise, *Winnipeg: An Illustrated History* (Toronto, 1977), 64.

[34] *Telegraph* (Berlin), January 20, 1905.

[35] Tiessen, *Berlin*, 196.

[36] P. Goetsch, "Canada in 19th Century German Travel Books," lecture series on Nineteenth-Century Germany, University of Toronto, October 8, 1981.

[37] Carl Berger, *The Sense of Power* (Toronto, 1970).

[38] *Mail* (Toronto), n.d., 1886.

[39] Leibbrandt, *Little Paradise*, 103.

[40] Gerald J. Stortz, "John Joseph Lynch, Archbishop of Toronto: A Biographical Study of Religious, Political and Social Commitment" (Ph.D. dissertation, University of Guelph, 1980), 22-23.

[41] This aspect of Berlin's culture has been treated extensively by Patricia Pearl McKegney, "Germanism, Industrialism, and Propaganda in Berlin, Ontario During World War I" (M.Phil. thesis, University of Waterloo, 1979), 26-45.

[42] H. K. Kalbfleisch, *The History of the Pioneer German Language Press of Ontario, 1835-1918* (Toronto, 1968), 81-90, is the source for much of the analysis of the editorial content of the German newspapers.

[43] Ibid., 108.

[44] Cited in ibid., 109.

[45] Pennsylvania Deutsch is basically a spoken language, although there have been several attempts to put it in written form using a phonetic system. As such, it served as a common language for those who had not been formally educated in German.

[46] A full account is given in Leibbrandt, *Little Paradise*, 95-98.

[47] Quoted in *Telegraph* (Berlin), February 12, 1901.

[48] We are indebted to Robert Cornish, one of our former students, for this information gleaned from an exhaustive study of assessment rolls, from newspaper research, and from interviews.

[49] Gladys Heinz, "German Immigration into Upper Canada" (M.A. thesis, Queen's University, 1938), 70.

[50] Tiessen, *Berlin*, 48, 89.

[51] Ibid., 196, 198.

[52] *Globe* (Toronto), August 3, 1889.

[53] We are indebted to Wendy Collishaw and Robert Cornish for detailed studies of the historical architecture of Berlin. For an overview of the architecture of this period, see Alan Gowans, *Building Canada: An Architectural History of Canadian Life* (Toronto, 1968).

[54] Ibid., 128.

[55] *Globe* (Toronto), August 3, 1889.

[56] Tiessen, *Berlin*, 89.

[57] See Wendy Collishaw and Bert Williams, *The Heritage Homes of Kitchener* (Kitchener, 1981).

[58] Uttley, *Kitchener*, 328.

[59] The following account is from the reports in the *Telegraph* (Berlin), February 13, 14, and 20, 1905.

[60] This phrase was the police chief's regular statement in his yearly report. For example, see *Telegraph* (Berlin), January 11, 1911.

[61] The following statistics are drawn from the police report for the final year before Berlin's elevation to city status. They are similar to the statistics cited in previous reports.

[62] An excellent account of these tensions and of the conflicts within Berlin's commercial and civic elite is found in George A. Borovilos, "The Evolution of the Town of Berlin into the City of Kitchener: A Period of Growth, Change and Response to Urban Industrialization, 1890-1925" (B.A. thesis, Department of Geography, University of Waterloo, 1977). See also the Board of Trade *Minute Books*, 1898-1902.

[63] For example, see the case of the attempted tax exemption and bonus for the Dennis Wire Company in 1905. In this case, the by-law received the support of a large majority of those who voted, but not the necessary two-thirds of the eligible voters. Mayor Kranz and Alderman Gardiner went so far as to request Premier Whitney to

introduce special legislation to ratify a by-law of the town in order to give a bonus to the Dennis Wire Company (*Telegraph* [Berlin], May 11, 1905).

[64] We are especially indebted to two former students, Bonnie Tough and Marianne Huber, who first brought to our attention the remarkable career of Allen Huber.

[65] *Telegraph* (Berlin), January 2, 1901.

[66] Ibid., December 31, 1901.

[67] Ibid., December 31, 1901 to January 8, 1902.

[68] Ibid., January 8, 1903.

[69] Ibid., September 14, 1907. The remainder of this account of Huber's mayoralty campaign and his conduct in the office of mayor is drawn from the *Telegraph* (Berlin) and, to a lesser extent, from the *News-Record* (Berlin). An interview with Mr. W. H. E. Schmalz (part of the Oral History Series at the Kitchener Public Library) also provided some details.

[70] *Telegraph* (Berlin), January 5, 1909.

[71] Ibid., January 2, 1909.

[72] Ibid., December 30, 1910.

[73] Ibid., January 4, 1911.

[74] This account is taken from Uttley, *Kitchener*, 307.

[75] For an excellent account of municipal ownership, see Tiessen, *Berlin*. The influence of municipal ownership in neighbouring communities, especially Guelph, was also noted. See L. A. Johnson, *History of Guelph, 1827-1927* (Guelph, 1977); and Paul Rutherford, "Toronto's Metropolis: The Urban Reform Movement in Canada," in Gilbert Stelter and Alan Artibise (eds.), *The Canadian City* (Toronto, 1977), 372-73. Borovilos' study cited above ("Evolution of the Town of Berlin") is also particularly useful. On "inland" fears, see K. C. Dewar, "State Ownership in Canada: The Origins of Ontario Hydro" (Ph.D. dissertation, University of Toronto, 1976).

[76] On this important question of technological innovation, see Nathan Rosenberg, *Technology and American Economic Growth* (New York, 1972).

[77] Tiessen, *Berlin*, 39.

[78] Dr. J. Amyot, "The Berlin Sewage Disposal Plant," Province of Ontario, Sessional Paper No. 36 (1908), 92-93, cited in Borovilos, "Evolution of the Town of Berlin," 40.

[79] Leibbrandt, *Little Paradise*, 135.

[80] H. Koch, *Kitchener-Waterloo Record*, November 24, 1981.

Chapter Four

[1] Paul Tiessen, "Introduction," in Paul Tiessen (ed.), *Berlin, Canada* (St. Jacobs, 1979). Tiessen's account is based upon Gordon Eby's contemporary diary.

[2] Gottlieb Leibbrandt, *Little Paradise, The Saga of the German Canadians of Waterloo County, Ontario 1800-1975* (Kitchener, 1980), 323.

[3] Berlin's troubles have attracted much attention from scholars, although there has been no comprehensive study of the period 1914-18 before this one. See Leibbrandt, *Little Paradise*, xii; Barbara Wilson, *Ontario and the First World War 1914-1918* (Toronto, 1977), Section C (an excellent account of the name change); W. H. Heick, "The Lutherans of Waterloo County During World War I," in WHS, *Annual Report* 51 (1962), 23-30; W. H. Heick, "The General Election of 1917 in Waterloo North," forthcoming in *Ontario History*; Marie Oswald, "The Zenith of Tension," unpublished paper; Gerhard Enns, "Waterloo North and Conscription 1917," in WHS, *Annual Report* 51 (1963), 60-69; Alexander Forbes, "Volunteer Recruiting in Waterloo County During the Great War, 1914-1918" (M.A. thesis, University of Waterloo, 1977); and Patricia McKegney, "Berlin, Ontario, 1914-1919" (M.Phil. thesis, University of Waterloo, 1979).

[4] *Berliner Journal*, August 26, 1914. Mr. W. H. E. Schmalz, a militia member and prewar Royal Military College graduate, has supplied us with details.

[5] "Eid ist Eid . . . aber das Herz läßt sich nicht aus der Brust reißen." Cited in Leibbrandt, *Little Paradise*, 326-27.

[6] W. V. Uttley, *History of Kitchener* (Waterloo, 1975), 49.

[7] *Telegraph* (Berlin), January 12, 1915.

[8] *Galt Reporter*, January 26, 1916. (I am indebted to Marie Oswald for this reference.) Also, interview with Mr. John Walters, Kitchener. Mr. Walters recalled that his German socialist father walked to work with a lead pipe to protect himself during the wartime troubles.

[9] Public Archives of Canada (hereinafter cited as PAC), John Lang Papers, MG30C54 clipping scrapbook; and *News-Record* (Berlin), January 31, 1916. For a fuller description of Dancey's activities, see Wilson, *Ontario and the First World War*, xxvi-xxviii.

[10] Detweiler Diary, Kitchener Public Library, February 1916. (Detweiler chaired the meeting which led to the name change resolution.) See also Wilson, *Ontario and the First World War*, xxviiff.

[11] Ibid., xxviii-xxix; Detweiler Diary, April 1916; and *Telegraph* (Berlin), April 17, 1916.

[12] Quoted in Wilson, *Ontario and the First World War*, 80-81. Originals of two inquiries are in PAC, RG 24, V.1256, file HQ 593-1-87. See also *Berliner Journal*, February 23, 1916.

[13] Full text of letters is in Wilson, *Ontario and the First World War*, 81-86.

[14] Quoted in ibid., 88. The description of the dragging of Tappert through the streets comes from interviews with observers. Wilson, following Lochead's report, says Tappert was "paraded." Contemporary accounts are contradictory.

[15] *News-Record* (Berlin), May 15 and 16, 1916. On the financial supporters of the Citizens' Leagues (opponents of the name change), see list in John Lang Papers. Largest donors were August Lang, Jacob Kaufman, George Lang, John Lang, Hartman Krug, William Roos, W. H. Breithaupt, Dumart's Meatpacking, Carl Krantz, M. Wunder, Baetz Brothers, Caspar Braun, Western Shoe, Dominion Button (David Gross), C. N. Huether, Rittinger and Motz (*Berliner Journal*), and W. T. Sass. Although later authors (e.g., Oswald) have said that the troubles were not strictly "English-German," it is worthwhile noting that every name or business listed was, in 1916 terms, "German." See also Robert Cornish, "Berlin 1916" (unpublished paper).

[16] See report of Lochead to Major-General W. E. Hodgins, May 20, 1916, in Wilson, *Ontario and the First World War*, 89-90.

[17] John Lang Papers, Scrapbook.

[18] Results were: Kitchener, 346; Brock, 335; Adanac, 23; Benton, 15; Corona, 7; and Keowana, 3; 163 were spoiled (Wilson, *Ontario and the First World War*, xxxi-xxxii).

[19] Detweiler Diary, October-November 1916; *News-Record* (Kitchener), September 11 and 16, 1916; and Leibbrandt, *Little Paradise*, 254. For biographies of Schmalz and Detweiler, see ibid., 254-56 and 241-42. Schmalz was second vice-president of the Patriotic Fund in Berlin. One of his harshest critics, S. J. Williams, was president. See Philip Morris (ed.), *The Canadian Patriotic Fund* (Ottawa, 1917), 216.

[20] Quoted in Wilson, *Ontario and the First World War*, 94.

[21] Ibid., 93-100; Forbes, "Volunteer Recruiting," passim; and W. H. E. Schmalz, interview.

[22] "Newspapers featured headlines such as '118th Battalion Arrives in England,' 'An Impressive Patriotic Affair,' and '$100,000 Mark Reached in Kitchener'" (Oswald, "Zenith of Tension," 8).

[23] See ibid., 16, for a full account.

[24] PAC, Laurier Papers, V.711, Euler to E. M. Goddard, July 25, 1917.

[25] *Telegraph* (Kitchener), November 17, 1917.

[26] We are indebted to Marie Oswald for drawing our attention to references in these two paragraphs. The original sources are *News-Record* (Kitchener), November 24 and 26, 1917; *News-Record*, December 1, 1917; and *Ontario Journal*, December 5, 1917.

[27] Henry Borden (ed.), *Robert Laird Borden: His Memoirs* (Toronto, 1938), vol. 2, 763.

[28] *News-Record* (Kitchener), December 13-15, 1917; and Detweiler Diary, December 12, 1917. Detweiler sat at City Hall "explaining" the telegrams.

[29] The report of the Weichel action and the coffin incident derives mainly from the *Galt Reporter* of December 18, 1917. Kitchener papers claimed the coffin slogan had been misread or misunderstood. The reference to "burying" referred, the Kitchener papers argued, to the vote total with which Euler buried Weichel (*News Record* [Kitchener], December 18, 1917).

[30] Cornish, "Berlin 1916"; and Oswald, "Zenith of Tension."

[31] *News-Record* (Kitchener), December 9, 1919.

[32] These figures are taken from Cornish, "Berlin 1916," who gleaned this information from an exhaustive study of assessment rolls, newspapers, directories, and interviews. The ethnicity percentages here cannot be exact because of the difficulties of working with surnames. They nevertheless present a clear picture of the balance in Berlin.

[33] Berlin's average manufacturing wages were lower in the early 1900s than neighbouring industrial cities such as Brantford and Guelph. The local press often mentioned this but did not explain it. The ethnic-cultural ties to Berlin may explain why Berlin workers were not willing to migrate.

[34] "Kitchener's Finances," *Saturday Night*, August 7, 1937, 30.

[35] John Lang Papers, Patriotic Fund Record.

[36] Interview with Mr. Walter Barrie, July 1979.

[37] John Carter, "Berlin-Kitchener" (unpublished paper).

Chapter Five

[1] W. V. Uttley, *A History of Kitchener* (Waterloo, 1975), 427-28; *Daily Record* (Kitchener), January 2, 1920. Interviews with Messrs. A. R. Kaufman, J. Walters, Walter Barrie, and W. P. Clement. On May 30, 1919, the Trades and Labour Council and the Board of Trade held a joint meeting (*Daily Record*, May 31, 1919).

[2] Information from Ernie Ronnenberg's profiles of significant persons in Waterloo region (Kitchener Public Library). Originally published in *Kitchener-Waterloo Record*.

[3] *Daily Record* (Kitchener), May 23 and 27, 1919.

[4] Ibid. Comparisons of wages with other centres is difficult because of the higher percentage of women in Kitchener's work forces.

[5] See T. Harevin's study of the textile town of Manchester, New Hampshire, which reveals that the traditional French-Canadian family suited best the needs of modern industrialism ("Family Time and Industrial Time: Family and Work in a Planned Corporation Town 1900-1924," *Journal of Urban History* 1 [1975]).

[6] *Census of Canada 1911* (Ottawa, 1915), vol. 6, 456-58; *Census of Canada 1921* (Ottawa, 1929), vol. 4, 37; and *Census of Canada 1931* (Ottawa, 1936), vol. 7, 49. In 1911, of 1,148 working women in Kitchener, 667 were in clothing and allied products and 306 in leather and rubber goods.

[7] *Daily Record* (Kitchener), June 5, 1919 and May 12, 1919. See also *Kitchener: "The Industrial City"* (Kitchener, 1928). In January 1920 the council was urged to promote more American industries.

[8] Sources for this paragraph are City of Kitchener assessment reports; *Kitchener: "The Industrial City"*; *Daily Record* (Kitchener), various issues in 1921; and *Saturday Night*, August 7, 1937.

[9] *Kitchener: "The Industrial City."* On the front page of this publication was the slogan, "Where Capital and Labor are on Good Terms."

[10] *Daily Record* (Kitchener), November 26 and December 6, 1929.

[11] The phrase is J. K. Galbraith's in *The Great Crash* (Boston, 1955), 113.

[12] Bernard Webber, "Kitchener in the Great Depression," Kitchener Public Library (n.d.), 4-6; Uttley, *Kitchener*, 415; Terry Copp and Blake Weller (eds.), *Industrial Unionism in Kitchener, 1937-1947* (Elora, Ontario, 1976); and Ronald Hands, "Kitchener: 1930-1933" (unpublished undergraduate paper).

[13] Copp and Weller, *Industrial Unionism*, ii.

[14] *Daily Record* (Kitchener), January 13, 1932. Webber, "Kitchener in the Great Depression," 10.

[15] Figures for relief expenditures for the years 1931-35 are as follows: 1931, $85,382; 1932, $225,601; 1933, $335,966; 1934, $343,935; and 1935, $356,736 (compiled by Webber, "Kitchener in the Great Depression").

[16] Total costs from 1930 to September 1939 were $1,096,000 (*Daily Record* [Kitchener], September 26, 1939).

[17] Copp and Weller point out that a family that had an income of $1,200 in 1929 could live at the same level on $900 in 1935 (*Industrial Unionism*, v). This pattern of recovery was national. See A. E. Safarian, *The Canadian Economy in the Great Depression* (Toronto, 1970).

[18] Canada, *Labour Organization in Canada 1923* (Ottawa, 1924), 258; and ibid. (1933), 191.

[19] See Copp and Weller, *Industrial Unionism*, vi. See also *Kitchener-Waterloo Record*, *Kitchener 125 Years* (Kitchener, 1979), 41.

[20] Ian St. John, "The Early History of the URW in Kitchener 1936-1939" (unpublished essay); Len Bruder, "URW History: Canada" (unpublished official history); and Copp and Weller, *Industrial Unionism*, chap. 2. This pattern of Canadian invitation to Americans was followed nationally. See I. M. Abella, *Nationalism, Communism and Canadian Labour* (Toronto, 1973).

[21] *Daily Record* (Kitchener), March 10, 1939. See also St. John, "The URW in Kitchener"; and Copp and Weller, *Industrial Unionism*, 2.

[22] See Elizabeth Bloomfield, "Town Planning Efforts in Kitchener-Waterloo, 1912-1925," *Urban History Review* 9 (June 1980), 8. Mrs. Bloomfield's excellent article gives full details of Berlin-Kitchener's early planning history. The *News-Record* (Berlin), November-December 1912, contains the various other criticisms.

[23] Ibid.; Detweiler Papers, Kitchener Public Library, W. M. O. Lochead to Board of Trade, December 5, 1912; and *Telegraph* (Berlin), December 12, 1912. To compare Kitchener's approach with city beautiful rhetoric elsewhere, see Walter Van Nus, "The Fate of City Beautiful Thought in Canada, 1893-1930," in G. Stelter and A. F. J. Artibise (eds.), *The Canadian City* (Toronto, 1977), 164-65. Detweiler's views on planning combined what was termed by contemporaries "the aesthetical school" and "the practical school." C. H. Mitchell, the speaker at the meeting, was an engineer and tended toward the latter school. For what he said in Berlin, see C. H. Mitchell, "Town Planning and Civic Improvement," *Canadian Engineer* 23 (December 26, 1912).

[24] Bloomfield, "Town Planning Efforts"; Detweiler Papers, "History of Planning"; Detweiler Diary, 1913-14, passim; *Telegraph* (Berlin), January 27, 1914; and for the impact of war on planning thought and action, see Van Nus, "City Beautiful Thought." Detweiler's energies were transferred to the more limited goal of establishing "Cressman's Woods" beyond the southern city limits as a conservation park. He was assisted in this by Homer Watson, who lived in the area, and A. R. Kaufman, who led Kitchener into its first official plan in the 1920s. George Rumpel expressed the fears about costs well: "Berlin is a big city, but small in some matters" (*Telegraph* [Berlin], October 2, 1913).

[25] Bloomfield, "Town Planning Efforts," 25-30.

[26] A. R. Kaufman, "Kitchener Town Plan," *Saturday Night*, August 7, 1937, 30; and "Kitchener Plan Becomes Law," *Journal of the Town Planning Institute* 4 (January 1925), 1-8.

[27] This evaluation reflects the conclusions of Bloomfield, "Town Planning Efforts."

[28] *Daily Record* (Kitchener), December 27, 1939 and October 29, 1940.

[29] Ibid., January 2, 1920. On the club, see Uttley, *Kitchener*, 427; see also interviews with Walter Barrie and W. P. Clement.

[30] *Daily Record* (Kitchener), December 24, 1920 and January 1, 1921.

[31] Ibid., December 24, 1921. The vote was Greb, 1,601; Eden, 947; and Bricker, 188.

[32] "Kitchener's Finances," *Saturday Night*, August 7, 1931, 30.

[33] *Daily Record* (Kitchener), November 26, 1928.

[34] Ibid., November 30 and December 1 and 4, 1928. On Clement, see *Kitchener-Waterloo Record*, August 26, 1967. Clement, in an interview in June 1979, admitted that the Young Men's Club was very much a political organization. In 1928-29 he had denied that charge when Bezeau made it.

[35] Hands, "Kitchener 1930-1933"; *Daily Record* (Kitchener), December 1930, passim; and clipping file "Bezeau," *Kitchener-Waterloo Record*.

[36] *Daily Record* (Kitchener), December 7, 1920. On the general subject of the 1920s as the first "modern" period, see Paula Fass, *The Damned and the Beautiful* (Oxford and New York, 1979).

[37] *Daily Record* (Kitchener), January 3, 1929. The Station and the Germania (or the "Last Chance") were charged after these raids. Also, an interview with Mr. R. Sattler, July 1979.

[38] Quoted in *125th Anniversary Reunion: Kitchener-Waterloo Collegiate and Vocational School 1855-1980* (Kitchener, 1980), 34.

[39] Maurita McCrystal, "The Parents Information Bureau" (unpublished paper, 1981).

[40] *Daily Record* (Kitchener), December 11, 1925.

[41] On the demise of the *Berliner Journal*, and of German-language publishing generally, see H. K. Kalbfleisch, *The History of the Pioneer German Language Press of Ontario, 1835-1918* (Toronto, 1968).

[42] *Statutes of Canada*, PC 1203 and PC 1204, 1919, 9-10 Geo. V. On the national mood which caused this action, see Donald Avery, *"Dangerous Foreigners": European Immigrant Workers and Labour Radicalism in Canada, 1896-1932* (Toronto, 1979), chap. 4.

[43] See Leibbrandt, *Little Paradise*, 283-316; and his *100 Jahre Concordia* (Kitchener, n.d.). See also Henry Paetkau, "A Struggle for Survival: The Russian Immigrants in Ontario, 1924-1929" (M.A. thesis, University of Waterloo, 1977).

[44] *Daily Record* (Kitchener), March 28 and June 13, 1933. We are indebted to Mr. Tom Schaefer for these references. See his "Kitchener and the New Germany 1933-1936" (M.A. research essay, University of Waterloo, 1978).

[45] *Daily Record* (Kitchener), July 9, 1933. On another occasion, Motz wrote: "Perhaps when we think of the conditions under which the Canadian election of 1917 was held, we should not be too critical of what is happening in other countries. Should Hitler fail in the coming contest, anarchy may result in his country and the present danger of Europe will be increased a hundredfold" (ibid., October 16, 1933).

[46] Ibid., August 14 and 15, 1933. See also Lita-Rose Betcherman, *The Swastika and the Maple Leaf: Fascist Movements in Canada in the Thirties* (Toronto, 1975), 55-57.

[47] On the *Bund*, see Betcherman, *Swastika and Maple Leaf*, passim; Schaefer, "Kitchener and the New Germany," chap. 6; Leibbrandt, *Little Paradise*, 260-68; Jonathan Wagner, "The Deutscher Bund Canada 1934-1939," *Canadian Historical Review* 63 (1977), 176-99; and John Offenbeck, "The Nazi Movement and German Canadians" (M.A. thesis, University of Western Ontario, 1970).

[48] Schaefer, "Kitchener and the New Germany"; and *Daily Record* (Kitchener), September 3, 1935.

[49] Leibbrandt, *Little Paradise*, 260-68. Using German sources Leibbrandt proves the connection between the Kitchener *Bund* and Berlin.

[50] On Euler's difficulties with Mackenzie King, see H. B. Neatby, *William Lyon Mackenzie King: The Prism of Unity* (Toronto, 1976).

[51] *Daily Record* (Kitchener), September 20, 1939. Only seven Kitchener residents were interned as enemy aliens. The *Daily Record* proudly contrasted this with higher totals elsewhere.

Chapter Six

[1] *Daily Record* (Kitchener), July 8, 1939.

[2] December 26, 1939.

[3] Monthly totals for Munitions and Supply contracts were: February, $47,680; March, $230,151; April, $79,275; May, $97,926; June, $77,732; July, $336,583; August, $669,670; September, $320,508 *Industrial Canada* [April-November 1941]). Obviously, these totals reflect only a portion of the war-generated economic activity in Kitchener.

[4] *Daily Record* (Kitchener), May 5, 1941. We are indebted to John Carter for this reference. Mr. Carter's unpublished paper, "War-time Labour Unrest and Industrial Conflict: A Case Study of Kitchener, Ontario 1941," has been of much assistance in writing this section. On these troubles, see also Terry Copp and Blake Weller (eds.), *Industrial Unionism in Kitchener, 1937-1947* (Elora, Ontario, 1976), chaps. 3-5.

[5] For an extended argument about wartime benefits which uses Kitchener as a case study, see John English, "Canada's Road to 1945," *Journal of Canadian Studies* (Fall-Winter 1981).

[6] The industries that showed the greatest relative increase were steel and iron products (444 per cent) and electrical equipment (371 per cent). In absolute terms, the greatest expansion was in the automobile equipment area (including rubber tires) which rose in sales volume from $15.5 million to $33.3 million.

[7] Copp and Weller, *Industrial Unionism*, 85.

[8] Ibid., 99. The Rubber Workers' official historian has recently confirmed this. "Prior to 1946," Led Bruder claims, "there were very few benefits [for rubber workers] to speak of." Quoted in *Kitchener-Waterloo Record*, *Kitchener: 125 Years* (Kitchener, 1979), 39. Kaufman remained unorganized despite attempts in 1950, 1952, 1954, and 1960.

[9] Bill Moyer, *Kitchener: Yesterday Revisited* (Burlington, Ontario, 1976), 73.

[10] See the university history, James Scott, *Of Mud and Dreams* (Toronto, 1967).

[11] This section is based on material in Moyer, *Kitchener: Yesterday Revisited*, in which numerous businesses have had their histories printed. See also *Kitchener: 125 Years*, passim; O. W. Klinck, *Uniroyal Canada, A History* (Kitchener, 1966); and the invaluable business columns in the *Kitchener-Waterloo Record* by Henry Koch.

[12] Robert Perry, *Galt, U.S.A.: The "American Presence" in a Canadian City* (Toronto, 1971), 3.

[13] Waterloo Area Local Government Review, *Report of Findings and Recommendations* (February 1970), 200-202. Kitchener showed 15.1 per cent in retail employment, Galt 13.5 per cent, and Guelph 10.7 per cent. Kitchener had 84 per cent of its labour force living and working within it, but Waterloo had only 55 per cent. Despite Waterloo's white-collar tinge, Kitchener and Waterloo were almost precisely the same in industrial assessment as a percentage of total assessment. Decentralization of manufacturing probably favoured Kitchener in the postwar era in comparison to other larger centres. See James W. Simmons, "The Evolution of the Canadian Urban System," in Alan Artibise and G. A. Stelter (eds.), *The Usable Urban Past* (Toronto, 1979), 25.

[14] Local Government Review, *Report*, 15 and 17. When the Kitchener extension of Highway 401 was opened, Kitchener's mayor claimed that it would mean as much or more to Kitchener's progress as the first railway did (*Kitchener-Waterloo Record*, November 18, 1960).

[15] J. E. Rea, "Political Parties and Civic Power: Winnipeg, 1919-1975," in Artibise and Stelter, *The Usable Urban Past*, 155.

[16] Interview with Jack Walter, October 1976.

[17] *Daily Record* (Kitchener), August 7, 1939; and an interview with Dr. Louis Lang, July 1979.

[18] *Daily Record* (Kitchener), September-November 1939. Also confidential interviews.

[19] *Daily Record* (Kitchener), November-December 1939, passim.

[20] Ibid., November 27, 1941, and December 2, 1941; and *Kitchener-Waterloo Record*, June 6, 1962 (obituary). In delivering the eulogy the priest said Meinzinger by his background and early years might well have been a juvenile delinquent. He was mayor between 1940 and 1945 and again in 1959, 1961, and part of 1962.

[21] PAC, King Papers, J1, v. 355, 308412-4, Breithaupt to King, September 23, 1944; and ibid., 308415-6, King to Breithaupt, September 25, 1944. In a later letter Breithaupt reflected two aspects of local politics, the jealousy of Toronto and the concern for patronage. "Toronto with all its sniping and unfriendly spirit to the government seems to get everything it wants, and good old North Waterloo is always bypassed." John Richardson, a former Conservative Association president, had been appointed to a Veterans' Affairs position, and "Not long ago, the Secretary of the Conservative Association here, Mr. Roy Trott, was appointed Retail Furniture Controller for Canada . . ." (ibid., 308417-8, Breithaupt to King, October 28, 1944).

[22] Interview with Norman Schneider, August 1979. Schneider was the president of J. M. Schneider, a war veteran, and sixty-four years old when first elected in 1952.

[23] *Kitchener-Waterloo Record*, December 8, 1953, and December 7, 1954.

[24] Ibid., November 24, 1956.

[25] The six elected in 1956 were Kieth Hymmen, Boyd Cressman, Wilf Bitzer, Milton Oswald, Harry Wambold, and Frank X. Weiler. The other four aldermen were Dr. Leavine, Joe Meinzinger (who finished first and second), and Fred Breithaupt and Mike Walters (who finished ninth and tenth). Walters, a lawyer, was publicly identified as a Labour-CCF candidate (*Kitchener-Waterloo Record*, December 4, 1956). Turnout was a relatively high 45.9 per cent. Meinzinger returned to his anti-union stance in 1960, running his election campaign against the city garbagemen who, he charged, were "drunk with power" (*Kitchener-Waterloo Record*, November 24, 1960).

[26] Weichel's margin of victory fell from 9,320 in 1958 to 3,500 in 1962, and 641 in 1963 (*Canadian Parliamentary Guide 1968* [Ottawa, 1968], 442).

[27] The 1975 provincial election saw the Liberals with John Sweeney capture the new riding of Kitchener-Wilmot which included part of the City of Kitchener.

[28] See Jack Pasternak, *The Kitchener Market Fight* (Toronto, 1975), 18-20, and especially W. E. Thomson, "Renewal in Downtown Kitchener—A Community Project," in A. G. McLellan (ed.), *The Waterloo County Area: Selected Geographical Essays* (Waterloo, 1972), 268-75.

[29] "Reflections of our Religious Heritage," in *Recollections of 125 Years* (Kitchener, 1979); *Ethnic Communities in Kitchener-Waterloo Region* (Kitchener-Waterloo Regional Folk Arts Multicultural Centre, 1979), 22-29; *Census of Canada 1941-1971*; and *Kitchener: 125 Years*, 17.

[30] Often new churches grew out of older affiliations. The Kitchener Gospel Temple (Pentecostal), for example, grew out of the Bethany Mennonite Church. The Mennonite Church itself divided into several fairly distinct groups, the usual distinction being between traditional and modern.

[31] *Kitchener-Waterloo Collegiate and Vocational School, 1855-1980* (Kitchener, 1980), 14.

[32] Social Planning Council of Kitchener-Waterloo, *A Social Profile of Kitchener-Waterloo* (Kitchener, 1981), vol. 1, 195-213.

[33] A more extensive history of cultural activities is found in *Kitchener: 125 Years*, 78-79. By the 1970s there were enough authors in Kitchener to form a branch of the Canadian Authors' Association. The best-selling author was undoubtedly Edna Staebler, whose Mennonite cookbooks have sold thousands of copies.

[34] Don Cameron, "The Sporting Life," in *Reflections of 125 Years*. See also *Kitchener-Waterloo Record*, November 27, 1957, for a vivid description of the Dutchmen's 2-0 victory when the Russians came to play in Kitchener.

[35] Another municipal course, the Doon Valley, was purchased by the city in 1974.

[36] See, for example, Alan Artibise, *Winnipeg: An Illustrated History* (Toronto, 1977), 176; and John C. Weaver, *Hamilton: An Illustrated History* (Toronto, 1982). Both of these books are in the Lorimer-National Museum History of Canadian Cities series.

[37] John Seeley, R. Alexander Sim, and E. W. Loosley, *Crestwood Heights: A Study of the Culture of Suburban Life* (Toronto, 1956), 45. On government involvement, see Robert Bothwell and William Kilbourn, *C. D. Howe: A Biography* (Toronto, 1979), 207-208.

[38] Thomas Ritchie, *Canada Builds, 1867-1967* (Toronto, 1967), 328.

[39] Ralph Krueger, "Towards Regional Planning and Regional Government in Waterloo County," in McLellan, *Selected Geographical Essays*, 296. In 1953 planning consultants Dryden and Smith deemed the "city-encircling" road as essential (*Kitchener-Waterloo Record*, December 10, 1953).

[40] Local Government Review, *Report*, 141.

[41] A subdivision plan for the St. Mary's area existed in 1912, as a plan in the Waterloo Historical Society archives indicates.

[42] *Kitchener-Waterloo Record*, November 17 and 27, 1956. See also Local Government Review, *Report*, passim.

[43] Two major reports appeared in 1956: "A Comprehensive Sewerage and Sewage Treatment Plan for Kitchener" and "A Study of Water Supply and Distribution Systems."

[44] *Kitchener-Waterloo Record*, November 18, 1960. See also Pasternak, *Kitchener Market Fight*, 17.

[45] *Kitchener-Waterloo Record*, November 21, 1962.

[46] For a description of those responsibilities, see Local Government Review, *Report*, 131-33. See also Krueger, "Towards Regional Planning."

[47] See Pasternak, *Kitchener Market Fight*, for a fuller albeit partisan account. The question on the referendum was as follows:

> Are you in favour of the City of Kitchener entering into an agreement with Oxlea Investments Limited which will provide as follows:
> 1. That the existing Farmers' Market will be moved from its present location into a new building to accommodate the market and public parking;
> 2. to convey the City Hall site and the present Farmers' Market site to this developer who intends to demolish the existing buildings and erect new buildings thereon;
> 3. a lease to the city for 15 years at an annual rental of $195,000 of 30,000 square feet of floor space for municipal offices;
> 4. a lease back arrangement for a public parking and market building at an annual rental to reimburse the developer in 20 years for the full cost including financing cost and at profit of one and one half percent?

[48] Ibid., 66-67.

[49] *Kitchener-Waterloo Record*, June 25, 1970.

[50] Official Plan of the City of Kitchener Planning Area, January 20, 1975, 2 and 6.

[51] *Kitchener-Waterloo Record*, September 9 and 12, 1939.

[52] Hildegard Martens, "Accommodation and Withdrawal: The Response of the Mennonites in Canada to World War II," *Social History* (November 1974), 306-27; *Daily Record* (Kitchener), July 3, 1942; and David Fransen, "Canadian Mennonites and Conscientious Objection in World War II" (M.A. thesis, University of Waterloo, 1977). See also Frank Epp, *Mennonites in Canada 1920-1940* (Toronto, 1982).

[53] The history of this organization is found in Gottfried Leibbrandt, *25 Jahre caritative und kulturelle Arbeit des Hilfswerkes der Deutsch-Kanadier* (Waterloo, 1972).

[54] See Gottlieb Leibbrandt, *Little Paradise* (Kitchener, 1980), 280-310. Most of this account is based on Dr. Leibbrandt's invaluable work.

[55] For the full text of the alliance's aims, see ibid., 371. The original reads: "Forderung der deutschen Tradition, Sprache, Gesang, Musik, Literatur, Sport, usw."

[56] The Portuguese and the Cypriot Greeks both formed social clubs in which they centred many of their collective activities. See also *Ethnic Communities in Kitchener-Waterloo Region* (Kitchener-Waterloo Regional Folk Arts Multicultural Centre, 1979), 6-7.

[57] Ibid., 15-16.

[58] Bruce Tudin and Sandra Roussakis, *A Social Profile of Kitchener-Waterloo* (Social Planning Council of Kitchener-Waterloo, 1981), 8-23.

SUGGESTIONS FOR FURTHER READING

The sources available for the reader who wants to learn more about the past of Berlin-Kitchener are not numerous. The major work is W. V. Uttley's *A History of Kitchener* (Kitchener, 1937; reprinted, Waterloo, 1975). Uttley's work contains much valuable information, but unfortunately it largely ignores the twentieth century and is not a continuous narrative. Bill Moyer's *A Unique Heritage* and *Waterloo County Diary* are folksy and interesting popular histories of the area. His *Kitchener: Yesterday Revisited* (Kitchener, 1979) follows the style and level of research in Moyer's other publications. A recent and unusual work deserves special mention: Dr. Gottlieb Leibbrandt has written a valuable history of the Germans of Waterloo County. Trained as a scholar, Dr. Leibbrandt reveals a thorough command of his sources and a sensitive appreciation of the experience of his own ethnic group in this area. The title of his work is *Little Paradise: Aus Geschichte und Leben der Deutschkanadier in der County Waterloo, 1800-1975* (Kitchener, 1977). Dr. Leibbrandt's book has recently been translated by G. K. Weissenborn and reprinted under the title, *Little Paradise: The Saga of the German Canadians of Waterloo County, Ontario, 1800-1975* (Kitchener, 1980).

Other important sources for those studying the history of Kitchener must be its daily and weekly newspapers and the annual reports of the Waterloo Historical Society. The first newspaper in Berlin was the *Canada Museum und Allgemeine Zeitung*. It was published in German and Berlin continued to have a weekly German newspaper until the federal government forced the *Berliner Journal* to close during the First World War. The first English-language papers, the Berlin *Telegraph* and the *Chronicle*, were founded in the 1850s but there was no daily paper until 1878 when the *Daily News* began publication in English with a German supplement. The *News-Record* and the *Telegraph* merged in the early 1920s, since which time the Kitchener (later *Kitchener-Waterloo*) *Record* has been the sole daily paper.

The reports of the Waterloo Historical Society begin in 1913. These are perhaps the richest source on the history of the area. There is an excellent index to these reports in the Kitchener Public Library. The reports contain both primary sources and secondary works. The Waterloo Historical Society also maintains archives in which some unique compilations can be found as well as documents relating to the history of the area. A good example of the former is M. H. Snyder, *Hannes Schneider: His Descendants and Times 1534-1939* (Kitchener, 1937). This work is not only a history of the Schneider family but also a source of considerable information on the development of the community.

Among manuscript sources are the D. B. Detweiler Papers, the E. W. B. Snider Papers (both valuable on hydro), the John Lang Papers, the W. H. E. Schmalz Papers, and portions of other collections such as the W. L. M. King Papers. One regrets very much that W. D. Euler left no papers; neither did the Breithaupt, Lackner, or Bowlby families. Similarly, municipal records are weaker than one would hope. The City of Kitchener does have council minutes as well as reports on various commissions, but in the case of commission records earlier volumes are often missing. Some private organizations have maintained their records more carefully. The Board of Trade minutes, held by the Kitchener Chamber of Commerce, are especially valuable for the prewar days when the board played such a large part in civic affairs. Many of the churches have also kept their records, the Lutheran and Catholic churches being especially notable in this respect.

The following sections indicate where one might look for information on specific themes. For further guidance, our notes should be consulted.

Origins of Kitchener

The Mennonite community has attracted much attention from historical scholars. The standard academic works on the Mennonites are Frank Epp, *Mennonites in Canada, 1786-1920* and *Mennonites in Canada, 1920-1940* (Toronto, 1974 and 1982). A popular work which is available in paperback is G. E. Reaman, *The Trail of the Black Walnut* (Toronto, 1975). Dr. Reaman's work offers a lively account of the emigration of the Pennsylvania Germans to Waterloo County. Also available in paperback is a novel originally published in 1942 by the outstanding Kitchener librarian Mabel Dunham, *Trail of the Conestoga* (Toronto, 1970). Miss Dunham's work is generally reliable and thoroughly charming in its depiction of the early Mennonite immigrants. Another highly regarded novel by Miss Dunham, *Towards Sodom* (Toronto, 1927), describes the movement of younger Mennonites away from the old ways during the nineteenth century. Although Ezra Eby, *A Biographical History of Waterloo Township* (Berlin, 1895; new edition with Eldon Weber, Kitchener, 1971) can scarcely be described as readable, it is nonetheless an invaluable compilation of biographical details about the early settlers and their kin. Other works on the early period include Orland Gingerich, *The Amish in Canada* (Waterloo, 1972); Gladys Heinz, "German Immigration into Upper Canada from 1783 to the Present Day" (M.A. thesis, Queen's University, 1938); and Heinz Lehmann, *Zur Geschichte des Deutschtums in Kanada*, Band 1: *Das Deutschtum in Ostkanada* (Stuttgart, 1931). An excellent source on mid-nineteenth-century Berlin is the reminiscences of Jacob Stroh, recently republished in the 1978 *Annual Report* of the Waterloo Historical Society, and Virgil Emerson Martin has produced a finely researched and well illustrated *The Early History of Jakobstettel* (St. Jacobs, 1979) which is especially useful for the new research which it provides into the disposition of the Indian land claims.

Economic Growth and Metropolitan Development

Despite the fundamental importance of industrial development to the history of Berlin-Kitchener, historians have tended to avoid the subject. The best sources remain primary sources, notably the "boosterish" publications of the pre-First World War period. The annual reports of the Board of Trade during this period are exceptionally rich in detail. Such works as *Busy Berlin*, *Berlin Today 1906*, and *Berlin: Celebration of Cityhood 1912* are not Board of Trade publications but they do reflect the ethos of the period. This last volume has been republished recently (St. Jacobs, Ontario, 1979). For the later period, a collection of essays edited by Terry Copp and Blake Weller, *Industrial Unionism in Kitchener, 1937-1947*, offers much useful detail and insight. So does a pre-depression pamphlet, *Kitchener: The Industrial City* (Kitchener, 1928). On the depression's effects, the best work remains Bernard Webber's unpublished paper, "Kitchener in the Great Depression," available at the Kitchener Public Library. Other unpublished works also deserve mention: G. H. Davey, "Kitchener: A Case Study and Industrial Geography" (B.A. thesis, Waterloo Lutheran University, 1970); Kenneth Dewar, "State Ownership in Canada: The Origins of Ontario Hydro" (Ph.D. dissertation, University of Toronto, 1976); and Elizabeth Haldane, "The Historical Geography of Waterloo Township" (M.A. thesis, McMaster University, 1963).

The reports of the Regional Planning Commission and especially the Fyfe Report on regional government give much detail on the recent past. An interesting and pioneering survey of social attitudes during the Second World War is the Kitchener Chamber of Commerce's "Post-War Survey" (Kitchener, 1944). Much work is being done currently on Kitchener's economic growth in the universities. One hopes that the products of this research will be available soon. Elizabeth Bloomfield's recent article is especially valuable on the early planning movement in Kitchener: "Economy, Necessity, Political Reality: Town Planning Efforts in Kitchener-Waterloo, 1912-1925," *Urban History Review* 9/1 (June 1980), 3-48. Unfortunately, Dr. Bloomfield's recent doctoral thesis on economic development in Kitchener-Waterloo is not yet available.

Ethnic and Cultural History

Because of the leadership Berlin-Kitchener offered to the German community in Ontario and because the city's Germanness caused the great controversies of the past, this area of history has attracted the most students. The outstanding work is Gottlieb Leibbrandt's *Little Paradise* which traces the history of the Germans in the area in expert fashion. His footnotes are a good guide to other resources on the subject. He has also written a history of the oldest German club, the Concordia Club, which is available from the club. Another notable work in the area is H. K. Kalbfleisch, *The History of the Pioneer German Language Press of Ontario, 1835-1918* (Toronto, 1968). This work has a broader scope than the title suggests; it discusses in some detail the character of the German community in Ontario before and during the First World War. On education, the best essay is Patricia McKegney, "The German Schools of Waterloo County," in Waterloo Historical Society, *Annual Report* (1970). The churches have several individual histories. Especially notable are W. H. Heick, "The Lutheran Church in Waterloo County" (M.A. thesis, Queen's University, 1964); J. B. Koegler, *St. Peter's*

Church (Kitchener, n.d.); John Schneider, *St. Matthew's Evangelical Lutheran Church, 25th Anniversary Report* (Kitchener, 1929); and Theobold Spetz, *The Catholic Church in Waterloo County* (Berlin, 1916).

The conflicts during the First World War were, of course, political as well as ethnic. Barbara Wilson's chapter, "Loyalty in Question," in her *Ontario and the First World War* (Toronto, 1977) is an admirably broad treatment of the troubles the war brought to Berlin-Kitchener. Other studies of wartime problems include Gerhard Enns, "Waterloo North and Conscription 1917," in Waterloo Historical Society, *Annual Report* (1963); Alexander Forbes, "Volunteer Recruiting in Waterloo County During the First World War" (M.A. thesis, University of Waterloo, 1977); and Marie Oswald, "The Zenith of Tension" (Kitchener Public Library). Ethnic tensions after the war are discussed in Lita-Rose Betcherman, *The Swastika and the Maple Leaf: Fascist Movements in Canada in the Thirties* (Toronto, 1975), and more accurately in John Offenbeck, "The Nazi Movement and German Canadians" (M.A. thesis, University of Western Ontario, 1970); and Tom Schaefer, "Kitchener and the New Germany" (M.A. research essay, University of Waterloo, 1979).

Art, architecture, and music in Berlin-Kitchener remain an area where much fascinating study might be done. The W. H. E. Schmalz collection contains an abundance of musical programmes from early Berlin. These documents testify to the richness of the musical life of Berlin. In the field of architectural history, Wendy Collishaw has opened up new paths with her "Inventory of Kitchener Historical Buildings" (Waterloo Regional Heritage Foundation, 1978) and her "Walking Tour of Kitchener." The quality of this work leads us to expect other contributions of major importance from Ms. Collishaw in the future. The standard work on Fraktur art (traditional Mennonite) is Michael Bird, *Fraktur Art* (Toronto, 1977). Mr. Bird and T. Kobayashi's *A Splendid Harvest* (Toronto, 1981) is a fine study of the impact of the Germanic tradition on the visual arts. One can find sections on Waterloo County furniture in most books on antique furniture. The most recent is Howard Pain, *The Heritage of Upper Canadian Furniture* (Toronto, 1978).

Kitchener's best-known painter was, of course, Homer Watson, although in terms of subject matter he did not come nearer Kitchener than the cattle flats at nearby Doon. Appreciations of Watson and his near-contemporary Berliner Carl Ahrens can be found in most histories of Canadian art such as J. R. Harper's *Painting in Canada* (2nd ed.; Toronto, 1977). There is also a biography of Watson, *Homer Watson, the Man of Doon* (Toronto, 1938) by M. Miller. The Kitchener-Waterloo Art Gallery calendars often provide information on art in the area.

Politics and Civic Life

Kitchener's politicians may have been garrulous during their careers, but they have been remarkably reticent in recollection. No politician, civic or otherwise, has left a published memoir, although Dr. J. F. Honsberger has recorded impressions of his distinguished municipal and provincial career. The biographies of Berlin-Kitchener's politicians can be best consulted in the collection of biographical essays by Ernie Ronnenberg at the Kitchener Public Library (originally published as articles in the *Kitchener-Waterloo Record*). Also at the library is

Ian MacNaughton, "A Historical Study of Political, Ethnic, and Religious Composition of Kitchener and Waterloo" as well as several essays written by our students which attempt to study Kitchener's political life using the community power model first developed by Robert Dahl. The fight to save Kitchener's old market and city hall captured much media attention. An historical analysis by a participant is Jack Pasternak, *The Kitchener Market Fight* (Toronto, 1975). This fight over development highlighted the importance of the planning department in civic affairs. Kitchener had long been recognized as a leader in planning, and in the 1920s and the 1930s its official plan was the subject of several articles: "Kitchener Plan Becomes Law," *Town Planning Institute of Canada Journal* 4 (1925); A. R. Kaufman, "Town Planning in Kitchener after Three Years Trial," ibid. 7 (1928); and A. R. Kaufman, "Kitchener Town Plan," *Saturday Night*, August 7, 1937.

As mentioned above, much of the material on ethnic conflict deals with political events. There are, however, numerous other articles in the Waterloo Historical Society's *Annual Reports* which discuss the earlier period. Some works which deserve special mention are: Frances McIntosh, "Our Man in Ottawa," in WHS, *Annual Report* (1967); John Carter, "The Reciprocity Election of 1911: Waterloo North, a Case Study," in ibid. (1974); Annamaria Tessaro, "Mackenzie King and Waterloo North," in ibid. (1978); T. A. Crowley, "Mackenzie King and the 1911 Election," *Ontario History* 61 (1969); and Pat Myers, "Prohibition in Kitchener" (unpublished paper, University of Waterloo). Joseph Schull's *Ontario since 1867* (Toronto, 1978) in the Ontario Historical Studies series is intended for the general reader as well as for the scholar. F. H. Armstrong et al. (eds.), *Aspects of Nineteenth Century Ontario* (Toronto, 1974) is a collection of essays honouring J. J. Talman, and it maintains the scholarly yet pioneering spirit of research exemplified in Talman's own work.

STATISTICAL APPENDIX

Table 7

The Growth of Manufacturing in Berlin-Kitchener, 1871-1971

Year	Population	No. of firms	No. of employees	Value of products ($)
1871	2,743	—	—	—
1881	4,054	73	896	749,915
1891	7,425	94	1,827	1,825,722
1901	9,747	68	2,758	3,307,513
1911	15,186	76	3,980	9,266,188
1921	21,763	121	7,089	28,000,000
1931	30,793	137	8,759	50,117,175
1941	35,657	154	9,137	40,295,471
1951	44,876	183	15,327	128,467,162
1961	74,485	196	15,200	232,151,746
1971	111,800	509	32,116	1,017,221,000

Source: *Census of Canada, 1871-1951*; The Dominion Bureau of Statistics; *The Canada Yearbook*.

Table 8

Berlin Industries which Received Tax Exemptions and/or Bonuses

To exempt from taxation for five years the Dominion Butter Works and Breithaupt's Tannery	February 6, 1871
To exempt from taxation for five years the Berlin Pioneer Tobacco Manufactory, C. E. Moyer's Woollen Manufactory, and Maude's Foundry	April 7, 1873
Exempt from taxation for five years Feick & Co. Felt Shoe Works, provided that not less than 30 hrs per week be employed in manufacturing felt goods	May 4, 1874
To exempt from taxation for five years the Ratz and Kaufman Planing Mill and Sash Door Manufactory about to be erected on lots 67, 68, 69 and 22 of the Grange Survey	December 3, 1877
To exempt from taxation for five years Ratz and Kaufman's, Bramm's Mill, Vogelsang's Button Factory, and Rumpel Felt-Boot Factory, provided that no less than 40 hands are employed	March 7, 1881
To exempt from taxation for ten years the Berlin Glove Factory	January 15, 1883
Repeal of by-law #303 and granting of exemption from taxation for ten years the Dominion Glove Factory	February 5, 1883
To grant the sum of $3,000 by way of a bonus to Williams, Greene and Rome Co. to remove their operation from Toronto to Berlin, providing that not less than 100 hands are employed in 1885 and not less than 150 hands in succeeding yrs.	November 12, 1884
To exempt from taxation for five years the Atlantic Glue Works, providing that no less than 8 hands be employed	June 11, 1885
To exempt from taxation for ten years a shoe factory about to be erected by Louis Breithaupt & Co. provided that 35-100 hands be employed	June 18, 1885
To exempt from taxation for ten years Williams, Greene and Rome Company	December 7, 1885
To exempt from taxation for ten years the proposed glove manufacturing by Charles Frederick Brown, behind his existing Brown and Erb mattress factory, provided that no less than 30 hands be employed	May 17, 1886
To grant the sum of $10,000 by way of a bonus to the Crompton Corset Co. of Toronto to Berlin, providing that 250 hands be employed on average	July 19, 1886
Exempt from taxation for ten years an addition to Simpson furniture factory	January 17, 1887
To exempt from taxation for 10 years the furniture factory of Hartman Krug about to be erected in Berlin	July 9, 1887

Table 8 — Continued

To provide that the manufacturing establishments about to be erected by Jacob Kaufman and by Hibner, Anthes and Groff, will be assessed at a rate equal to that assessed upon their present factories, for a period of ten years	September 5, 1887
To authorize the issue of debentures to the amount of $80,000 for the purpose of paying for shares in the capital stock of the Berlin and Canadian Pacific Junction Railway Company	November 22, 1887
To grant the sum of $5,000 by way of a bonus to J. E. McGarvin and Co., manufacturers of trunks, to locate in Berlin	October 29, 1888
To exempt from taxation for three years the piano business about to be erected by Rainer, Rake, Risch and Rake, provided they use Bingeman's old glove factory; seven more years exemption will be added if they then construct a new building	May 20, 1889
To exempt for ten years the knitting factory about to be erected by Frederick Knell	March 11, 1890
To grant aid by way of a bonus of $5,000 to the firm of Jackson and Cochrane, manufacturers of woodworking machinery, to locate in Berlin	June 2, 1890
To grant aid by way of a bonus of $10,000 to the Berlin Piano Co., about to be formed by persons in Berlin, providing that 40 hands be employed during the first year, and five additional hands each year for the ten succeeding years	June 2, 1890
To exempt from taxation for ten years the addition to R. Lang & Son Tanners	August 4, 1890
To exempt from taxation for ten years the furniture factory of Jacob Greiner and Co. about to be erected, provided that not less than 20 hands be employed	March 14, 1891
To exempt from taxation for five years the shoe factory about to be established by Thomas Foster, provided that not less than 15 hands be employed in the first year and at least 30 hands thereafter	May 4, 1891
To authorize J. M. Schneider to carry on a pork shop in Berlin, to afford a better market for the farmer and an advantage to the consumer	May 4, 1891
To exempt for ten years an addition to the Brown and Erb mitt and glove factory, for the purpose of tanning and dressing glove leather; and to exempt for five years the addition to J. T. Huber's glue factory, providing that 5 extra hands be employed	October 5, 1891
To exempt from taxation for five years the Messer Shirt and Collar Company about to be established in Berlin, provided that not less than 25 hands be employed	January 11, 1892

Table 8—Continued

To exempt from taxation for ten years an addition to the Berlin Felt Boot Co.	June 7, 1892
To authorize Adam Wagner to carry on a pork shop in Berlin	July 4, 1892
To exempt from taxation for ten years an addition to the D. Hibner factory	July 4, 1892
To exempt from taxation for eight years Jackson, Cochrane and Co., provided that 25 hands are employed; To exempt from taxation for ten years the shoe factory of G. V. Oberholzer about to be built, provided that 25 hands are employed	March 6, 1893
To exempt from taxation for five years, except school taxes, the new box factory of A. & C. Boehmer, provided that 25 hands be employed; To exempt from taxation for ten years Joseph Bingeman's Brush factory, provided that 10 hands be employed	August 8, 1893
To exempt from taxation, except school taxes, for ten years the Hartman Krug furniture factory, provided 50 hands be employed	April 2, 1894
To exempt from taxation for ten years, except from school taxes, the glue factory about to be erected by John Wintermeyer, provided that he employ at least 10 regular adult male hands, and "provided also that such exemption shall cease if and when it shall be found that John Wintermeyer is in any degree whatever polluting the water of Schneider's creek with sewage or refuse from such manufacturing establishment"	August 6, 1894
To exempt from taxation for ten years, except for school taxes, Eby, Cairnes and McBrine factory	October 8, 1894
To exempt from taxation for ten years, except school taxes, certain extensions to be made to the Eagle Tannery	April 10, 1895
To exempt from taxation for eight years, except school taxes, the tannery about to be erected by George Rumpel	August 22, 1895
To exempt from taxation for eight years, except school taxes, addition to C. H. Doerr & Co.	October 7, 1895
To exempt from taxation for eight years, except school taxes, the John R. Stouffer factory about to be erected, provided that not less than 10 hands be employed and that the site "shall be assessed during such period at the sum of $1,000, the present cost thereof"	December 2, 1895
To exempt from taxation for eight years, except school taxes, the new D. Hibner factory about to be rebuilt, provided that not less than 50 hands be employed	December 15, 1896
To authorize the granting of a $5,000 bonus for the rebuilding of the D. Hibner factory destroyed by fire	December 23, 1896

Table 8—Continued

To exempt from taxation for seven years, except school taxes and local improvement taxes, the proposed bicycle factory of Arthur Pequegnat, providing that not less than 10 hands be employed	July 5, 1897
To exempt from taxation for ten years the proposed addition to the Lang Tanning Co. Ltd.	February 7, 1898
To exempt from taxation for five years, except for school taxes and local improvement and frontage rates, the Diamond Furniture Co. of J. C. Klippert, providing that not less than 10 hands be employed	September 5, 1898
To exempt from taxation for ten years, except for school taxes and local improvement and frontage rates, the addition to the Berlin Felt Boot Co., provided that no less than 25 additional hands be employed	October 3, 1898
To exempt from taxation for ten years, except school taxes and local improvement and frontage rates, water rates, and interest on waterworks debentures, the new factory of Von Neubronn and Co., provided that not less than 40 hands be employed	November 7, 1898
To exempt from taxation for ten years the proposed Berlin Rubber Co., provided that not less than 25 hands be employed	March 13, 1899
To exempt from taxation for ten years the proposed Alpha Chemical Company of W. J. Moody and Hambly Pearce, provided that not less than 10 hands be employed	April 3, 1899
To exempt from taxation for ten years L. McBrine and Company provided they employ not less than 10 hands	April 21, 1899
To exempt from taxation for ten years an addition to C. H. Doerr & Co. biscuit factory, provided that not less than 25 hands be employed	April 22, 1899
To exempt from taxation for five years the Berlin Piano and Organ Co., provided they continue to give employment to not less than 20 hands	May 1, 1899
Amendment to by-law #630, extending taxation exemption granted to Diamond Furniture Co. to include not only present buildings and machinery but also any additional buildings and machinery	July 7, 1899
To grant aid by way of a $25,000 bonus to the Ontario Sugar Company to establish in Berlin	December 2, 1901

Table 9

Population Growth of Urban Areas in the Region, 1871-1971

Year	Berlin-Kitchener	Waterloo	Brantford	Galt	Guelph	Hamilton	London
1871	2,743	1,594	8,107	3,827	6,878	26,716	15,826
1881	4,054	2,066	9,616	5,187	9,890	36,661	19,746
1891	7,425	2,941	12,753	7,535	10,537	48,959	27,891
1901	9,747	3,537	16,619	7,866	11,496	52,634	37,976
1911	15,196	4,359	26,617	10,299	15,175	77,072	46,300
1921	21,763	5,883	29,440	13,216	21,763	114,151	60,959
1931	30,793	8,095	30,107	14,006	21,075	115,547	71,148
1941	35,657	9,025	31,948	15,346	23,273	116,337	78,264
1951	44,867	11,991	36,727	19,207	27,386	208,321	95,343
1961	74,485	21,366	55,201	27,830	39,838	273,991	169,569
1971	111,800	36,677	64,421	38,897	60,087	309,173	223,222

Source: *Census of Canada, 1871-1971*.

Table 10

Number of Males Per Thousand Females in Berlin-Kitchener, 1871-1971

Year	Males	Females	Ratio
1871	1,379	1,364	1,011
1881	2,008	2,046	981
1891	3,600	3,825	941
1901	4,630	5,117	905
1911	7,383	7,813	946
1921	10,602	11,161	950
1931	15,212	15,581	976
1941	17,424	18,233	956
1951	21,815	23,052	946
1961	36,822	37,663	978
1971	55,245	56,555	977

Table 11

Urban Population Growth of Berlin-Kitchener and Ontario, 1871-1971

Year	Population of Berlin-Kitchener	Urban population of Ontario[a]	Percentage
1871	2,743	355,997	.8
1881	4,054	575,848	.7
1891	7,425	818,998	.9
1901	9,747	935,978	1.0
1911	15,196	1,328,489	1.1
1921	21,763	1,706,632	1.3
1931	30,973	2,095,992	1.5
1941	35,657	2,338,633	1.5
1951	44,867	3,251,099	1.3
1961	74,485	4,941,228	1.5
1971	111,800	6,343,630	1.8

[a] Figures for the urban population of Ontario are according to the latest definition of urbanized areas as included in each census.

Source: *Census of Canada, 1871-1971*.

Table 12

Population Growth in Berlin-Kitchener, 1871-1971

Year	Population	Numerical change	Percentage change
1871	2,743	—	—
1881	4,054	1,311	47.8
1891	7,425	3,371	83.2
1901	9,747	2,322	31.3
1911	15,196	5,449	56.0
1921	21,763	6,567	43.2
1931	30,793	9,030	41.5
1941	35,657	4,864	15.8
1951	44,867	9,210	26.0
1961	74,485	29,618	66.0
1971	111,804	37,351	50.1

Source: *Census of Canada, 1871-1971*.

Table 13

Birthplace of Berlin-Kitchener's Canadian-Born Population, 1871-1961

Birthplace	1871		1881		1911		1921	
	No.	%	No.	%	No.	%	No.	%
Maritimes	1	.0	3	.1	27	.18	36	.2
Quebec	4	.1	17	.4	26	.17	119	.5
Manitoba	—	—	—	—	7	.05	30	.1
Saskatchewan	—	—	—	—	—	—	30	.1
Alberta	—	—	—	—	7	.05	33	.2
British Columbia	—	—	—	—	—	—	16	.1
Yukon/Territories	—	—	—	—	—	—	0	.0
Ontario	1,578	57.5	2,623	64.7	12,156	80.00	17,331	80.0
Not given	—	—	—	—	2	.01	18	
Total Canadian-born	1,583	57.7	2,643	65.2	12,225	80.46	17,613	81.0
Total population	2,743		7,425		15,196		21,763	

Source: *Census of Canada, 1871-1961*.

1931		1941		1951		1961	
No.	%	No.	%	No.	%	No.	%
42	.1	128	.4	994	2.2	1,804	2.4
169	.5	198	.6	593	1.3	903	1.2
65	.2	155	.4	316	.7	537	.7
80	.3	324	1.0	662	1.5	857	1.1
52	.2	101	.3	176	.4	305	.4
27	.1	33	.1	84	.2	142	.2
—	—	—	—	0	.0	3	.0
23,603	77.0	34,071	76.0	53,241	71.5	53,241	71.5
16	.0	4	.0	—	—	—	—
24,054	78.1	29,709	83.3	36,898	82.2	57,797	78.0
30,793		35,657		44,867		74,485	

Table 14

Birthplace of Berlin-Kitchener's Foreign-Born Population, 1871-1971

Birthplace	1871		1881		1911		1921	
	No.	%	No.	%	No.	%	No.	%
Great Britain	207	7.5	214	5.3	748	5.00	1,454	6.7
United States	117	4.3	143	3.5	413	2.70	636	3.0
Scandinavia	—	—	6	.1	5	.03	22	.1
Germany	807	29.4	999	24.6	1,258	8.30	976	4.5
Russia	2	.1	—	—	228	1.50	162	.7
Poland	—	—	—	—	—	—	363	1.7
Italy	—	—	—	—	19	.10	49	.2
Asia	—	—	—	—	43	.30	60	.3
France	14	.5	9	.2	9	.10	14	.0
Other/Not given	13	.5	40	1.0	248	1.60	414	2.0
Total foreign-born	1,160	42.3	1,411	34.8	2,971	19.63	4,150	19.1
Total population	2,743		4,050		15,196		21,763	

Source: *Census of Canada, 1871-1971*.

1931		1941		1951		1961		1971	
No.	%	No.	%	No.	%	No.	%	No.	%
1,677	5.4	1,516	4.3	1,714	4.0	2,736	3.7	4,785	4.3
658	2.1	686	2.0	756	2.0	874	1.2	1,265	1.1
17	.0	19	.0	24	.1	111	.1	—	—
1,209	4.0	723	2.0	825	2.0	4,048	5.4	4,550	4.1
531	2.0	566	1.6	1,105	2.5	1,405	2.0	1,250	1.1
755	2.5	811	2.3	1,351	3.0	1,824	2.4	1,995	1.8
38	.1	32	.1	74	.2	203	.3	490	.4
54	.2	29	.1	45	.1	76	.1	580	.5
14	.0	23	.1	—	—	—	—	—	—
1,174	3.3	2,075	5.0	—	—	5,411	7.3	7,760	7.0
6,739	22.0	6,317	17.7	7,969	18.0	16,688	22.4	22,675	20.3
30,793		35,657		44,867		74,485		111,800	

Table 15

Ethnic Origins of Berlin-Kitchener's Population, 1871-1971

Ethnic group	1871		1881		1901		1911		1921	
	No.	%	No.	%	No.	%	No.	%	No.	%
Austrian	—	—	—	—	—	—	—	—	—	—
Asian	—	—	—	—	—	—	—	—	—	—
British	662	24.1	813	20.1	1,667	17.1	3,416	22.50	6,292	29.0
French	34	1.2	30	.7	53	.5	102	.70	592	2.7
German	2,002	73.0	3,053	75.3	7,562	77.6	10,633	70.00	12,094	55.6
Italian	—	—	—	—	17	.2	39	.30	85	.4
Jewish	—	—	—	—	10	.1	226	1.50	298	1.4
Netherlands	—	—	16	.4	30	.3	36	.20	356	1.6
Polish	—	—	—	—	—	—	342	2.30	852	3.9
Russian	5	.2	8	.2	134	1.4	42	.30	90	.4
Scandinavian	—	—	9	.2	18	.2	7	.04	57	.3
Ukrainian	—	—	—	—	—	—	—	—	—	—
Hungarian	—	—	—	—	—	—	—	—	—	—
Indian and Eskimo	—	—	—	—	—	—	1	.00	—	—
African	13	.5	6	.1	—	—	—	—	—	—
Others/Not given	27	1.0	119	2.9	256	2.6	352	2.3	1,037	4.8
Totals	2,743	100.0	4,054	100.0	9,747	100.0	15,196	100.00	21,763	100.0

Source: *Census of Canada, 1871-1971*.

1931		1941		1951		1961		1971	
No.	%	No.	%	No.	%	No.	%	No.	%
—	—	—	—	200	.4	1,061	1.4	440	.3
—	—	154	.4	163	.4	324	.4	290	.2
9,601	31.2	12,355	34.6	14,538	32.4	24,691	33.1	50,365	45.0
702	2.3	1,002	3.0	1,385	3.1	2,799	4.0	5,150	5.0
16,345	53.8	17,086	48.0	20,258	45.2	31,791	43.0	35,920	32.1
112	.4	123	.3	266	.6	640	.9	1,200	1.1
411	1.3	425	1.2	345	.8	225	.3	725	.6
212	.7	559	1.6	408	.9	1,187	2.0	1,570	1.4
1,909	5.0	1,893	5.3	2,463	5.5	3,547	5.0	4,170	4.0
257	.8	322	.4	222	.5	493	.7	255	.2
44	.1	100	.3	104	.2	573	.7	545	.5
—	—	—	—	820	1.8	1,225	2.0	1,860	2.0
—	—	466	1.3	276	.6	875	1.2	1,050	1.0
—	—	4	.0	12	.0	39	.0	195	.2
—	—	—	—	—	—	—	—	—	—
1,491	5.0	1,168	3.3	3,257	7.3	5,075	7.0	8,065	7.2
30,743	100.0	35,657	100.0	44,867	100.0	74,485	100.0	111,500	100.0

Table 16

Major Religious Affiliations of Berlin-Kitchener's Population, 1871-1971

Religion	1871		1881		1891		1901		1911	
	No.	%	No.	%	No.	%	No.	%	No.	%
Anglican	280	10.2	266	6.6	473	6.4	433	4.4	907	6.0
Baptist	267	10.0	405	10.0	267	3.6	421	4.3	662	4.4
Brethren	5	.2	71	1.8	100	1.3	114	1.2	17	.1
Evangelical	94	3.4	—	—	—	—	—	—	—	—
Greek Orthodox	—	—	—	—	—	—	10	.1	12	.1
Jewish	—	—	—	—	—	—	10	.1	225	1.5
Lutheran	1,184	43.2	1,700	42.0	2,963	40.0	3,685	37.8	5,100	33.6
Mennonite	—	—	—	—	—	—	412	4.2	518	3.4
Methodist	178	6.4	307	7.6	891	12.0	977	10.0	1,542	10.1
Presbyterian	143	5.2	285	7.0	419	5.6	509	5.2	968	6.4
Roman Catholic	358	13.1	581	14.3	1,283	17.3	2,035	20.9	3,560	23.4
Swedenborgian	111	4.0	—	—	—	—	—	—	—	—
United Church	—	—	—	—	—	—	—	—	—	—
Other and No religion	123	4.5	439	11.0	1,029	13.9	1,141	11.7	1,685	11.1
Totals	2,743	100.0	4,054	100.0	7,425	100.0	9,747	100.0	15,196	100.0

Source: *Census of Canada, 1871-1971*.

1921		1931		1941		1951		1961		1971	
No.	%	No.	%	No.	%	No.	%	No.	%	No.	%
1,740	3.0	2,350	7.6	2,862	8.0	3,435	7.7	5,592	8.0	9,085	8.1
922	4.2	1,427	4.6	1,907	5.3	1,940	4.3	2,772	4.0	3,715	3.3
286	1.3	207	.7	226	.6	—	—	—	—	—	—
1,203	6.0	1,773	5.8	2,429	6.8	2,713	6.0	1,988	3.0	—	—
141	.6	56	.2	140	.4	225	.5	432	.6	1,470	1.3
298	1.4	411	1.3	423	1.2	391	.9	525	.7	655	.6
6,559	30.1	8,735	28.4	9,499	27.0	10,764	24.0	18,236	24.4	19,780	18.0
635	3.0	1,214	6.0	1,472	4.1	1,646	4.0	2,194	3.0	2,545	2.3
2,045	9.3	—	—	—	—	—	—	—	—	—	—
1,572	7.2	1,834	6.1	2,016	6.0	2,663	6.0	4,428	6.0	6,990	6.3
5,521	25.4	8,626	28.0	10,246	28.7	13,891	31.0	24,681	33.1	39,995	36.0
234	1.1	—	—	—	—	—	—	—	—	—	—
—	—	3,001	9.7	3,122	8.8	4,676	10.4	8,014	11.0	15,695	14.0
607	2.8	1,159	3.6	1,315	3.7	2,523	5.0	5,627	8.0	11,870	11.0
21,736	100.0	30,793	100.0	35,657	100.0	44,867	100.0	74,485	100.0	111,800	100.0

Table 17

Labour Force of Berlin-Kitchener by Industry, 1911-1951

	1911 No.	1911 %	1921 No.	1921 %	1931 No.	1931 %	1941 No.	1941 %	1951 No.	1951 %
Primary: Agriculture, forestry, fishing, trapping, mining	96	1.5	69	.7	123	1.0	89	.6	115	.5
Manufacturing	3,816	60.2	5,292	57.0	6,883	54.0	9,295	60.0	8,227	38.0
Construction	498	7.9	561	6.0	881	7.0	693	4.4	1,097	5.0
Transportation and communications	149	2.3	418	5.0	504	4.0	440	3.0	1,033	5.0
Trade	792	12.5	933	10.0	1,484	12.0	1,884	12.1	n.a.	
Finance, insurance, real estate (professionals for 1911)	311	4.9	261	3.0	506	4.0	600	4.0	161	.7
Community, business, and personal service	493	7.8	1,200	13.0	1,877	15.0	2,355	15.1	1,663	8.0
Government employees, all levels	187	2.9	272	3.0	329	3.1	n.a.		n.a.	
Other or unspecified	0	0.0	279	3.0	276	2.1	223	1.4	9,492	44.0
Total classified	6,342		9,285		12,863		15,579		21,788	

Table 18

Age Composition of Berlin-Kitchener's Population, 1871-1971

Year	0-15		16-40		41-60		61		Total population
	No.	%	No.	%	No.	%	No.	%	
1871	1,275	46.5	909	33.1	429	15.6	127	4.6	2,743
1881[a]									7,425
1891[a]									
1901[a]									
1911[a]									
	0-14		15-44		45-64		65+		
1921	6,563	30.2	10,695	49.1	3,481	16.0	995	4.6	21,763
1931	8,519	27.7	15,591	51.0	4,992	16.2	1,687	5.5	30,793
1941	8,290	23.2	18,408	51.6	6,687	18.8	2,272	6.4	35,657
1951	10,499	23.4	21,706	48.4	9,240	21.0	3,422	7.6	44,867
1961	23,131	31.1	32,399	43.5	13,698	18.4	5,257	7.1	74,485
1971	31,855	28.5	52,200	47.0	19,475	17.4	8,270	7.4	111,800

[a] Data not available.

Source: *Census of Canada, 1871-1971*.

INDEX

253